A TIME
TO
LEARN

Also by George H. Wood

Schools That Work

A TIME TO LEARN

CREATING COMMUNITY IN AMERICA'S HIGH SCHOOLS

George H. Wood, Ph. D.

A DUTTON BOOK

DUTTON
Published by the Penguin Group
Penguin Putnam Inc., 375 Hudson Street, New York, New York 10014, U.S.A.
Penguin Books Ltd, 27 Wrights Lane, London W8 5TZ, England
Penguin Books Australia Ltd, Ringwood, Victoria, Australia
Penguin Books Canada Ltd, 10 Alcorn Avenue, Toronto, Ontario, Canada M4V 3B2
Penguin Books (N.Z.) Ltd, 182–190 Wairau Road, Auckland 10, New Zealand

Penguin Books Ltd, Registered Offices:
Harmondsworth, Middlesex, England

First published by Dutton, an imprint of Dutton NAL,
a member of Penguin Putnam Inc.

First Printing, August, 1998
10 9 8 7 6 5 4 3 2 1

 REGISTERED TRADEMARK—MARCA REGISTRADA

Library of Congress Cataloging-in-Publication Data:

Wood, George H. (George Harrison)
    A time to learn : creating community in America's high schools /
George H. Wood.
        p.   cm.
    Includes index.
    ISBN 0-525-93955-5
    1. High schools—United States—Administration—Case studies.
2. High school principals—United States—Case studies   3. School
improvement programs—United States—Case studies.   I. Federal
Hocking High School (Stewart, Ohio)   II. Title.
LB2822.2.W66   1998
373.12'00973—dc21   98-2674
                                                         CIP

Printed in the United States of America
Set in New Baskerville
Designed by Leonard Telesca

This book is printed on acid-free paper.

Many people talk about what a difficult job it is to be a high school principal. But it's a much harder job to be a father or a husband, and probably harder still to be the wife or child of a school principal. For the past six years my wife, Marcia Burchby, has picked up all the loose ends and, more important, reminded me how much I love my work. My sons, John and Michael, have been forgiving of the meals missed, the books not read, the weekends without their dad. I hope that dedicating this book to them, in honor of all the things they do to make this a better and more humane world, makes up a little bit for what we have missed together.

Contents

ACKNOWLEDGMENTS

Since 1992 I have had the great privilege of working with the staff, students, parents, and community members of Federal Hocking High School. As principal of FHHS I have profited from their counsel, support, and loyalty. Most of what is found in the pages of this book I have learned from them, and to all of them I offer my sincerest thanks.

I have also had the great pleasure of trying out the ideas herein on a wide range of friends and colleagues. Among them, special thanks to Marcia Burchby, David Lackey, Joe MacDonald, Carl Glickman, Ted Sizer, and Fred Wood.

I have been fortunate to work with an agent, Denise Marcil, who believes that words can change the world; with an editor, Deb Brody, who insists (in a very kind way) that such words be worthy of being read; a typist, Debi MacMillan, who forces me to be sure I want to say what I am saying; and a copy editor, Ann Marlowe, who unmixes my metaphors and goes beyond the call of duty in checking my facts. To all four, my heartfelt thanks.

Finally, Dick Streedain, Deborah Meier, and Dennis Littky provided me with the model of what a school principal could do. After watching them work, I wanted to be a school principal—and since becoming a principal, I have wanted to live up to the standard of their work. For the inspiration you have provided so many school leaders my sincerest thanks.

Introduction

The book you have in your hands is written from the vantage point of a high school principal. I should probably mention now that I never intended to occupy such a position. In fact, prior to becoming principal of Federal Hocking High School in Stewart, Ohio, I was rather comfortably in place as a professor of education at Ohio University. But when, after twelve years of work inside the "ivory tower," the chance came to take the job at FHHS, I jumped at the opportunity. It was one of the best decisions I have ever made. And it is from this experience that I have learned how important it is to rethink our high schools—to transform them from the institutions they now are to the communities they should be.

I started my career in education as a junior high school social studies teacher. Having no aspirations to move into the principal's office, I did everything I could to keep myself from being identified as "leadership material." My lesson plans were always lacking some detail, I avoided suits and ties, and I never made a meeting on time. When I moved on to graduate school I continued to avoid the front office. My course work was filled with John Dewey and George Counts, not with Buildings and Grounds or Financial Management. I escaped from grad school without having sat through a single lecture on principalship, superintending, or local backslapping (also called School Politics). I was interested only in the classroom and had, I must admit, a fair amount of disdain for school administrators.

Much of that attitude was hard earned. My experience as a classroom teacher had introduced me to school administrators who offered little or no help in improving instruction or developing curriculum. At best I was given a few tips on bulletin board layout or what movies to show. At worst I had found administrators to be more interested in sports scores than test scores, committed to the status quo whether it worked or not, and dedicated to the principle that the main task in a school is to make kids sit down and shut up.

But experience was also what changed my attitude toward the principal's office. In the late 1980s I undertook a project designed to offer a counterpoint to much of the bad news we were hearing about schools. Believing that schools could and would improve only if educators, parents, and students had models upon which to base their efforts, I spent five years traveling to and researching outstanding schools. My goal was to find schools that made a powerful difference in the lives of children, schools that had a positive impact upon the communities within which they were located. I found schools like this around the country and was able to tell their stories in my book *Schools That Work*.

While writing that book I ran into three people who changed my mind about what school principals can do—Dennis Littky, Deborah Meier, and Dick Streedain. Littky had, in rural New Hampshire, turned Thayer Junior/Senior High around, helping it gain the reputation of one of the best schools in the country. Meier was the founder and leader of Central Park East Secondary School (CPESS), a beacon of hope for the children of Harlem and for urban educators everywhere. Streedain carried on the tradition of the progressive educator Carleton Washburne at Hubbard Woods School in suburban Chicago, an elementary school that is about as child-centered as a school can be.

In many schools I visited, teachers or parents had provided the push for change or had been its staunchest defenders. At Thayer, Central Park East, and Hubbard Woods it was the principals that seemed to me to have made the difference. Littky, on arrival, began to turn around a school in crisis by pulling the staff together around a plan that would build closer personal and academic ties between students and teachers. Meier was the designer of Central Park East (as she had been of several elementary schools in New York City) and had built the school from the ground up. Streedain urged his faculty and staff on, beyond their already good reputation, to find new ways to meet the needs of every student.

Each principal had also been fundamental to the survival of the school's program. When Littky's plans seemed a bit too radical for a conservative New Hampshire town and he was fired, he rallied the faculty and community in a successful effort to elect a new school board that reaffirmed Thayer's program. In New York City's political labyrinth, Debbie Meier has fought and won battles on almost a daily basis to maintain Central Park East's autonomy. When an intruder brought violence to bucolic Winnetka and Hubbard Woods School, it was Streedain who led the healing process and refused to let the school abandon its openness.

As I followed Denny, Debbie, and Dick, I became more and more convinced that the principal's office could be a genuine force for positive change in schools. In fact, I found myself actually drawn to the job. While it had its drawbacks—too many meetings to attend, endless forms to fill out, an impossible range of publics to please—it did appear to be, as Dick called it, "the best job in the world."

Wanting the job was not enough. First there was the question of certification: I didn't have it. Like most states, Ohio has an unnecessarily difficult procedure leading to a principal's certificate. A long list of courses, many of them only vaguely connected to the day-to-day work of school administration and few addressing the larger issues of school change and/or purpose, must be taken. Add to that an internship, and you have quite a series of hoops to jump through before you can be called a principal. Even if I wanted to do all that, when would I, busy being a college professor, find the time to go back to school?

Of course all of this was a moot question—no one had really asked me to be a principal yet. There had been opportunities, and I'd even interviewed once, but most of those were far away from our home in Amesville, Ohio, thus holding little appeal. My wife, Marcia Burchby, loves teaching kindergarten here, and our sons, Michael and John, just cannot imagine life in any home other than the one they have always known. I too had grown to love Amesville and Athens County. A small town influenced by nearby Ohio University, Amesville offered everything I wanted. So with moving out of the question, finding a principal's job seemed nothing more than an idle dream.

All of that changed in the summer of 1992. For several years I had worked with our local school district, Federal Hocking Schools, in a variety of capacities. I had spent time in my children's classrooms as a parent volunteer, been involved in research projects, helped build a partnership between the district and Ohio University, and begun working with the high school staff on a curriculum project. It was that relationship that led me to volunteer my help when it was time to recruit a new high school principal.

The search turned up one outstanding candidate who had a record of building strong programs in rural schools. I had known him for several years and was anxious to see him interview. However, upon arriving at the interview one Wednesday evening in June, I was surprised to find his name scratched off the list of candidates. As it turned out, a family crisis had led him to withdraw. This left the search committee without much to choose from. After interviewing the remaining candidates, we agreed they were fairly lackluster.

The committee then did what many do in these situations. Finding ourselves out of time (it was already late June) and options, we recommended the candidate who appeared likely to do the least harm.

Employed by the school board on a Thursday, the following Tuesday our new high school principal turned in his keys and resigned. He gave no reason for his actions, though I now realize there were plenty of signs I should have seen indicating what a mess the previous FHHS administration had left. Now, in early July, Federal Hocking High School was only six weeks from a new school year and had no principal.

It was at this point that Tim Lairson, then superintendent of schools, approached me with an interesting offer: Would I care to apply for the principal's job? It was hard to believe; something that I assumed would never be possible now was. Without giving it nearly enough thought, I dusted off my resume, checked with my family, arranged a leave from the university, obtained a waiver of principalship certification, and, by the first week of August, found myself putting up bookshelves in the principal's office at Federal Hocking High School.

*   *   *

To say the very least, I have learned a great deal since becoming a principal. The unexpected lessons have included how to load and service soda machines (we are a poor school and we need the money for field trips), how to schedule athletic events, and (after a cold snap featuring forty-two below temperatures) how to fix school heating units. I've also been introduced to strategies for staying awake during school board meetings that drag into the early morning hours, ways of making fewer than a dozen computers serve nearly four hundred kids, and methods for remembering the names of not only all our kids but their parents as well (though I still struggle with this).

More seriously, I've also learned or in some cases relearned some fairly important lessons. Right up front, it has been great to be reminded how wonderful teenagers are to work with. For most of them, the world is still their oyster, and they are always ready to share their dreams. They laugh and cry with ease, are one minute a sophisticate and the next a pouting infant, can charm you with a smile that only moments ago was a grimace. As long as we remember they are kids and are entitled to make mistakes, we can enjoy watching them struggle to grow separate from us while at the same time checking over their shoulders for reassurance. To me, it's the best age to work with, and when my job as principal goes the way it should, I get to spend a lot of time with them.

I've also become ever more convinced that the most important mission before our public schools is not, as we so often hear, getting kids jobs. Much more important is the task of helping young people develop the habits of heart and mind that will make them good citizens. When I think about what we choose to teach, what I hope the young people with whom we work will learn, it usually all boils down to one thing—what type of neighbors they will be.

Certainly I want them to be able to find, hold, and perhaps even create decent jobs that will provide for their material needs and contribute general prosperity. But that is only part of it, because employment is also only part of our lives. Equally, if not more, important is their ability to be a part of a community. This means performing a wide range of tasks, including using leisure time well, paying attention to and getting involved in public decision making, being committed to the general welfare of society, and dozens of other things that make our communities habitable. When I think about what we do in our schools with the young people entrusted to our care, I keep returning to the fact that they come to us as students and children and leave as fully enfranchised citizens and neighbors. To ignore this transition is to forfeit much of what public education stands for in our society.

Living these lessons has also afforded me the chance to learn yet one more. It is simply this: We must not underestimate the urgency of our task and the importance of using well every minute of a student's school life. In four years the average high school student will spend five thousand hours inside our halls. This is time the kids never get back—time they cannot use to talk with their parents, learn to play the banjo, or ponder life's mysteries with a good book. It is valuable time. It is, in fact, the most important time kids will spend during their teenage years. We must use it well.

Unfortunately, I am convinced that in too many high schools we are not using our children's time well at all. There is much talk about our schools being in crisis. Anecdotal stories on radio talk shows about metal detectors to keep weapons out, graduates who cannot fill out a job application, or increased drug use among teens make up much of the discussion about our high schools. In response politicians call for dressing our children in uniforms, requiring them to pass more tests, and finding quicker ways to expel the noncompliant. All of this misses the point.

It is easy to understand why we become preoccupied with this sideshow. For one thing, adults have always struggled in their relationships with teenagers. Witness how uncomfortable adults become when surrounded by a large group of these children in adult bodies at the local mall. Adults have always seen the years between thirteen and eighteen as a time when their formerly lovable children turn into strangers who dispute everything from the station on the family car radio to the length of their hair or skirts. When we are at our best with this time of rebellion, we hold our tongues and our position, knowing in the end this time of struggle makes us all better people. At our worst we insist that schools should somehow toughen up, enforce rules we ourselves would have fought against, and basically take responsibility for our failures as parents.

Today the cry for more control over our kids is even shriller because the stakes are higher. We see an epidemic of violence and gunplay, drugs that addict with just one use, and sexually transmitted diseases like AIDS that do not merely inconvenience but actually kill. We see more and more teenagers who seem to have been turned loose, to wander the streets, by parents who are either unwilling or unable to supervise their own children's behavior, and who do little to support the efforts of their kids' schools. The easy answer to all this is to simply ask that schools "get tough" when the rest of the community is unable to provide the support and nurture that our children—and, yes, even teenagers are children—need.

Aside from our usual adult clumsiness when it comes to dealing with teens, there is another reason for the misguided reforms of schools today. As is often the case in the world of sound-bite politics, solutions such as tests and toughness are deceptively concrete-seeming. Rather than dealing with the complexity of what it means to educate democratic citizens, politicians and pundits tell us to measure schools by standardized tests. Rather than seriously tackling how much money should be spent on schools, the statehouse mantra is "Spend what you have more wisely, we're too busy building prisons." Rather than sitting down with communities and figuring out what it is our children need to be able to do in order to contribute to the general welfare of our villages, towns, and cities, state education bureaucrats simply add on more credit requirements for kids to earn a diploma. It is politically expedient to reach for the quick fix. But it is the quick fix that has landed us in the mess we are in today.

The real crisis in the American high school is our inability to connect all our students to learning communities that can assist them in being more democratically engaged, more able to meet the demands of our changing workplaces, and simply more well rounded in what they gain from life. Over the last eighty years we have engineered, through a series of quick fixes, a high school structure that often simply *spends* our kids' time rather than *using* it, and that is the crisis of the high school. It is this wasting of the five thousand hours that every American teenager spends in high school that should concern us. The issue is not test scores or dress codes, the issue is connection. Connection is what this book is about.

*   *   *

have been dismayed over the past decade by the slow, often ponderous pace of school reform. It was more than a decade ago, in 1983, that then president Reagan's Department of Education released the seething critique of American public education *A Nation at Risk*. The country was supposedly awash in poor schools generating a "rising tide of mediocrity." The call was for all-out war on poor schooling. Quick on the heels of this slim booklet were mountains of reports from business groups, think tanks, citizens' groups, and others outraged by the supposed poor state of public schools. "Education" governors, representatives, and mayors were elected by the score to set things right. And yet today, after all the sound and fury, so little seems to have changed in our secondary schools. In fact, the typical high school day described in chapter 1 will probably sound very familiar to all readers, regardless of age.

Before I became a principal, my frustration over the slow pace of reform was mostly out of sympathy for teachers. My teacher-education students worked to learn new strategies to reach children but could find few places to put them into classroom practice. My teaching colleagues felt that their best intentions and programs were consistently thwarted by the way schools were organized and run. It was as if we had deliberately designed schools to insure that no one could do a good job in them.

Now, from my vantage point at FHHS, I have an even deeper source of frustration with our nation's unwillingness to rethink our high schools: the time we are losing with our kids. For adults there always seems to be more time to get schooling "right." After all, if our ninth-grade program doesn't work this year, we get to do it again next year . . . and the next, and the next, and the next. But the freshmen at FHHS get just one chance at a ninth-grade year. If it isn't right, if it doesn't work for them, they never get to do it again. Watching them grow up and move so quickly through school has brought home in a very personal way the urgency of doing our job well right now, not waiting for some far-off future.

It is for that reason that calling for improved schools by the year 2000 seems like such a crime. My first freshman class at FHHS graduated four years before the year 2000. My older son, Michael, will graduate from my high school that very year. What are these kids to do while we meander our way along to improving schools? Are we willing to write off their education while we take our time getting things right? Are we willing to allow any part of the only five thousand hours young people will spend in high school to be less than excellent?

Let us hope everyone's answer to those questions is "Of course not, but where do we start to make our high schools places where our children do quality work?" It is for people who respond in that way that this book has been written. Based on what we are doing now at FHHS and other high schools, this book is about how to change our high schools in ways that will provide for all American teenagers an education that genuinely reflects a commitment to our kids. A commitment to provide an education that equips them with the tools to find, keep, even create productive work. An education that encourages them to keep on learning, that lights in them the fire to ask why things are the way they are. An education that equips every young person with the habits of heart and mind that make democratic life possible.

What is provided is not a recipe to be slavishly followed in every instance. Rather, these pages present some general guidelines, some practical plans, the advice of those who have tried and succeeded, and failed as well. As you read them it must always be with one eye on your own school, your own community. Change happens in real places, not on the printed page. What can happen in your place with these ideas is for you to figure out through trial and error, not for any commission or report writer to dictate.

This book is also about hope. I cannot imagine our high schools not getting better. They are filled with children who want to do well and with adults who feel that they can make a difference. They are places where young people spend a significant amount of their time, often more than the required five thousand hours as they march in the band, play on an athletic team, act in a play, compete with the debate team, write and edit the newspaper and yearbook, among hundreds of activities. Our high schools are places that can, and indeed do, make a difference in the quality of their lives, if we let them.

For that to happen means rethinking virtually everything we do in our high schools today. The rethinking can only be done in a climate of hope for a better future. Hope comes from know-ing that change is possible, that we do not have to settle for the status quo, that others who have gone before us have succeeded, and that it is worthwhile to try. This book is built upon stories that should give us that hope, stories of real schools and real changes happening today. Our job is to turn hope into action, because high school should be the best five thousand hours of a teenager's life.

CHAPTER ONE

Five Thousand Hours

For nearly two decades Americans have been deluged with numbers about high schools. Test scores, dropout rates, money spent (or not spent), teacher-student ratios, and on and on and on. From this parade of numbers a wide array of "experts" on education have tried to draw a recipe for fixing the American high school. We've been fed a steady diet of new tests, plans for school choice, new certification requirements for teachers—one quick fix after another, all in the name of changing the numbers. The problem is that the numbers are not the problem.

The real issue confronted by the American high school is how to change the day-to-day experience of students so that they are connected to the academic and social agenda of the school. This means creating, nurturing, and sustaining a school community where every young person feels valued. It means doing more than nudging up test scores or requiring teachers to attend one more workshop, fiddling with an occasional new textbook series or making school uniforms mandatory. If we are to get serious about having the high schools that our children and communities deserve, we must rethink the entire culture of high school in our attempt to make it a place where young people can develop the habits of heart and mind that are required of citizens in a democracy.

This book is about the work it will take to reinvent our high schools, moving them from institutions to communities. It starts where any honest discussion of schools must start—the experience of the students. For all our talk about improving schools, this is the only real issue that matters: What is the daily experience of high school like for our kids, and does that experience cause young people to do the best work possible?

Six years ago I returned to the real world of the public high school when I was fortunate enough to be offered the principalship of Federal Hocking High. During my first year back, after twelve years as a university professor, I relearned what it means to teach high school. From this vantage point what struck me most was how many teachers went home exhausted and came to school already behind in their preparations for the day. Working side by side with a group of dedicated but overwhelmed teachers, I came to see that something about high school was deeply wrong—something that wasn't reflected in test scores but showed up clearly in the worn expressions of our teachers.

It wasn't just the work lives of the teachers that rang warning bells. When I watched our students make their way through the school day, a more pressing case for rethinking how we do high school emerged. The daily life of our students presented us with a paradox. On one hand, it was fairly easy to "slide" through the day, doing minimal work, just getting by in class. On the other, it was almost impossible to do quality work in all areas as students were herded through eight classes a day, in forty-two-minute chunks, with two-minute breaks. It was as if we had intentionally designed a system to prevent learning rather than enable it.

This is not to say that nothing was going well in our high school, or in the classrooms of high school teachers around the country. In fact, brilliant lessons often went on, only to be cut short by the changing of classes, and students often did outstanding work, even if it meant doing less competent work in another class or subject.* The problem was that most of this work went on *in spite of* how the school was structured rather than because of it.

The daily reality of how school worked (or didn't work) was what caused our teachers, students, and community to begin

---

*The first of Ted Sizer's three outstanding books on school reform, *Horace's Compromise* (Boston: Houghton Mifflin, 1984), gives an excellent description of how teachers accommodate current school structures.

asking ourselves some serious questions about our school. Did we really believe that a teacher could actually teach more than 145 children a day, prepare effective lessons for six or seven different classes, and provide adequate feedback on literally scores of student papers? Did we really think young people used their minds well when confronted by six to eight different subject areas daily? Did learning really take place in forty-two-minute chunks, with two-minute breaks to use the toilet and a thirty-seven-minute lunch break to meet friends and catch up on the gossip of the day? Did every subject we taught really need the same 120 hours of instruction yearly? Most important, did organizing a school around clocks, bells, credit hours, and grades really prepare young people to become citizens, employees, and neighbors?

Questions like these caused my colleagues and me to begin rethinking many of our automatic assumptions about how our high school operated. Along with teachers, administrators, parents, and students at scores of high schools across the country we found ourselves face to face with one central question: Is our high school organized so that our students can do their best possible work? Quality student work is what must be at the center of how we organize our schools; after all, the work our students do is the only reason we have schools. But so much of the way we set up high school seems to work against young people using their minds well in order to do quality work. So much of what we do is built around the *institution* of high school. What we wanted instead, we knew, was to create a *community* of learners.

In the pages that follow I want to draw from my experiences at a school that is trying to rethink itself as well as from the experiences of others to argue for a different way of making high schools work. What is presented is not a panacea, as different schools require different programs. Like children, schools have their own personalities and needs, and attempting to raise them all in the same way would be a horrible mistake. What is presented is also not easy. A host of skeletons make it difficult to clean out this closet. There are state laws that insist the high school curriculum be doled out in chunks of 120 hours. University programs for the preparation of high school teachers continue to focus on developing content-matter specialists who know little about the whole child or school. A public mind-set has been so conditioned as to what high school should be that it is hard to convince parents, the general public, and even educators that we could do high school any other way. Colleges and universities say they want school reform, yet continue to ask for high school transcripts that reflect the very school structures they claim to want changed.

In spite of all this, my daily work at Federal Hocking High School and my observations of the work of other committed high school educators leave me convinced that we can rethink the American high school experience. We can make our institutional high schools into genuine learning communities. But to do that requires not merely *reforming* the institutional high schools we have now. If we are to help our children learn to use their minds well, we must set about the task of *transforming* our high schools into learning communities. By doing that we can make the five thousand hours that high school students spend in school one of the most meaningful experiences of their lives.*

At 7:10 A.M. every Monday through Friday from late August to early June a large yellow school bus pulls up in front of the Amesville Elementary School and opens its door. Onto bus number nine file about a dozen kids, some still munching on a hasty breakfast, others barely awake, one or two busily copying the homework they forgot the night before. The bus swings out of the school lot and follows the winding lanes of Ohio State Routes 550 and 329 toward the old frontier town of Stewart. Along the way the driver stops several times, warning flashers on, to pick up a couple dozen more kids, ranging in age from fourteen to nineteen. The new passengers grunt in greeting and make their way to their seats, the same ones that by habit they sit in every day, glaring at anyone who might have mistakenly sat in another's chosen place.

The ride is not too long, only twenty-five minutes or so, just long enough for a nap or some gossip about who is dating who. In that respect these kids are lucky (other students ride the bus

---

* While the primary focus of this book is high school, I believe the lessons in it are easily applied to middle and elementary schools as well. In a previous book, *Schools That Work* (Dutton, 1992), I discussed elementary and middle school education in more detail.

for more than an hour), so they don't complain much about the ride or hassle the driver. At the end of the trip the door of bus nine swings open, depositing its now full load of strangely quiet and still sleepy adolescents at the door of Federal Hocking High School (FHHS). Named after the confluence of the Hocking River and Federal Creek, Fed-Hock High (as it is often shortened) stands silently awaiting these first occupants of the day. Dozens of other buses and scores of cars fill the parking lot until, when the first class starts at 7:30 A.M., nearly four hundred kids in all shapes, sizes, and colors fill our building.

This same scene is repeated in every state of the Union. Every county, town, village, and city provides a free high school education to all comers. It matters not whether a young person is male or female, black or white or brown, rich or poor, physically whole or impaired, we bring them all to high school. The kids that walk up the front steps of FHHS are welcome to walk in the doors of the high school wherever they might live. But, of course, just opening the doors is not enough. Having guaranteed that all can attend, we must make sure we spend wisely the time our students have with us.

Because of the way high school calendars and schedules are organized, we usually do not think of a student's total time spent in high school when considering what schools should be like. Rather, we think of one year (freshman, sophomore, junior, or senior) or one subject (algebra, English, industrial technology) as defining a high school experience. It is precisely that way of thinking, the breaking apart of the school day as opposed to the pulling together of the total high school experience, that prevents us from rethinking how to more effectively use the time our children spend in school. We devote so much effort to tinkering with the pieces of the high school experience that we have little effect on the whole. But it is the entire experience that students have, not just individual courses or grades, that makes them high school graduates.

Compare our ways of thinking about high school to the construction of a jigsaw puzzle. Both have pieces that lead to a finished product. With a jigsaw puzzle we start with the finished product—the photograph of a painting, a landscape scene, or some other interesting design. We then disassemble that picture, taking care that each piece will fit with the others to create again and again the picture we see on the box.

Now consider how we put together a high school program. Indeed, most schools start with some general, quite bland statement about well-rounded, well-informed students. But the statement is promptly forgotten as we turn to the little pieces of a child's education. The school is broken up into individual units which we call courses, and each of these units vies for time in the student's day. Usually this means that the individual units have little if anything to do with one another. So the English teacher first period is unaware of the health report being written second period, for example.

In effect, what we do in organizing a high school program is spend tremendous effort on the size, shape, and color of the individual pieces of the jigsaw puzzle while the teacher or teachers working on each piece have only the most general idea where their piece fits in the finished puzzle. It is, at best, left to the student to figure out how to make the pieces come together, perhaps within the framework of a college or technology preparatory curriculum. At worst, this way of looking at high school cuts the student adrift to just fill up a schedule as a way of killing time.*

If we could change our thinking about high school, if we could consider the entire school experience vis-à-vis the picture or graduate we want at the end of the experience, we could then move on to make the changes necessary in our high schools. The changes we need to make are not to be found in tinkering with the parts; rather, they require rethinking the very assumptions that guide how we organize the time our kids spend in school.

I've referred several times to the five thousand hours students spend in high school. To begin our exploration of how best to organize our schools, let's start by examining how this time is currently utilized. Up until now I have spoken of the need to restructure the high school experience as an article of faith. On examining what we currently do with the time allotted for high school, the case for restructuring becomes all too clear.

First, the big picture. Over a four-year period students in American high schools come to school for an average of 180 days,

---

* Having been a university professor for more than a decade before coming to FHHS, I know that most colleges and universities are at least as unthoughtful as high schools (if not worse) when it comes to the undergraduate curriculum. Undergraduate programs make little sense to students who chose electives from broad lists that have little to do with their career paths or broadening their cultural or intellectual

seven hours a day. A little simple math and we find that this equals just slightly more than five thousand hours of a young person's life.* How do we spend this time? On average, roughly a thousand hours are devoted to such things as lunch and time to walk from class to class (known as passing periods). That leaves some four thousand hours of instructional time, which is broken down into units of 120 hours each, or about thirty-two units in the course of four years.† At first glance one may be impressed by these numbers. University students average eight to ten courses a year; kids in high school take a similar course load. Their seven-hour school day is slightly shorter than an eight-hour workday, but kids do spend about 5.6 hours a day actually in the classroom, with added time for homework at night.

So far, so good. But this is only looking at the pieces of the puzzle. They may look fine in isolation, but fit them together and the picture makes little, if any, sense.

Begin with the number of credits required for graduation. At our high school, for example, until 1996 we required students to amass twenty credits for graduation. That is, they had to pass an average of five courses a year to earn their diplomas. In this respect we were similar to most schools in Ohio and to those around the country that have students meet state-mandated graduation requirements. However, we were not happy with this way of looking at high school completion, for several reasons.

First is the simple fact that requiring only twenty units for graduation means that students need to pass only two-thirds of the courses they take. Back to our hours per unit, twenty units equals only 2,400 of the 4,000 academic hours kids spend in school. In other words, the message is that a student may do little or nothing with 1,600 of the 5,000 hours (s)he spends in school and still earn the title of high school graduate.

Look closely at this big picture and more surprises await you.

It takes twenty units to graduate, but twenty units of what? Since it is similar to most states', Ohio's list of required credits is a good example of what courses the aspiring graduate must take.

---

* National figures on time spent in school can be found in *Prisoners of Time: Report of the National Education Commission on Time and Learning* (Washington, D.C.: U.S. Government Printing Office, 1994).

† The picture is somewhat more complicated than 120 hours equaling one credit. For example, in Ohio 120 hours of Physical Education class equaled ¹/₂ unit.

Specifically, Ohio law requires students to complete four units of English, two units of math, two units of social studies (including $\frac{1}{2}$ unit of American History and $\frac{1}{2}$ unit of American Government), one unit of science, $\frac{1}{2}$ unit of PE, $\frac{1}{4}$ unit of health and $10\frac{1}{4}$ additional nonspecified "elective" units. That's it. Meaning that fewer than ten units, or some 1,170 hours of student time, are required in specific courses for a student to graduate from high school. Said another way, the core academic curriculum for a high school student may take up less than a quarter of the total time (s)he spends in high school. When we allow ourselves to look at just the pieces, the good English or tough chemistry course our child is taking, it's easy to be satisfied with this state of affairs. But pulling back, looking at the whole picture, we become frustrated by the sense that the young people being handed diplomas have spent so little of their precious time on the intellectual skills and concepts we claim to value.

GRADUATION BY CREDIT

The following is a sample four-year schedule that students could follow in order to graduate from most high schools if they took only the required courses.

9th Grade	10th Grade	11th Grade	12th Grade
English	English (course	English (course	English (course
Civics	chosen by	chosen by	chosen by
Biology or Earth	student)	student)	student)
Science	U.S. History	7 electives*	7 electives*
Math (General	Math (General		
Math or Alge-	math or Geo-		
bra)	metry)		
PE	Health		
3 electives*	4 electives*		

---

*Remember that out of the 21 possible electives students only have to pass $10\frac{1}{4}$. Most students opt for at least one study hall period each year.

It was frustration with this state of affairs that led our faculty, as it has many others, to begin rethinking how we organize our school. But it wasn't just the low expectation of how much work it takes to graduate that goaded us on. Once we stepped back to look at the total high school picture, we also became aware of how disjointed and uneven the high school experience can be.

Go back a bit and look again at the list of requirements for graduation. Now remember that each unit equals 120 hours of class time. A bit of history here is useful in understanding why 120 hours equal one unit. The unit in question is known as the Carnegie Unit. It was back in 1893 that the National Education Association, then an organization of school administrators, appointed a committee to study creating uniform high school standards that would lead to college admission. Among the recommendations of the Committee of Ten (as it had come to be known) was that an academic unit be uniform from high school to high school. It was their recommendation, more than a century ago, that these units consist of 120 hours of class time.

Of course the Committee of Ten had no legal authority to impose this requirement. However, in 1910 Andrew Carnegie's charitable trust, the Carnegie Foundation for the Advancement of Teaching, made an offer to colleges that would dominate the way high schools are organized to this day. The offer was simple. The foundation would fund college professors' pensions if (among other criteria) college admissions were based upon high school students' having completed sixteen set units. And each unit was to equal 120 hours of instruction—or what we know today as the Carnegie Unit. While we would never settle for driving a car made in 1910, or running a factory at 1910 productivity levels, or even being supplied water from sanitation facilities that meet 1910 health standards, we still expect our kids to earn school credits based on an accounting system developed at the turn of the century.*

Whether or not 120 hours of seat time spent in a classroom add up to having actually learned something is a question to which we will return later. Note, however, that this system of accounting fragments what young people study in high school.

---

* A detailed history of the Carnegie Foundation's effect on public education can be found in Henry J. Perkinson, *The Imperfect Panacea*, 4th ed. (New York: McGraw Hill, 1995).

Given a mandate that 120 hours equal one unit, high schools do the logical thing: they divide the 120 hours by the number of school days in a year (around 180) and come up with the simple conclusion that each class should meet for approximately forty minutes a day. The school day is then broken into anywhere from eight forty-minute periods to six fifty-odd-minute periods and instantaneously the accounting problem is solved. Rather than discuss what should be learned in algebra to equal a high school credit for graduation, the issue becomes just insuring enough time spent in the math classroom to fulfill the 120-hour criterion.

Consider for a moment the way such a system hands out knowledge. Assume an eight-period day for most students. This means that in the course of just one day a student may be faced with learning English, math, U.S. History, biology, French, music theory, and typing, all in discrete, time-divided blocks. There is no formal mechanism for any of these subjects to be tied to any others, though enterprising teachers may find connections on their own. Imagine how difficult a task this intellectual juggling would be if we really expected students to do high quality work in each of these areas.

One student raised this very issue with me during a conference we had about what his teachers perceived to be his lack of effort in class. "You know, Doc, I work harder than the teachers do, actually." A bit taken aback by this comment, I asked him to elaborate. "Well," he continued, "how many different courses a day do teachers teach?" "Seven," I replied. "But some of those are the same course. How many *different* courses per day?" I checked the schedule and, on average, our teachers had three different preparations. "Well, I have eight separate classes that I am supposed to be ready for every day. Right now I'm getting As in three of them, Bs in two, one C, and only failing two classes. Come on, Doc, I'm passing seventy-five percent of my classes— not bad, really." While I was not convinced that he worked harder than our teachers, it is true that he worked hard at more separate tasks than most of us ever face after high school.

The important point here is not whether students work harder than teachers. It is instead that we ask kids to do something most adults need never do—learn and use academic content and skills in discrete, disconnected blocks of time—all for the sake of earning Carnegie Units. At very best, this system would produce a young person who knows a little bit about a lot of things. At worst, it produces young people who memorize bits of information for examinations, information quickly forgotten because it is never required again in any meaningful context. This may be a good strategy for preparing masters of trivia games. It is a lousy way to prepare citizens and neighbors.

A low level of expectation and a fragmented educational experience. Certainly these are reasons enough to rethink how we spend our kids' five thousand high school hours. Yet even within this system some kids have a good high school experience. They leave able to write well, show a good sense of history, handle complex math formulas, and perform scientific inquiries. It is the fact that only *some* kids leave so well prepared that raises one more reason to be concerned with the way we spend our children's time in high school.

Within the structure of credits for graduation hides the unfortunate truth that there are huge differences from student to student in what counts as a credit. Take, for example, the English credit. For students whom we identify as college material we organize a "college prep" curriculum where these students will read Hemingway, Shakespeare, Angelou, and Keats, write essays on symbolism, culture, and voice, and use the library to prepare research papers on war and peace, capital punishment, and the lives of great authors. For the rest of the students, who we guess will not grace the halls of the university, the same English credit is earned reading autobiographies of sports stars, writing business letters, and visiting the library only to find a magazine article on a topic of interest. The best that can be said of such a program is that it is designed to "meet the needs" of each student. However, it also greatly limits the range of citizen and vocational skills some students get from school. Multiply this across all the curricular areas—some students get Algebra and Geometry while others get General Math, some take Chemistry and Physics while others take General Science, some take Advanced Placement Western Civilization while others take Great American Heroes—and it becomes clear that even within the credit structure there is no standard high school curriculum.

It is not hard to see why teachers, parents, and students who are serious about what is learned in high school want to rethink the way things are currently done. When we look at the fragmentation of the day into credits or units, the multiple tasks at which we expect kids to excel, and the unevenness of the curriculum various young people experience, it should be clear that what is needed is an overhaul of the entire system. It was stepping back and looking at the total high school experience that caused the faculty at FHHS to reconsider how our high school is organized. As with our colleagues in many other high schools, ours was not a theoretical discussion like those that often take place in statehouses or universities, far removed from the day-to-day life of the high school experience. Rather, we began with what we know best, the daily experiences of teachers and students in our own school. When we looked at what a school day was like, at how it limited what students learned and their relationships with teachers, we knew it was time to do something very different.

To bring that picture into closer focus I'm going to share with you a typical day at our high school *before* we began to change the way we work. Follow students Sharon McMullins, Jake Delone, and Nina Mitchell and teachers Reba Theiss, Leon Talbert, and Donna Bennett from class to class as they try to teach and learn in an eight-period day.[7] While you might not be surprised, you should be disappointed by the system we've created for our children.

---

[7] All of these individuals are composites and their names are invented.

EIGHT PERIODS: ON YOUR MARK, GET SET, GO . . .

We will follow these teachers and students through their school day. To help you follow along, their complete daily schedules are reproduced here.

Teachers

		Reba Theiss	Donna Bennett	Leon Talbert
Homeroom	7:30–7:37	HR	HR	HR
First Period	7:40–8:23	Biology 2	U.S. History	Algebra 1
Second	8:26–9:09	Planning Period	U.S. History	Algebra 1
Third	9:12–9:55	Biology 1	Practical Law	Remedial Math
Fourth	9:58–10:41	Biology 1	U.S. History	Planning Period
Fifth (includes lunch)	10:44–11:57	Biology 1	Planning Period	Pre-Algebra
Sixth	12:00–12:43	Chemistry	Practical Law	Pre-Algebra
Seventh	12:46–1:29	Biology 2	Ancient Cultures	Algebra 1
Eighth	1:32–2:15	Physics	U.S. History	Pre-Algebra

Students

	Sharon McMullins	Jake Delone	Nina Mitchell
Homeroom	HR	HR	HR
First Period	U.S. History	Mythology	Algebra 1
Second	Drama	PE	Spanish 1
Third	Spanish 2	Study Hall	Civics
Fourth	Geometry	Parenting	English
Fifth	Health	PE	Biology
Sixth	Biology 2	Study Hall	PE
Seventh	Study Hall	Consumer Math	Study Hall
Eighth	Band	Industrial Technology	Typing

Monday morning, 7:00 A.M., at Federal Hocking High School. Reba Theiss and Donna Bennett are in their classrooms making last-minute preparations for the seven classes they will teach over the next seven hours. Reba will begin with a Biology Two class, followed by a forty-minute planning period. She'll then have three Biology One classes and finish the day with Chemistry, Biology Two, and Physics classes. Donna will teach four classes of

American History, two sections of Practical Law, and one section of Ancient Cultures.

At about 7:20 Leon Talbert comes in. While teachers do not have to report until 7:30, Leon, like Donna and Reba, likes to beat the kids through the door. The peace and quiet gives him a moment to recover from racing around his home getting his two preschoolers ready for their day. In the time he has, he checks through his folders to make sure he has graded and recorded the seven sets of homework papers from his three sections of Algebra One, three sections of Pre-Algebra, and one section of Remedial Math. Sometimes he finds he missed more than a few of the assignments he tried to grade between nine and midnight.

The day starts early for Sharon McMullins, Jake Delone, and Nina Mitchell as well. Sharon's bus picks her up at 6:50, Nina's at 6:45. Jake drives, but he tries to get to his girlfriend's house by 7:00 because his future mother-in-law always has breakfast ready for him. Sharon is out of bed by 6:00, planning on nearly an hour to shower, put on her makeup, and do her hair. Breakfast is not included in her morning routine. Nina, on the other hand, rolls out at 6:15, plenty of time to comb out her straight hair and munch on some bagels and cream cheese while reading one of the novels she always keeps nearby.

This Monday Jake is well rested. The Sunday night football game on television was a blowout and he fell asleep at 10:00 with the TV still on in his room. This was unusual for him, however, as he is usually up until 1:00 A.M. or so, figuring on plenty of time to catch up on his sleep at school. Nina, as is usual, heads for the bus well rested. Too young to have a part-time job and not involved in any activities at school, she is usually in bed by nine, spending an hour reading herself to sleep. Sharon arrives at the bus stop just on time, her eyes bloodshot as they often are on Mondays from not enough sleep. A member of the marching band, she spends her Friday evenings at football games and her Saturdays at competitions. She sleeps in on Sunday morning and it is only by Sunday evening that she finds the energy to tackle her homework—a task that usually keeps her up until the late hours.

By 7:30, Sharon, Jake, and Nina have made it to school, Jake always slipping in the door just as the first bell sounds. That bell

signals to Reba, Leon, and Donna that it is time to take attendance (a task they'll repeat seven more times) and read the
morning announcements to their homerooms. For seniors, like
Jake, announcements include the ordering of cap and gown and
plans for the class trip; most of the homeroom dozes. Sophomores like Sharon pay a bit more attention as the announcements include testing dates and plans for the dance on Friday.
Nina, like most freshmen, listens to all the announcements
closely, having not yet installed the filter that will soon begin to
screen out many of the least relevant items.

The teachers find themselves mentally doing other chores
while attending to the homeroom monitoring. This time doesn't
really feel like a class, the kids are only there for seven minutes,
and it is a new set of kids each year. Leon wonders why the time
couldn't be better spent, even just adding a minute to each class,
as he slips out to get to the office to copy a set of handouts he forgot for the Pre-Algebra classes. Reba and Donna also do not find
much useful in the homeroom period, but there's always been
one, and at least this way attendance can be taken by grade level.

At 7:37 the bell rings again (it will ring twenty more times in
the next six hours and forty minutes) and the three-minute dash
to first period begins. Reba, Donna, and Leon all know they
should be out in the hall during passing time, but it doesn't
always work that way. Today Reba wants to spend every available
minute getting the Biology Two dissection lab set up. Since
classes only meet for forty-three minutes, every second counts.
Last Friday the students were briefed on the cow heart dissection
they would do, assigned a lab partner, lab table, and equipment,
and given the lab assignment sheet. Reba knows she'll have to
remind at least half of the seventeen students which lab table
they are assigned to, and she has enough extra lab sheets to
replace the ten or so that will be left in lockers or with other
books. She's always frustrated by the number of students who
forget materials, and she knows that it would teach them responsibility if she made them go back and get their materials. But
with so precious little class time, that lesson is forsaken for the
larger academic lesson that needs to get started the moment the
bell rings. Of course, while she scurries to get the final touches
on the lab set up, she doesn't notice the homeroom attendance

form sitting on her desk which she forgot to send to the office. The oversight will cost her precious minutes of her first-period class when she is interrupted twice by office personnel who come looking for it.

Leon and Donna meet after the homeroom bell at their usual place—the locker area between their classrooms. Here they start their daily ritual of keeping track of the FHHS romances. Jake gets there first, slipping out of the library where his homeroom meets a minute or two early so he can be waiting for his girl-friend at the locker they share. When Maria shows up, they lock arms and wander out of the teachers' gaze to steal kisses that belie the fact that they have only been apart for less than ten minutes. Sharon and Nina just casually drift through the lockers. They both shoulder book bags that weigh more than thirty pounds as they carry all their books and assorted necessary mate-rials—magazines, makeup, address books, combs, curlers taken out on the bus, and gym clothes. It is quite a load, but with only three minutes between classes they would rather spend the time talking with friends than sorting through a locker. Gathering up two or three companions, each of them heads off in the direc-tion of her first-period class.

Almost by instinct, with about thirty seconds left before the bell signaling first period, teachers and students alike begin drifting toward their classrooms. Reba sets out the last of the jars of cow hearts, Donna starts checking off attendance, and Leon begins handing back graded homework from the day before. Sharon sits down in Donna's room and turns to talk to Laura, her best friend, who sits behind her. Jake lingers outside Maria's first-period Typing class until the bell begins to sound and then skips inside his English class as the teacher is pulling the door shut. Nina gives Leon her assignment in Algebra One and gri-maces as she is handed back a homework paper with fewer than half of the answers marked correct.

As the first-period bell finishes ringing, students scurry into classrooms, teachers take roll and post it on the door, last-minute makeup is applied, gossip is hushed but contin-ues, papers are shuffled, dropped, turned in, tossed out. Everything to this moment has been preliminary. School is about to begin.

*   *   *

"Ms. Theiss, I forgot my lab sheet."

"You'll find additional sheets at your station."

"But I forgot which station to go to."

"Those are on the board. OK, everyone should be getting their samples out and pinned down. Remember, key dissection today, then put the heart back in the jar. Tomorrow we finish and will take the rest of your hearts apart."

"Isn't that a country song, takin' my poor heart apart," croons one of the first-period juniors.

"Funny, funny. Let's go, you've only—"

"We know, forty minutes and counting," a chorus back to Reba as the students and teacher scurry about their jobs.

Meanwhile, on the other side of the building, Donna addresses her class on a favorite topic, the causes of the American Civil War. Notes are neatly printed on the board, and her comments richly supplement and add life to the dry treatment the topic receives in the text. Donna loves this era and tries to transmit that passion to her students. Today, for the most part, it works. The discussion of the role of black soldiers in the Northern army and their second-class status has been assisted by the showing of the film *Glory* the past week.

Leon has started the first-period Algebra class in his usual way, checking in with the class about their homework, asking which problems were especially difficult. He gets the usual response as well, silence. The Algebra One class first period is made up of freshmen, a group of fourteen- and fifteen-year-olds who are still a bit more than shy about admitting they don't know something. Leon knows that. He also knows, from just a casual glance at the papers turned in, that almost half the class missed the most difficult homework problems. The question he faces now, as he does every day, is whether to spend time getting those right with every student or to move on. It's his call and, like virtually every call a teacher makes, it is made in isolation and with one eye on the clock.

Jake has his eye on the clock too—at least his open one. His first-period Mythology class is not his favorite. He needed an English course for graduation, however, and this was the only one first period that did not require much writing. He is dozing peacefully in the back of the room as he does so often at the start of the day. The front of the room is filled with kids who are turned on to the topic, and the teacher focuses attention there. With a class of thirty, many who, like Jake, are there just for the credit, the teacher is happy to have so many students involved in today's discussion of Sisyphus. Jake, meanwhile, dozes on, figuring he knows just enough from skimming the reading to pass the exam.

Sharon is fascinated with the question Mrs. Bennett is raising about the role of the black Civil War soldier. She wonders to herself: Could the Civil War have been motivated by other things, things other than freeing slaves, if black soldiers were so mistreated by their supposed liberators? If only Donna could read Sharon's mind. This is precisely the question she hopes will come out of the discussion. But Sharon never raises it, knowing that if Mrs. Bennett finishes her lecture early the class will be given the remaining five or ten minutes of class time to use as they please. Third period will feature a Spanish Two test for which Sharon is not prepared, so every little minute helps.

Nina fidgets under Mr. Talbert's gaze as he waits for questions about the homework she just turned in. She wants to raise her hand, she wants to say, "Wait, I don't have any idea how to do half of those problems." She wonders why Mr. Talbert even asks if they understand. She obviously doesn't understand, given that she did not pass the homework from last week. She starts to get warm around the neck. Doesn't anyone else have trouble? Am I the only one who doesn't understand? I'm getting further behind, maybe I should just drop math? Mom said she could barely balance the checkbook, so why am I doing algebra? "Well, if there are no questions, let's go on to the next section"—Mr. Talbert's voice penetrates her chain of thought—"and we will plan for a quiz over this chapter for, say, Friday." And I'll plan on explaining another F to Dad, Nina thinks.

Back in the biology lab, time is running out and Reba races from group to group to help them get their samples ready to go back in their jars. "I know you're not finished with that ventricle, but get to class early tomorrow and catch up." "Make sure to stabilize the sample, don't let it fall apart as you put it in the jar." "Give me your lab sheets, I'll set them out for you tomorrow."

Donna has finished what she has always felt is her best lecture of the year and is waiting expectantly at the board for questions. There aren't any, and on one hand she feels good about that, because she knows the kids understood. But she is disappointed too. This is controversial stuff, and the film not only popularized it but helped kids see what she was talking about. Why don't any of the kids ask about the connection between the treatment of black soldiers and the North's supposed commitment to freeing slaves? "Well." She hesitates. "If there are no questions, use the last few minutes for review. Remember, test on Thursday." With that, Sharon pops open the Spanish book she has been surreptitiously glancing at beneath her notes all period.

Leon has finished the chalkboard explanation of the distributive property in polynomials and has answered a couple of questions. When no more come forward, he assigns the even-numbered problems to be turned in tomorrow and tells the class to use the last five minutes to get started. Nina closes her book and begins to gather up her materials. Second period is study hall and she will start then.

Jake is still snoozing in the back of English class when the bell rings signaling the end of first period. He wakes with a start and heads for the lockers and Maria. Reba uses the luxury of her second-period planning time to let the class go without finishing cleanup. She'll do it herself and still have time for coffee and a trip to the teachers' rest room. Leon realizes that once again he's only been able to help four out of the twenty-two students in Algebra One get started on their homework, and they were not even halfway to the toughest problems. Donna heads down the hall to the teachers' lounge with, as is always the case, two or three students following her asking questions about the assignment for tomorrow or the test or trying to schedule a makeup session for work missed last week.

The picture from first to second, third, and on through to eighth period doesn't change much for our students or teachers. All of them, in their own ways, figure out how to accommodate the system within their daily routines. Jake takes the easiest route. A senior who has no real plans past high school, he has signed up for courses that demand little of his attention. Two study halls, two sections of Physical Education, Parenting (which will prove to be most useful as his girlfriend Maria will be pregnant before the end of the year), Consumer Math, Industrial Technology, and the Mythology course. He has already earned before his senior year the twenty total credits he needs to graduate. The only courses he needs to pass this year are English and math, and in both cases he has chosen courses that figure to take little effort on his part. By the end of the year he will have passed those courses, with Ds. He will also have failed most of his other courses, concentrating on Maria and his car more than on school.

Nina would struggle her entire year with her courses. She had signed up for the traditional college prep sequence which included Spanish, Algebra One, Civics, English, Biology, the required Physical Education course, and Typing, her one elective. Algebra was her Achilles' heel, and once she fell behind in it, there was never enough time for her other courses. As the year progressed, her continuing struggle in math began to consume her to the point where her mother came in to talk with me. Nina had always enjoyed school, but now, according to her mother, she was frequently sick and wanted to stay at home. In fact, periodically Nina would show up in the office during first period complaining of stomach cramps and calling home for someone to pick her up.

Nina was unaware that her mother had been in. I arranged to see her one day during second period. "I want to drop algebra" were the first words out of her mouth when we sat down. "I can't do it, I'm too far behind, and when I work on it I don't have enough time for my other classes." I probed awhile, asking why she didn't like algebra, what it was about it she couldn't do. It has always seemed to me we should help kids master difficult challenges and not avoid them, so I wanted to make sure Nina was doing all she could to get through the course. In exasperation she finally blurted out, "Look, Dr. Wood, it's really very simple. I can't do algebra because of problem sixteen." Puzzled, I asked what she meant. "Well, in class we always learn a new thing. Then we all work the sample problem and I'm always sure I understand. Then Mr. Talbert assigns homework, the even-numbered problems. I start in class and get through a couple, but when I get home I get as far as problem number sixteen when they change the problem. I can't do any more, my parents can't help me, and I miss the rest of the assignment. See, problem sixteen." After one more week of trying, I approved Nina's dropping of Algebra One and moving to Pre-Algebra. Her attendance and grades picked up for the rest of the year, but I'm still not sure it was the right decision.

Sharon visits my home frequently. I had lived in Amesville, one of the several small towns that feed our school, for more than a decade before becoming principal, so I knew a number of the kids like Sharon quite well. One evening she stopped by the house for a recipe around 8:30. She had stayed late after school for marching band practice and to work on a skit her Drama class was putting together. After dinner and a couple of phone calls to friends she had begun her preparations for the next day, which included a cake for lunch with a favorite teacher and friends. The recipe in hand, she was headed out the door when I said, "Have a nice evening." "I won't," Sharon shot back. This was not like her, so I held her up for a moment to ask why not. "Oh, well, let me see. Tomorrow I have a test in U.S. History, a vocabulary quiz in Spanish, a monologue to have memorized for Drama, my usual Geometry homework of twenty problems, and I need to review my Bio Two notes because Ms. Theiss is giving one of her killer exams on Friday. See ya." With that she was gone.

A week or two later in a casual conversation with her mom I asked how Sharon managed to handle her load and the rest of her life. "Well, she doesn't sleep much, except Sunday when she sleeps all day. And I know she could do more in her courses, but her grades are pretty good." Sharon, in conversation with me at graduation where she was serving as a sophomore class marshal, had much the same to say when we were talking about the upcoming summer vacation. "I look forward to catching up on my sleep and really getting into some of the stuff we studied this year. I never had enough time to really get into the good stuff during the school year."

It is sixth period and Reba's lecture on chemical bonding is interrupted by a question from one of the seniors. He has noticed the lab materials left at the stations in the other part of the room and wonders when the Chemistry class will do another lab. She knows that part of the motivation behind the query is to slow down the class, perhaps preventing her from covering the chapter that is to be quizzed early next week. But she also knows it has been quite a while since the last chemistry lab and that she really should do another one. In fact, the labs are her favorite part of the class, giving her time to work directly with each student and to observe how well the kids can use what they are learning.

But how can she do any more? With classes lasting only forty-three minutes, the average lab takes five days—one day to discuss procedure with the class, one day for setup, one or two days to conduct it, and a day for writing out notes and observations. The room can accommodate only one set of labs at a time, so when it is tied up with a biology lab, students in chemistry, physics, and even the other biology classes have to wait their turn.

Reba has done the math in her head all too many times—180 school days, divided by five days per lab, divided by seven classes, equals about five labs per class *if* there are not too many days lost to bad weather. Five labs a year. Five labs that have to be carefully chosen to make sure they illustrate the key concepts in the field. Reba knows it just is not possible that five labs will have the impact on the students' way of thinking that she wants. Her only other choice is to increase the labs in one class at the expense of the others, another bad choice in her mind. So she supplements classroom labs with demonstrations and homework assignments that include extra credit for bringing in materials from home (insect collections, snakes, and fossils fill the room). Every day as she heads home she knows there are better ways to connect kids with science.

Leon gathers up the day's homework and packs it into his briefcase to be graded that night. Even before he starts on it, he knows that fewer than three-fourths of the students will earn a passing grade and a scant one in ten will receive an A or B. The problem is really very simple. Like Nina, many of the students do not get much help with math at home. Thus, while they feel they understand the concepts when working the sample problems in class, when they get home and the work gets harder they either do it wrong or don't do it at all. Of course, Leon never finds that out until Tuesday night when he is grading the homework done on Monday. By then he has usually moved on to new material, and the students are doing the Tuesday assignment even though they may not totally understand what went on before. He knows this confuses a lot of them, but he also feels pressured to cover the material so the classes are ready for the next course in the math sequence. Nothing in his teacher education program ever prepared him for this dilemma.

At the end of the year Donna surveys her final grade sheets. With a few exceptions, she is generally very pleased. Students do well in her courses, they enjoy her as a teacher, and she works hard to bring high-interest materials in to illustrate periods of American history. Yet she knows that she isn't able to reach her students as she wants. Donna loves her content; she is a student of the Civil War, and she makes annual pilgrimages to the sites she teaches about in the Ancient Cultures class. Every year her Law classes organize a mock trial team and every year they bring home awards for their performance. She wants to pass on her love for the field, her interest and desire to learn more, and that does happen for some students, but not enough. Obviously, it isn't that she doesn't try, but the obstacles to connecting in depth with every student seem impossible to overcome.

The first challenge is the sheer number of students she faces each day. Her four sections of the required American History class are always full, as are her three elective courses. She is a popular teacher who can never say no when another student asks to get in her course. This means she now teaches 182 students per day, one of the heaviest loads in the school. She knows that to get kids to really use their minds well, to really think about what she is teaching, she should assign more essays and have them do more research papers. But she cannot figure out how she would ever grade them. If she spent just 30 minutes per student reading their work every other week, that would be more than forty-five hours a week of grading alone, not to count the hours spent planning and preparing for her teaching. So she settles for multiple-choice and short-answer exams, hoping each student at least hits the main points and knowing many will go into more depth with things like the mock trial team.

There's the other obstacle, the time to do things like mock trial. Donna knows the large projects like mock trial and field trips such as the one she conducted to a visiting Egyptian exhibition in Cleveland are vital to motivating students to learn. These real-world connections to the academic material help her students see how the past connects to the present, how what they learn in school matters in their daily lives. But finding the time to carry out these activities within the confines of forty-three-minute periods is next to impossible. An extended practice period with the mock trial team requires that Donna get a colleague or myself to cover other classes. A field trip means time lost with all her other classes, as a substitute is usually more of a baby-sitter than anything else. Showing a film takes two or three days, good discussions just get started when the bell rings, student presentations have to be shoehorned to fit into the limits of the clock.

All things considered, it wasn't a bad year, she decides. But there has to be a better way; there has to be some way to teach for understanding, not just coverage. Yet coverage seems to be the best she can hope for when teaching 182 students a day, seven periods a day, for forty-three minutes each.

Donna, Reba, and Leon are good teachers. They care deeply about the education young people receive and work harder for the money they are paid than their counterparts in any other profession.* Sharon, Jake, and Nina, in their own ways, want to get something out of high school—a job, a ticket to college, or just knowledge about things they care about. Unfortunately, the way we organize high school prevents all six of these people, teachers and students alike, from doing the good work of which they are capable.

When I joined the staff of FHHS as principal during the 1992–93 school year I was convinced of one thing: that teachers like Donna, Reba, and Leon could do a good job with students like Sharon, Jake, and Nina *if* the structure of the school allowed it. I was also convinced, as was most of the staff, that the current way of organizing the institution we call high school did more to prevent learning than to assist it. The task we faced together was to imagine and then put into place a way of organizing our school that would enable all of us to do our best work.

---

* The starting salary in our district is $20,049. The most a teacher can make is $38,093. This means that teachers at FHHS are paid from $15.73 to $29.90 per hour—with no pay at all for the ten to forty hours a week they put in on lesson planning, research, grading, meeting with students after school, and similar tasks. Additionally, teachers are expected to provide their own tools, pay for their own professional development, and attend a wide range of after-school functions including sporting events, concerts, school board meetings, and graduation. Clearly this is the poorest-paid profession in America.

We began with our students. We wanted to know how they experienced high school, what they should be like when they graduated, how we could make the school a place where teachers and students knew one another well enough to work together. Institutions are built around formal roles: teacher, student, principal each playing a set part. We wanted a community built around personal relationships: students working with and for teachers who they knew were committed to their best interests.

This is where every good high school starts. Listen in to the conversation in the teachers' lounge and it will be about trying to understand kids; drop by after school and you'll see teachers spending extra time helping students with their work; read through lesson plans and you'll find references to students' experiences in what is being taught. The goal is to build the high school community around the kids. As opposed to much of the talk about school reform that starts with the needs of business or the economy, genuine school restructuring starts with the needs of the kids. They are the ones we are creating a community for, and it's with them that any effort to rethink schools must start.

CHAPTER TWO

Starting with Kids:
The Case for Community

Each day as I watch the students of Federal Hocking High School walk through our doors I am reminded of the many different stories they bring with them. Several of the staff and I make a point of standing on the wide walkway our kids use to enter the school in order to greet them as they start a new day. It's a good time to pat one or two of them on the back for a classroom achievement, congratulate an athlete or artist, set up appointments for the day, inquire about a family member, or check in to see how things are going for any student we're concerned about. For me it's like watching one of my children wake up and start the day—I can tell a lot about how school will go by watching how our kids come into the building.

As each of the classmates of Jake, Nina, and Sharon walks by me, either alone or with a circle of friends, I am reminded that no two of our students are the same. Past me strides the young man who is president of his class and the star of almost every athletic team, and who lives within the care of an extended family that shows obvious pride in the As he has earned in every class he has taken. On his way in he passes another young man who shares his age but little else. This student clearly carries the burdens that come from calling a string of foster placements home, trying to kick a drug addiction, and struggling to pass one out of every three courses he takes—burdens from which he finds refuge by sleeping in class whenever he can. Later a young woman who lives with her mom and her mom's string of live-in boyfriends, some more interested in her than in her mom, comes in. Walking with her is her best friend, a young woman who is on the cheerleading squad and who, along with her mother, father, and brother, is about to move into a brand-new home. A freshman walks by, head down, almost as if he wants not to be seen, a common posture for young people still unsure of who they are and where they are going. Past him pushes a classmate full of bravado and cheer, attempting to hide the frustration and pain of watching his parents fight through a messy divorce. Behind them both a pair of female freshmen stroll in, books cradled in their arms, heads bent together as they share secrets, laughing and enjoying a friend-ship that has lasted through years of small-town life complete with the security of parents with jobs, grandparents who visit regularly, and neighbors who are there whenever mom or dad can't be.

Thinking about what high school should be must start with knowing who our students are. This was one of the great plea-sures of joining the FHHS staff: the commitment to start with the kids. Unlike the avid discussions of policymakers, politi-cians, and (I'm sorry to say) university faculty, the talk among teachers and staff at our high school began with a focus on kids. How could we create a school program that would engage the minds of each and every one of our students? What sort of daily life in school would encourage the young adults with whom we work to do their very best? How might we use our stu-dents' stories to connect them to the academic agenda of the high school?

Our point of departure, in short, was the welfare of our stu-dents as opposed to the needs of the economy (How can we pre-pare better employees?) or the universities (What should schools do to prepare students for college?). Focusing first on students is the approach any genuinely good high school takes. Not that we are unconcerned about our graduates finding jobs or succeeding in college. Of course we are. But these are rela-tively low-level aspirations for a school. Consider seriously what skills it actually takes to do well in most entry-level jobs in the American economy. After you learn to read at about the sixth-grade level, do basic math, and follow directions, there isn't much else needed to get and hold a job serving hamburgers or assembling televisions.* Getting ready for college is only slightly more difficult. Know how to find information, write in well-constructed sentences with appropriate footnotes, do some higher-order math (depending on your field), take notes, and use your time well, and you can succeed in most undergraduate programs.

High school is about much more than that. It is democracy's finishing school—the last shared experience that all Americans will enjoy, the place where the skills and dispositions that citizens in a democracy need should be secured and nurtured in all of our youth. Our children leave high school as fully enfranchised citizens, not only able to take a job or go to college but also to vote, to engage in debate over public issues, to buy the house next door, to become our neighbors. To live up to this task, the place we call high school should be thought of not as a compilation of courses, grades, athletic teams, and band concerts. Instead it should be considered an experience that teaches each student, through example, what it means to be part of a democratic community.

I had just finished speaking at a high school in northern Ohio. Two students and two teachers from our high school had gone along, and their talks about the effects of the changes we had made in our school had held every member of the audience in rapt attention. While I was putting away my notes, a young woman approached me to thank us for our comments. She felt encouraged by the talks, especially the presentation by the students. In the middle of only her third year as a business teacher, she was dejected and defeated. She was, she said, already looking for a new line of work.

When I asked her why, I was taken aback by her answer. "It's the kids. They don't want to learn, they don't even show up more than half the time, and their parents don't help. Now, if I just had kids like yours, I might keep teaching." When I assured her that our students were not innately better than hers and that, in fact, they may have had even more to overcome, she just

---

* If there were more skills required, maybe I would get more requests from employers for the high school grades of our graduates. In the past five years, with more than five hundred graduates, I have not had a *single* employer ask for the academic record of a student.

mumbled something about it being "different here" and wandered off to lunch.

Like so many other Americans, our business teacher believes that the problem is not with schools, it's with our kids. Rather than try to make high schools fit our kids, we want kids to fit our high schools.* If they don't fit, we might run an alternative program or two for them, but the basic shape of high school goes unquestioned. Unquestioned and unchanged, in fact, for nearly ninety years, because we would rather blame the kids than take on the hard work of restructuring our schools.

The nature of life in high school is virtually the same today as it was at the turn of the century. If it were possible to take some residents of your town or city in 1910 and somehow "time travel" them to the present, there is very little they would recognize of their hometown. Some of the houses might be familiar, but the roads in front of them would now be filled with automobiles, not horse carts. Even in those familiar homes, electric lights would glow strangely from every window, a sign of a world of wonders including microwave ovens, electric refrigerators, stereos, televisions, and computers, just to name a few, that would totally disorient our guests. They would stumble in and out of stores, banks, even the post office unable to make much sense of how the town now operated. Looking for a familiar landmark, your time travelers might ask you to take them to the local high school.

On the surface the school would appear as different as anything else: a new building, with televisions and computers, filled with teens arrayed in strange costumes. But if you were to linger with your guests, it would not take long for them to become comfortable with a routine they remembered from their own teenage years. Children sitting in desks while teachers talk, bells ringing frequently demanding that students move from room to room, teachers presiding over their classrooms in splendid isolation, the principal patrolling the halls enforcing order and quiet. These are things the visitors would remember and understand as they settled into desks in the back of a classroom, happy at least something hadn't changed over the past nine decades.

---

* My elementary school colleagues have over the past two decades worked to make their schools fit students. The efforts to create "developmentally appropriate" elementary schools could teach those of us working in high schools a great deal.

None of the differences our visitors might notice would have seriously altered the traditional high school. Indeed, the only ongoing attempt to change high school has consisted of various campaigns to add to the existing program. Over the decades we've added more chapters in history books, more math, new discoveries in science, and volumes of new poets and authors. Those who pine for the "good old days" of schooling, believing kids learned more back then, might well find themselves amazed if they took a serious look at all we ask kids to learn today in school.

We've also added a wide range of topics that were, historically, not the purview of the school. In order to combat each problem we perceive kids to have, we add a new "educational" program: sex education, drug education, driver's education, vocational education, and so on. It is not without reason that the high school program is often referred to as the "add-on curriculum."

Finally, we've added all sorts of kids to our schools. The children of the poor, who had to leave school to join the work force; children of minorities who were denied entry to the school; young women whose place was thought to be in the home. All these young people now come to school. Just getting everyone in the door, however, is only half the battle. The second, just as crucial, effort must be about making sure the high school experience connects in a powerful and meaningful way with those children who attend. In order to do that we have to begin with who our kids are and be willing to recognize something most proposals for reform ignore—that the kids we educate today don't necessarily fit in yesterday's school.

Before alarm systems and safety checks, coal miners in our area would take canaries with them into the shafts. More sensitive than humans to the loss of oxygen or the presence of dangerous gases, the miner's canary by its illness (or death) warned of hazardous conditions. Similarly, children are society's canary in the coal mine. When social conditions begin to sour, we first see it reflected in the lives of children. And the first to notice that children are struggling for air are classroom teachers.

For the past two decades teachers have become ever more conscious of a growing illness among our children. Imagine a nation in which in one day 27 children—a classroomful—die from poverty, 788 babies are born at very low birth weight, 1,340 teenagers have babies, 2,860 children see their parents divorce, 5,703 teenagers are victims of violent crime, 8,189 children are reported as abused or neglected, and more than 100,000 children are homeless. This, according to the Children's Defense Fund, is the condition of children in America today. Children reflect back at us one of the highest poverty rates in modern American history, where one out of every four children is born into a family that lives below the poverty line. They signal the danger of living in a country where child nutrition programs struggle for funding while tobacco subsidies float through Congress with only limited debate. They bring home to us that if we spend less than $4,000 a year per school child while we spend $25,000 per prisoner, we'll only have more prisoners, not safer streets. It is in our schools that we first hear the alarms as more and more students come to class tired, hungry, uninterested, and, quite often, angry.

Our classrooms and schools are not only hearing and seeing the illness generated by poverty and violence. Even among students whose families are free from want, we see children who are gasping for breath. Spending an average of more than twenty hours a week before a television, they are bombarded with images of wise-guy heroes, violence as a reasonable answer to conflict, alcohol as an accepted tool for relaxation or friendship, and fleeting family relationships as the norm. Watching adults in public life offers our children little that is better than commercial television. Politicians bicker over who lies the most rather than address carefully the issues of the day. We spend millions of dollars paying professional athletes to play games and only a tiny fraction of that on teachers or ministers, while relations among adults of different ethnicity or culture deteriorate on the streets of our major cities and the avenues of our small towns. And the behavior kids observe in their so-called role models—from athletes spitting at or physically assaulting referees to movie stars being caught with prostitutes or drugs to politicians discredited by charges of sexual harassment or taking bribes—doesn't provide much of a model for a meaningful adult life.

It should be absolutely no surprise to anyone when teachers tell us that the students of today are somehow different from those of an earlier era. Bombarded with unproductive media images, surrounded by adults who seem unsure and disagreeable, and living in an uncertain world, our kids are only reflecting back to us what we ourselves look like. As one teacher put it, "I don't know of many children who aren't spoiled. They want gratification now, they want things their way. So few of them think of what is good for the whole group, they just want what is good for them. I'm afraid that if adults have taught them anything, it's how to look out for number one."

It's not that our children are innately less capable or more evil than we were when we went to school. It is simply that they live in a different world, a world that was created for them, not by them, a world they are trying their best to make sense of. It is that world that schools compete with for teenagers' attention and loyalty. We ignore it only at the peril of making high school irrelevant in the lives of many of our students.

It is important to stop here for a moment and caution ourselves to avoid the traditional blame-the-victim strategy Americans often embrace when confronted with social problems. Just like our business teacher at the beginning of this chapter, we could easily throw up our hands and abandon our concern with high schools by blaming kids for our schools' failures. This is a temptation I fight every day. When I watch a gifted student choose an "easy" project in order to protect a grade-point average, when I see a difficult child in my office once again because she has disrupted class, when I have to expel a youngster from school because of the threat he is to other kids, or when an obviously intelligent young person chooses just to "get by" rather than really work at school, I am often tempted to wash my hands of the affair and fall into the "Well, if Bobby had only tried harder" syndrome. Fortunately, it just isn't that easy.

Kids who do well enough but don't excel are really just responding to what we ask of them. It is no secret that most young people are happy to try and live up to the expectations of adults whom they trust. If you doubt this, look at the work of kids in all types of out-of-school activities—sports, work, Scouts, church, etc. While a few certainly don't live up to expectations, for the most part, kids are able to learn quickly and improve their performance with the appropriate training and support. One of the biggest problems we face is that, for these young people, the formal standards of schooling simply do not demand a great deal in terms of actual performance.

Of the kids who struggle in school I am, quite honestly, surprised that many of them do as well as they do in our classrooms. They don't have the childhood I had. My parents stayed together until my father's death, providing rides to every school event and a quiet room in which to study (and insisting that I did), never asking me to work to help support the family. I grew up around people who valued an education and were willing to sacrifice to make sure I had a good one. Even though my father never finished high school (the Depression intervened), he always preached its virtues, as did my mother, who worked her way through Iowa State Normal School in order to teach in a one-room schoolhouse on the Midwestern plains.

Today's world is making that sort of childhood increasingly rare. With both parents working just to make ends meet, many children are saddled with the care of siblings if they themselves do not have to work. As the number of entry-level jobs for which a high school diploma is required decreases, the value of doing well in school goes down as well. Faced daily with having to provide for themselves the things so many of us took for granted as children (from wake-up calls to getting to school, to buying and fixing meals), it shouldn't surprise us that high school as we now know it has little holding power for many kids. Sometimes its only holding power is as a source of the help with personal problems that we used to expect would be found at home. If it often seems in high schools that we spend more time on personal than on academic issues, this should come as no surprise—some kids simply have nowhere else to turn.

We should not fault kids for a world they did not create. They didn't ask for high schools run the way they are, families in crisis, the diminishing of decent entry-level jobs, or communities that provide few of the social structures and supports we used to take for granted. In fact, maybe we should pat them on the back for the job they are doing in a society that adults seem to have made quite a mess of. Beyond that we should take a good hard look at the high schools in which we want kids to spend five thousand hours, and make sure they are places where the young people of the late twentieth century can gain the skills and abilities to undo some of the harm we have already done.

But in fact, the vast majority of the proposals offered in the name of high school reform will do little to affect the high school experience of students like Jake, Nina, and Sharon. Currently, the lives they lead outside of school mean that the form high school takes today has at best a limited effect on them. Competition for their attention and engagement comes from all directions. Bombarded with media images, struggling to hold together families, sometimes even raising kids of their own, our children have plenty of things on their minds. We should not be surprised, then, that when we run high schools the way we do— structured as a series of infomercials some forty minutes in length, with nothing linking the subject matter of one to another, and at a pace that virtually prevents any meaningful human contact—today's students are at a loss as to why they should buy into our agenda.

As was suggested earlier, little in what is currently being offered in the way of high school reform will bring our schools into the twenty-first century. The approach is to reform children and their teachers, blaming them for the inadequacy of our secondary schools. Somehow we are to force them to learn more and teach harder, but not at the expense of our current school norms. Perhaps the best example of this blame-the-victim type of reform is the current rush to add more and more tests as ways of certifying kids to graduate. The scant positive effect this has on the daily lives of students demonstrates clearly the failure of nonstructural changes in high schools.

It is 8:00 A.M. on March 10, and there is a strange, almost unnatural silence in the halls of our school. In the cafeteria seventy students are hunched over test booklets stamped **State of Ohio: Ninth Grade Proficiency Test** in bold letters. Another eleven students, all seniors, are taking the same test in the library. They are given a separate space and separate attention, because for them the stakes are very high: either they pass the test on this, their eighth try, or they will not be given a diploma. The test runs all morning long. Today is the math test, a combination of computation, measurement data analysis, algebra, and geometry questions that has proved to be the hardest test to pass.

In the cafeteria the sophomores and juniors deal with the test in a variety of ways. A significant number finish the test in less than forty-five minutes, having rushed through knowing that they will have several more chances to take it. Others, especially the juniors who have not yet passed it, take a bit more time, knowing that their chances are running out. They bite erasers, figure and refigure problems, and many times just simply pray for divine guidance where all else fails.

In the library the scene is very different. The eleven seniors, four boys and seven girls, work so hard on the fifty multiple-choice questions before them that some of them break a sweat. The tension in the room is palpable even though our guidance counselor met them all before the test with juice, donuts, and a pep talk. Just one wrong answer too many, a question misread or a decimal point misplaced, and no matter what a student has done to this point, the student will not graduate.

For the week prior to the test my office has been occupied by these eleven kids and their parents. Rosemary's father cannot believe that his daughter, after passing all the required math classes, will not be allowed to graduate. His temper swings from anger at past math teachers to anger at the State of Ohio to genuine grief that his daughter, who has never crossed a teacher or skipped a day of school or failed a test, could be denied the diploma for which she worked so hard. So far she has missed a passing score by fewer than three questions. The last two times one more correct answer would have passed her. Rosemary cannot even speak during these meetings. She sobs every time she tries to talk. She is so distraught that for the two weeks prior to the test she comes to school only for math class and a special tutoring session. We excuse her from the rest of her classes, as she is unable to concentrate.

Julian is confident that he will pass the test. He claims that his girlfriend is tutoring him, and besides, just two more correct answers this time around and he's there. His easygoing demeanor disappears, however, when we discuss in earnest what will happen if he fails this time. Simply put, he promises that if he earns a failing score it will be the last we see of him, as he intends to drop out. He cannot see the point of continuing in his courses if it will not earn him a diploma. In fact, his teachers report that he has already begun to do very little in his classes, foreshadowing, perhaps, his potential rejection of the school that may, on the basis of one test score, reject *him*.

It would be wrong to think that for the rest of our students at FHHS life goes on as normal during testing week. Most classes grind to a halt all morning during the five days of testing. From day to day different groups of students are absent to take either the reading, writing, math, science, or citizenship test, and with as many as ten students missing from a class of twenty-five, teachers know that to cover new material is a mistake—they'll just have to reteach it the next day. Even those students who are not preoccupied with concerns about taking one of the tests during the week find it hard to concentrate as they worry about friends who have yet to pass. Afternoon classes are not immune from the Proficiency Tests' effect either. Students drained by the rigors of taking a test upon which their diplomas depend are about as ready to take another class that day as a law student who just finished the bar exam would be. During the October testing session the problem is magnified by the fact that more students test, including the entire freshman class taking the test for the first time.

A little math will demonstrate this loss of time. For the students to be gathered and given instructions, receive the test booklets and answer sheets, take the test, and be issued passes back to class, they will be involved in the Proficiency Tests for approximately two and a half hours. Repeated for five days, twice a year, this means that twenty-five hours, nearly four full school days annually, are given over to the tests. (This does not count the time lost to tutoring students, disruption of other classes, or counseling time for students struggling with the test.) Put another way, in the course of four years every student will lose sixteen school days to the tests. Sixteen days we will never have again, just to see if we can withhold diplomas from students who miss one question too many.

Rosemary made it. When she was called into my office with her father, the tears flowed again. They were tears of joy this time, however. Not so for Julian. Once again he fell two questions short of a passing grade. I broke the news to him, he uttered a few profanities and walked out the door, and I haven't seen him since.

The Ohio Ninth Grade Proficiency Test (conceived by the Ohio General Assembly in the early 1980s and first used to deny about five hundred diplomas to Ohio students in 1994) is one of those highly touted school reforms with which politicians and bureaucrats are so enamored. The assumption was that adding these tests to the credits required for graduation would force schools to improve. The reality is that very little has changed as a result of these tests. After nearly a decade of such testing programs across the country, the public perception of the quality of our graduates is unimproved, we still hear calls for school reform, and everyone knows our high schools could be better. The most glaring flaw in this reform has been that it does not cause high schools to change their basic structures in ways that would build the types of learning communities we need to help today's teens do quality work in school. This is best illustrated by seeing how the five students we have met so far have been affected by the Ohio Ninth Grade Proficiency Test.

For Sharon the effect has been almost unnoticeable, as she passed all the tests on her first try in her freshman year. Most certainly she lost five days of school to testing and several more as the years went on, as large numbers of her classmates missed class to take the test again, leaving her teachers with little to do but wait until class returned to full strength. But the basic structure of school, the way they spend five thousand hours, has not changed for her or for the thirty-five percent or so of her fellow students who also took just one try to pass the test. Some of them, in fact, place way too much importance on having passed the test, more than one challenging a teacher with "I've already passed the Proficiency Test, I don't need any more math [or English or social studies]." What was meant to be a minimum standard has become the maximum achievement.

Julian lost, during the four years of his high school career, thirty days of schooling to the Proficiency Tests. He also spent a fair amount of time with tutors who were trying to drill facts into his head so he might pass on the next try. (In some schools he might have also found himself placed in a remediation class geared to the test.) But for the most part the only real effect on Julian was to increase his cynicism about school. "What it all boils down to, Doc, is that I have to pass this test and then I am done with school, right?" he pointed out one day in my office. I agreed that was one way to look at it. "Enough pencil marks on the right little dots on one piece of paper . . . not much to show for twelve years of school, is it?" In his own way, he was a very insightful young man.

Rosemary and Jake carried the Proficiency Tests around with them like a weight on their backs. Each year they passed one more test, and each year they failed several others. As with so many kids, failure often meant just missing one answer too many. Jake would stop by and ask if he really would be denied a diploma because of just one answer. Rosemary always looked scared. Each time she took the math test it was a different sub-part of the test that failed her. She would study hard for that section, and the next time she took the test she'd fail a different section.

Nina does not seem to even notice the tests. She rips through them in record time, never checks her answers, and fails miserably. While she knows that someday there may be a consequence of her poor work, it doesn't seem to bother her now.

If the tests have done little to improve the daily experience of students, they have done even less to improve the conditions of teaching. Teachers are held accountable for preparing students to pass a test that they did not construct and have never seen. School after school has altered its curriculum in an attempt to "teach to the test." In many cases this has meant abandoning previously successful classes or experiences and replacing them with a course designed to drill students in all the possible correct answers. Any change in scheduling, curriculum, or school organization that does not immediately yield an improved Proficiency Test score is branded a failure. It matters not if students write or read better, demonstrate more skill in debate or discussion, or can analyze more carefully a mathematical proof or chemical reaction. If it doesn't help them guess which of the five multiple-choice answers is the correct one, it will be cut as soon as possible.

Increasing the number of tests has virtually no positive effect on the daily lives of kids in high school. Launched without any real sense of what needs to change in the basic structure of high school, the tests merely ask kids to do *more* of what is already not working. We have always tested kids, but the reason we test has almost nothing to do with kids.

Is This All That High School Is About?

As noted, one of the biggest reforms pushed in the State of Ohio is the state-mandated Ninth Grade Proficiency Test. This test, the passing of which is required for graduation, has done little, if anything, to change the high school experience for students. In fact, by causing teachers to "teach to the test," the net effect of the test may be a "dumbing down" of the curriculum. A few of the questions from the sample test (it is against the law for anyone other than students to see the actual test) demonstrate how mundane and trivial is most of the knowledge that the tests cover. The point is not that young people shouldn't know this material. Rather, it seems hard to believe that making them pass one more test such as this will really help them be better prepared in math or a more active democratic citizen.

From the Math test:
1. During their last vacation, a family took a train trip. They traveled 594 miles in 9 hours. What was the train's average speed?
    A. 56 mph
    B. 60 mph
    C. 66 mph
    D. 585 mph
2. Which is the correct order to show capacity from smallest to largest?
    A. pint, cup, quart, gallon
    B. cup, pint, gallon, quart
    C. pint, cup, gallon, quart
    D. cup, pint, quart, gallon

From the Citizenship test:
1. If Mariko wanted to serve her community, in which of the following activities should she be most actively engaged?
    A. read a book on constitutional law
    B. buy a national news magazine
    C. get a job in a local supermarket
    D. collect canned food for a local food drive
2. Yevgeny was born in Marion, Ohio, although his parents are not citizens of the United States. Yevgeny's parents came to the United States from the Ukraine. Which of the following is true of Yevgeny?
    A. Yevgeny is a U.S. citizen because his parents came from a foreign country.
    B. Yevgeny cannot become a U.S. citizen until his parents do.
    C. Yevgeny will not be a U.S. citizen until he is naturalized according to the procedure required by the Bill of Rights.
    D. Yevgeny is a U.S. citizen because of the 14th amendment to the United States Constitution.

Try this sometime. Ask a bunch of high school students what scores they earned on a recently administered standardized test. Then ask what the score means. Usually the first question will be answered quickly, some number or percentage rapidly offered. The second, however, will get you nothing more than a mumbled response about knowing more or less than other students or, more often, a simple "I don't know." Kids don't know what the scores mean because the scores are not for them. These numbers are for adults, so we can decide who goes to college, who gets a diploma, who goes into the most advanced programs. Rather than take the time to study the work of students, to really see what they can and can't do, we opt for a quick and easy numerical score to tell us whether or not a student should graduate.

Most of what we are seeing today in the guise of high school reform operates in the same way as requiring more tests does. Leaving unchanged the basic nature of the high school, reforms just call for more of what we are currently doing. Have kids in school for more and longer days, give them more homework, raise standards, let parents choose schools. The list goes on, but the more things change the more they seem to stay the same.

There are three reasons for the predictable failure of school reforms like the Proficiency Test, reasons that echo the similar failure of the Carnegie Unit imposed more than a hundred years ago. First, such mandates are not based on a genuine understanding of day-to-day life in our public schools. They do not start by calling into question the age-old assumption of how high school operates. Rather, these reforms begin by accepting the way high schools function and merely ask us to do more of the same. So we pile yet another task on the already overburdened school, usually fragmenting the school day into yet smaller and smaller pieces. And of course there is never any additional funding offered to help take on the new testing program or other, similar initiative.

Second, such mandates do not pause to consider the way in which students view the high school experience. One more requirement on top of those that our students are already choosing to ignore, avoid, or merely accommodate will not cause them to make better use of their minds or be more involved in their education. If anything, such a plan will only cause them to be more cynical about the high school experience, believing that one standardized test equals a high school diploma. Furthermore, such standardized reforms do not take into consideration that we do not teach standardized children. They all come with their own stories, needs, abilities, hopes, dreams, and fears, and if we are to reach them, we need to understand them and meet them where they are before we can take them somewhere new. As I have tried to point out, high schools are competing with a wide range of social forces for the attention of our kids. To compete with these forces and reach every student will require building a whole new sense of community in high schools to make up for the loss of community many of our children experience. Just adding a test here or there will not make this happen.

Third, reforms such as proficiency tests overlook any serious consideration of what we want our schools to do for our children. Is the result of twelve years of schooling to be nothing more than the ability to answer thirty-four out of fifty questions on tests of math, citizenship, and reading and to write a single essay or business letter? What do we want from our schools? What can we reasonably expect of high school graduates in terms of their contribution to our society? These questions, never asked when so many of the quick-fix reforms are adopted, are essential to any discussion of school change.

Once again, the point to remember is that while our children and our world have changed, our schools have not. For a variety of reasons we cling to outmoded ways of running high school, and our changes proposed for schools simply keep that system afloat. Meanwhile, our high schools continue to graduate students who have been only marginally changed by the experience. To be sure, they have been motivated by a teacher or two and have heard and seen new things. But the payoff for five thousand hours of their time has been limited. Beyond that, many of us are unsure that the young people leaving our high schools are the neighbors for which we had hoped. As I've said, the American high school is democracy's finishing school. It is the last common experience we all share on the road to becoming neighbors, coworkers, and fellow citizens. Reforms that do not address this core mission, that do not lead to providing our young people with the experience of community, will fail to bring about the meaningful change we seem to desire in our high schools.

I am certain that our high schools can be restructured to provide something much more for Jake, Nina, Sharon, Rosemary, Julian, and their friends. I am also certain that the changes required to have the impact we want on our future neighbors and community members will require diligent and difficult work on all of our parts. We will have to challenge every single one of our assumptions about school. How we use time and staff, how we organize kids, what and how we teach, how we know what kids know, absolutely everything must be questioned. In each case the only constant should be the quality of the work our children do. Everything can and should change in the name of improving what our kids can do as a result of the time they put in at school. And the centerpiece to such change should be creating a sense of community in each high school.

We continue to flounder in trying to create high schools that would genuinely connect with our kids. We accept the institutions as they are and do little to change their orientation. However, as we see with the continuing failure of reform agendas, what is wrong with our high schools is that they are simply not structured to connect with our kids. In settling for this institutional approach to high schools, trying only, on occasion, to fix things up by adding on a few extra programs, tests, or governance structures, we have left unchanged the basic outline of the high school.

For high school to be meaningful in a student's life it must gain that student's loyalty. Having worked closely with teenagers for most of my adult life (to say nothing of having been one and now raising one), I am absolutely convinced that you cannot make a high school student learn anything. Rather, teenagers must willingly assent to learn, they must volunteer, if you will, to give up all sorts of other pursuits—both legal and illicit—to learn from their teachers. They do this for one of three reasons.

The first, one we have used for years, is effective with a small and increasingly smaller group of kids—we threaten them. The typical threat is grades: either do this or your grade will go down. The latest set of threats comes in the form of high-stakes testing as with the Ohio Ninth Grade Proficiency Test; you pass this test or you don't graduate. We can continue to rely on such threats, adding more and more hurdles for kids to clear, but with little change to ways they experience high school each day.

But there are two other reasons high school students learn, reasons that will connect with all our children, not just a few. Both of these ways, which get students to volunteer to learn, have to do with loyalty.

One loyalty is to teachers. When young people build connections to teachers, connections based on trust that what the teacher asks the student to do is in the student's best interest, they can and will commit to the school's agenda. The second relies on the appeal of the material. When young people see that what they are being asked to learn is useful or in their best interest, they are likely to join up with the effort to learn.

Institutional settings do not encourage such loyalties. Devoted as they are to serving the needs of the organization and not its members, they tend to treat people as interchangeable parts. It does not matter, for example, who works for an institution, because the institution will go about its business whoever works there. Take the case of our large automobile manufacturers. It would be hard to imagine these institutions deciding henceforth to make cars only in consultation with their employees' wishes. No, they are going to make cars no matter who works for them, and if an employee does not like that agenda, he or she can always work somewhere else. The same is likely to be true of any institution, be it a university, social service agency, industry, or governmental department; the institution serves its own ends and the people who work within it only provide a means to that end.

Our high schools today are just as much an institution as our automobile manufacturers. Beginning with the push to large, urban secondary schools at the turn of the century, the orientation of all we do has been to serve the needs of the institution, not its members. Take time, for example. Why did we come up with the Carnegie Unit? To provide a quick and easy accounting method for college admissions. To make the Carnegie Unit work, we divided up the school day into the small isolated chunks of time described in chapter 1. The institution's need for a uniform accounting system of student credits was met. Simultaneously, however, the needs of the people in the school, both student and teachers, for the time it takes to do the work well have been largely ignored. The focus is not on what kids learn or how teachers teach, it is on how the school accounts for the time spent on each segment of subject matter.

There are dozens of other examples, both profound and mundane, of how our high schools are oriented toward institutional management at the expense of student achievement. Take the textbooks from which we teach. We have all seen students who love to read, yet reject any involvement at all with school textbooks. Even the most exciting events in the social sciences can be turned into boring, detailed yet fleshless accounts of past events in the hands of a textbook author. So why do we use them? Simply put, because then we can control what everyone teaches. Assigning a textbook to a course simplifies the answer to the question "What should we teach?" and gives control of knowledge to school authorities. Individual students, teachers, or even administrators often have little choice in what is to be taught—a topic we return to in chapter 4. The point here is the way in which knowledge serves the organization, not the individual.

A similar institutional orientation prevails around the rules for teacher certification. High school teaching has evolved into a field of specialists. Every teacher has to hold a certificate, earned through amassing college (you guessed it) credits, to teach in a particular field. Within each field subcertification rules apply, with some science teachers able to teach Biology but not Chemistry, some social studies teachers able to teach U.S. Government but not U.S. History, and some English teachers allowed to teach Advanced Composition but not Journalism. Again, all is based not on actual competence but based on certificates granted based on courses taken in college. Even though these certification requirements create scheduling nightmares as we lose faculty flexibility owing to the certification limits, we continue to decide who is capable of teaching what on the basis of paper credentials rather than genuine expertise or the ability to inspire the loyalty of students. It is the need of the institution to be in charge of people rather than to be responsive to people that dictates these rules.

Nothing points up our institutional orientation toward high schools more clearly than their size. Institutions love large numbers, as largeness justifies all sorts of things: big administrative staffs, elaborate buildings, specialization of roles—and, most of all, the many-layered and impersonal rule making that so typifies the modern institution. Confronted with thousands of daily interactions between staff and clients or customers, institutions do not know enough about individuals to trust in their good judgment or reasoned decision making. Rather, in the name of insuring consistency (or the oft-abused concept of "fairness"), policy manuals and standardized rules guide all behavior and dictate all decisions. The watch phrase "It's just the rules" echoes through every institution as organizational rules override personal needs.

When we think about the institutional focus that our high schools have adopted, it's important to note how little of what we do helps young people learn. The way we use time, the textbooks we choose, the certification requirements and policy manuals and a host of other rules, structures, and regulations have little if anything to do with how well students use their minds. But that isn't the point anyway. What is really at issue in our high schools is how to keep control of kids while doling out a standardized curriculum that certifies (not qualifies) their acceptability for the next phrase of their life, be it a job or college. That the high school experience might be of value in and of *itself,* that it might be more personalized so that it connects with every student, is simply not possible within the institutional structures that we have built around our high schools.

There is an alternative. We could embark on an entirely different way of thinking about the high school experience for Sharon and her friends. Instead of reforms that seem designed only to keep our institutions running, we could abandon our institutional approach to high school altogether. In its place we could put a learning experience that would not only better meet the needs of our children today but would also help us nurture the habits of mind and heart that make a democratic society possible. We could choose to have our schools be learning communities rather than settle for educational institutions.

In what follows I draw upon the experiences of the faculty and students at FHHS and other high schools that have been working to build learning communities. It was a process that we began in the 1993–94 school year at FHHS, following the lead of other schools that had dared to dream that their high school might become a community rather than remain an institution. It seems to me that three common factors emerge from this work that every high school faculty could, in its own way, adopt and adapt to restructure their institution as a community. The first of these has to do with structure and size, as genuine communities control their size in order to closely connect with every member. The second has to do with what is taught, and an orientation toward helping every member of the community to do good work now, not in some far-off future. The third is a commitment to supporting every member of the community in making meaningful connections with the world beyond the community, and in so doing enabling each to learn that one person can make a difference in the world.

Given the world our kids face, I am convinced that organizing high schools as learning communities is our best chance at gaining and holding their attention. My sense is that Jake, Nina, Rosemary, and all the rest want to belong, want to be considered important. The challenge they face is finding someplace where what they do makes a difference. High school could be that place, and we now turn to how to make that happen.

CHAPTER 3

Getting to Know Kids: The Power of Smallness

We should begin rethinking the five thousand hours kids spend in high school by admitting the obvious—our high schools are simply too big. Most American high schools house more than a thousand students, and most American high school students share seven to eight teachers with more than two hundred peers every day they are in school. Such numbers clearly spell out the impersonal nature of the places in which we expect the most personal act of learning to take place. It simply will not happen. Having our high schools become learning communities will have to begin with making them small enough to personalize each student's experience.

We have accepted large schools for a variety of reasons. Bringing together large numbers of kids would create, we were told, "economies of scale." One facility, with one gym, a large shop, and several science labs, could replace several facilities that all had to maintain each of these expensive spaces. Furthermore, bringing together large groups of students would mean that more specialized courses could be offered. With a thousand students you are more likely to fill up an Advanced Chemistry or Wood Shop Three class. By reducing the number of schools, we were told, we could have more specialized attention for less money.

We were lied to.

Specialized attention to young people as learners does not come from having the latest lab facilities or biggest school auditorium. In fact, our high school students today receive much less personal attention than they did in the small high schools of four decades ago. What they do get from our large schools are fancy swimming pools, big-name athletic teams which attract college recruiters, and a wider selection of courses—along with longer bus rides, less time with each teacher, and fewer opportunities for individual students to have an impact on their school or their school to have an impact on them.

Beyond being too large in terms of total numbers, high schools create size problems by the way they organize their schedules. The constant treadmill of changing classes every forty to fifty minutes multiplies by seven or eight times the number of teacher-student pairings. This means that even in small high schools we have created a setting where too many students get too little attention.

Time and time again at FHHS we have seen the effects of schools that are too large for students. During the year we receive a number of transfer students, many from larger schools. Often these students have not been successful at their former school for a variety of reasons. But at FHHS within weeks we notice a difference, and the parents often call to make sure that it really is true that their son or daughter is doing so well.

Charity was one such case. Transferring in from a school of more than sixteen hundred students with a traditional eight-period day, she was defiant and noncommittal when she met with the guidance counselor and myself. A sophomore, she had failed most of her courses and was under the court system's supervision for truancy. Rather than rehash her previous difficulties, we thought we would start at the end and ask her what she would like to do when she graduated.

"Buy a van and follow the Grateful Dead," Charity responded.

The guidance counselor and I exchanged surprised looks. Usually beginning with what a student wanted to be able to do upon graduation led to a productive discussion of an academic plan. But there wasn't a lot the school could offer that would help a student become a member of the Dead's entourage.

Charity wouldn't say much more to us. We were, in her mind, a "hick" school. Little about school interested her, and now she was even worse off, banished from the fast-paced life of the city to our small country school. Without much help from Charity we pulled together a schedule and sent her out with a student escort to learn the ropes.

For the first several weeks Charity was a regular feature in my office. She would either do nothing in class or cause a disruption of some sort. Her teachers met with me and the guidance counselor, and we all met frequently with Charity. We worked hard to find some way to get her to connect with the school. Then, suddenly, she stopped showing up in the office. I heard fewer concerns about her from teachers. In fact, I almost forgot that she was new and had had such a rocky adjustment time.

Several weeks later one of her teachers dropped in to see me. "By the way, are you coming to the Roaring Twenties celebration we're having Wednesday night?"

I indicated that I would be there, as it was an event the entire school seemed wrapped up in, even though it involved only two classes.

"Well, keep an eye out for Charity. I think you'll be pleased."

Indeed I was. There she was that evening, center stage, playing a famous movie actress of the time and being called back for an encore—quite a change from the kid who would have nothing to do with our "hick" school and staff. Later that evening I had the opportunity to talk with Charity's father. I let him know how pleased I was with her performance, and how much better she seemed to be doing in school. In fact, I said, we were seeing none of the behavior that seemed to have been such a problem in her former school.

"That's because she's convinced you people really care about her," he replied.

I remember how struck I was by that answer. Charity's father said that, indeed, Charity at first had hated it at FHHS. "They're always bothering me," she would complain to her dad. "Why don't they just leave me alone?"

"But," he went on, "when she knew the teachers weren't going to go away, when she had been as difficult as she could be and still they wouldn't give up on her, well, that's when it started to change. We're not there yet, but we're getting there." And with that he went off to find his daughter.

Indeed, we were not there yet with Charity. In fact, the very next day she skipped out of school for part of the day. We're not there yet with a lot of kids, and we know it. But we get closer to being there with every kid because we are small enough to make contact with each and every one of them. Charity's lack of success at her prior school was not because teachers or administrators didn't care. She wasn't successful because it was too hard to care about too many kids. She had become anonymous, she wasn't noticed. And when she failed to attend, she was just one fewer student in an already overcrowded school.

Charity's story is repeated again and again in high schools that are simply too large to connect with the young people who attend them. Too large not only by total number but too large in everything, from the number of students teachers try to teach to the number of teachers from whom students try to learn. As in so many places in our society, the people in our schools have become mere numbers, known as test scores, identification numbers, or client counts for special services. This has happened to our kids at the very moment in our history when they need more, not less, adult contact in schools.

What strikes me as the fundamental difference between the lives of high school students today and the lives of the children I grew up with is the influence of peer pressure. For a wide variety of reasons our young people have fewer adults upon whom to model their behavior. Almost forty-five percent of school-age kids do not live with both biological parents, and more parents have to work as the poverty rate grows.* Both of these trends mean that kids spend less time with the people who were traditionally their most important role models, their parents. One replacement for this influence has been the adults children do spend a great deal of time with, those on television—adults who are, for the most part, fairly irresponsible and rather poor role models. By that I mean they are unable to delay gratification, using sex and alcohol to solve most problems; they seldom hold any job that requires long hours of hard work; they only spend, never save or give to charity, all the money they "earn."† For

* See *Education Vital Signs* (Alexandria, Va.: National School Boards Association, 1994).
† It is also interesting to note that students' scores on the National Assessment of Educational Progress go down with each additional hour of television the students say they watch per day.

example, think of Roseanne as teaching manners, Al from *Married . . . With Children* as teaching a work ethic.

When our kids are not taking messages from television they turn to their peers. Lacking the experience that is necessary to make long-term decisions, they encourage one another to engage in risky behavior that often challenges their health and well-being, such as the use of drugs or alcohol or practicing unprotected sex. Academically, they lack a context within which to judge the value of what they are learning. Having never voted in an election, attended college, or held a full-time job, they either accept or reject the school's agenda in accordance with their short-term interests.

Young people have always been under the influence of other young people. Part of growing up is learning how to choose friends, sorting out whose advice to trust, and knowing that there are times when the past experiences of others limit or expand the quality of the advice they give. But the limitations of relying on peers for induction into the adult world have, in the past, been mitigated by the presence of adults—adults who can prevent young people from making sometimes disastrous decisions, who can counterbalance inexperience with experience, who demonstrate that the rights and privileges adults enjoy are coupled with responsibilities and obligations to the community and family.

Because our children seem to have such diminished interaction with adults, teaching in our schools has become more difficult. The long-term value of using one's mind well and developing the skills to be a lifelong learner is difficult to convey to teenagers who see athletes make millions, watch television heroes ridicule their parents, or live in a home where no one holds a job. We compound this challenge by having teachers work with more kids daily than they can possibly get to know well.

To connect with students and to get them to use their minds well in solving difficult problems requires that the adults in high schools play a more significant role in students' lives. In a sense, we need to structure high schools today in ways that recapture the best of the early school experiences in cities and villages. In the days of small one-room schoolhouses, teachers lived among their students, often visiting the families. They taught not only academics but the relationship of schooling to their students' communities and future work. In the settlement schools of the early twentieth-century urban tenements, teachers worked to help children and their families find ways to combat the daily ravages of poverty. Additionally, they helped young people develop the skills to find jobs and organize politically to oppose the graft and greed that kept them in substandard living conditions. While the shortcomings of these schools were many, their strength was the bond built between teacher and student. We need similar relationships between students and teachers today.

For some kids who lack the family support many middle-class students enjoy, this close tie between teacher and student is the best chance they will have to learn what it means to hold a job and to see that education can make a difference. Living in homes where they are often the only one that has to get up and go somewhere in the morning, they don't have the familial support needed to connect current decisions with long-term consequences. The rationale for even the most basic academic tasks, like writing a business letter or figuring a percentage, escapes them as they seldom see such activities in their own homes. For example, in a conversation I had with one young man, he told me he had never eaten in a restaurant with a menu or silverware on the table, had never seen a magazine come in the mail, and did not know what a resume was.

These students are rarely exposed in their everyday lives to the use of the tools they could gain in school. They don't see their parents or other adults whom they trust and respect reading for pleasure or information, engaged in trying to make sense of the issues of the day, or making a contribution to their community by teaching a Sunday School class, volunteering at the school or food bank, or serving on a city council or citizens group. These are the more intrinsic virtues of school, but the kids we are discussing lack the extrinsic motivation as well. They do not live with anyone who holds a job that offers any advancement or fringe benefits, and thus the schooling that such positions require holds little allure. They simply have not seen how working hard at schooling can pay off.

Therefore, if kids with limited horizons are ever to value the mission of the school, it will take more than revamping the curriculum or offering more stimulating activities (topics we explore later). It will also require putting them in close touch with an adult role model who can demonstrate that engaging in the hard work of learning is worthwhile. This is a task the current size of many high schools cannot accommodate.

For students who come from more affluent homes and neighborhoods, this close connection with their teachers is just as valuable, albeit for somewhat different reasons. Each of these young people is also influenced by the messages of the media. While these are mitigated by family members who work and who take an active and important role in their lives, the students still harbor doubts about what they are asked to learn in school. (Some of the doubts, I will argue later, are very well founded.)

Consider the cases of three such students, William, Beverly, and Clifton. William, a junior who is also captain of the basketball team, president of his class, and in the top ten academically, shrugs those doubts off and presses ahead, doing whatever it takes to keep his grade-point average high enough to enter the top-flight college he has his sights set on. Beverly, a senior cheerleader, popular and pleasant to be with, is already assured of a place in the local technical college and does no more than necessary to maintain a B average so that school does not interfere too much with her social life. Clifton is also a senior and currently giving his parents fits, as he has decided that school is just not worth the effort and he has little to do with it.

In each case a lack of connection between teacher and student limits what school can do for the child.

William always turns in good work—but from year to year it is remarkably the same. His writing follows the same conventions, his interpretations of history are seldom expanded by new readings, his science experiments seldom explore anything outside of the text, even in math he is always more comfortable with the practice drill and struggles when mathematical operations are used in new ways. But he does well at what he does, his grades stay up, and so he never ventures beyond the formulas, never tries an approach that could be a dead end, and rarely reads a book of his own choosing out of interest or curiosity. His teachers, who see him for just one or maybe two courses throughout his high school career, view him as an ideal student, never knowing that he is not finding out new things, just giving them what has worked before.

Beverly has found that little effort is required of her to do school well enough. The high school diploma is, after all, just a ticket to college. Now that that ticket is punched, there is not much that high school offers her besides a place to meet her friends. She tolerates it for that purpose, complaining whenever a teacher suggests she could take some work home or study for an upcoming test. Beverly has never really found out how much she could do. Getting by on her promptness, neatness, and just raw ability, she rests comfortably in her ranking in the middle of her class. Teachers know her for her steady work and leave her to her own devices as they spend more time with struggling classmates.

Clifton would surprise his teachers and parents if they knew just a bit more about him. For example, by Wednesday of each week he's read almost the entire Sunday *New York Times,* which supplements his views gathered from *Rolling Stone* magazine and *U.S. News and World Report.* He's an avid reader of comic books and the novels of Douglas Adams, listens to Nirvana and Garth Brooks, and is sure that the year 2000 will not arrive for humans on earth. School, it seems to him, is largely irrelevant. While he knows he would struggle to learn math and his spelling is poor, he could ace the other courses. But most of what school offers seems of interest only to teachers. The American History text is his favorite example. "Can you possibly imagine a book more boring than that?" he loves to ask. But what Clifton cares about goes unnoticed, and he in turn takes little notice of what the school cares about.

If the high school is to have an impact on the lives of our children, that impact will have to begin with a close connection with teachers—teachers who know what matters to their students, what strikes their interest, what would take them beyond the routine. These things can only be discovered through working closely with a student. All of our technology, textbooks, and tests will never replace the impact one human being can have upon another. Rethinking our schools requires finding ways to reclaim the educative, guiding function significant adults can play in the lives of young people. This means making prolonged contact between learner and educator a priority in restructuring our high schools.

The first step in building high school communities where these close ties can be developed, nurtured, and sustained is in rethinking the size of our schools. In a genuine community no one is anonymous. Everyone knows everyone else, and no one feels left out. Even more important, in communities members come to trust one another. They are willing to do things simply because someone they have come to know over time has asked them to. These personal connections can only be built in places small enough that everyone can meet face to face. So it should be in high schools.

Earlier I suggested that high schools had opted for bigness ostensibly because of the supposed benefits of size. I also mentioned another reason: The large, at times huge, size of our high schools justifies the institutional approach we have taken toward them. Largeness in any organization justifies layers of bureaucracy (and the jobs that go with that), standardized rules uniformly applied, and authority centrally held by the few people who (claim to) know what is best for the entire organization. So it is in large schools. They require multiple administrators, each with an area of specialization—student discipline, curriculum, athletics, staff development, etc. Life is organized around a set of rules that, because of the large number of students, have to be uniformly applied to nonuniform students. And above it all towers one individual, the principal, supported by assistants, whose control is often predicated upon knowing what is best for a school too large for anyone to know about all its parts.

In our oversized, impersonal schools we lose daily the attention of thousands of students. Most certainly there are niches carved out that accommodate some kids—drama clubs, sports teams, bands, and debate squads. But many of our children, far too many, are just drifting through. Like shoppers wandering through the local mall, once in a while spending enough time in a store to make a purchase but for the most part ambling aimlessly, using up time, hoping something might strike their fancy, so the teenager may find a lecture intriguing or a lab fascinating but for the most part merely wanders through the daily experience of school.

Rethinking our high schools as learning communities means opting for smaller schools. It is in smaller schools that we can enjoy the face-to-face relationships community requires. But just controlling absolute size is not, as we shall see, enough. We must also use smallness to our advantage. We must afford teachers the time with students to get to know them well enough to teach them. We must afford students the time to come to know and trust their teachers enough to be willing to learn from them. Deborah Meier, a leader in building small schools in New York City, put it this way: "Small schools mean we can get to know a student's work, the way he or she thinks. If it's thinking that we're seeking, then it's thinking we must get to observe, and this requires seeing children over time. . . . This close knowledge helps us demand more of them; we can be tougher without being insensitive and humiliating. It . . . means that every adult in the school feels responsible for every kid."*

When we began thinking about how to restructure FHHS several years ago, we began, like many other high schools, with time and size. The faculty were committed to doing whatever it would take to build closer connections to students like William, Beverly, and Clifton. Realizing that teachers could not connect with the 140 or more students they saw only in batches of twenty to thirty for forty-two minutes daily, we first attacked the issue of how to restructure time. When we decided that time *was* flexible, we discovered there were a variety of ways to build close teacher-learner connections that also reduced the number of students with whom teachers interacted. Some of these strategies we adopted immediately, others we have gradually implemented, and still others we have either tried and abandoned or decided not to use.

There follows five strategies any high school could use tomorrow in becoming a learning community with close ties to its students. All it takes is the will to be more meaningful in the lives of our kids.

Strategy One:
Reduce the overall size of high schools so that no student is anonymous

Anonymity is the enemy of community. Building connections between members of a community relies upon face-to-face contact. Authority in a community is based on trust, on believing

---

* From Deborah Meier, *The Power of Their Ideas* (Boston: Beacon Press, 1995), p. 111.

that the leader is someone worthy of being followed, not just a name and a title. Feeling valued in a community requires making a genuine contribution to the life of the community, knowing that the community would not function as well if you were not present. These are the reasons that communities are small, so that everyone plays a part and no one is anonymous.

To make high schools into learning communities requires committing ourselves to schools small enough that every student knows (s)he is of value. Phil Schlechty, who leads the Center for Leadership in School Reform in Louisville, Kentucky, points out that schools frequently employ substitute teachers, substitute janitors, substitute aides, even substitute principals when a staff member is missing. But no one ever brings in a substitute student. The message, to too many kids, is that it just doesn't matter whether or not they are in school. Imagine spending five thousand hours of your life in a place where no one knew you well, where you seemed to have almost no impact, and where those with authority over you were mainly strangers. Certainly it is hard to conceive that in such a place young people would do their very best work. But in a community of reasonable size, good work occurs for a variety of reasons.

The first reason for this is that in a small school there is more face-to-face contact between students and teachers. Learning is, above all else, a human endeavor built around human connections. To change the way we perceive something, to learn a new skill, to go beyond rote repetition and actually use new information, requires motivation. Such motivation comes from other human beings who are able to convince us that the effort required to do a task is worth it. For that, students and teachers in a learning community must build close connections—connections that say to students that their teachers care about them and are committed to their welfare, and that what students are being asked to do will make a difference in the long run. These connections are not a product of just labeling someone a teacher and telling kids to learn. Instead they are the product of ongoing, daily close work together where teachers can demonstrate their commitment to knowing their students well.

Authority at all levels of a learning community is personal and not positional. We have in our large high schools people vested with a variety of titles: principal, assistant principal, supervisor, department head, dean of students, and so on. We have then imagined that authority goes along with those titles. In fact, some authority does get passed along, in terms of who gets to sign all the paperwork. But authority anywhere is only possessed by individuals to whom we grant it. In a school, perhaps the most important granting of authority is from students to teachers: we will allow you to teach us, we will try to learn from you. This authority is granted on the basis of personal experience, not on who happens to be called a teacher. Following upon the connections that can be built in a small school is the granting of the authority to teach. Repeatedly testing out what they have learned from a teacher, observing the teacher's commitment to them as learners, and building a personal relationship with the teacher are all necessary steps in granting the teacher the authority to teach.

Beyond the connections to individual teachers, what helps make learning possible is students' connection to the overall school. Institutions are things we tolerate, sometimes being forced to join (as with the Internal Revenue Service), sometimes joining because there are no other options (often the case with employment). But communities are places where we feel we belong. We know that without us the community would not work as well, and that the community values us. We choose to "join up," we are not forced to. Students will only join up with the mission of school when they feel that they genuinely belong to the school. That sense of belonging comes from being important, from making a contribution that no one else can make. It also comes from being known well, having people call you by name, having teachers connect what you do in school with the life you live after school hours.

These are the reasons that the size of a high school matters. From observing a wide variety of schools, it seems to me that when a school tries to serve more than four hundred students, the personal contact and ability to make a difference is lost. In a high school of four hundred, or approximately a hundred students per grade level, it is likely that at least one person, usually the principal, will know every student by name. It is also more likely that each student will be able to find a place within the school to make a meaningful contribution. It is hard to get lost, to be just a face in the crowd, among four hundred students.

What is to be done, then, with our schools that house five or nine or fifteen hundred, even five thousand high schoolers? Certainly we cannot just abandon the school buildings that are in place, in the name of creating smaller schools. Too much is at stake—not only financial investment but community identification with our large schools—to just shut them down.

Well, we *could* think of large school buildings as places that house multiple schools.

Let's take, for example, a high school of sixteen hundred students. Wanting to connect with all students, we could think of such a place as actually four schools of four hundred. These schools could share the advantages of a large school: a big auditorium, extra library resources and laboratory space, and large numbers of students from whom to draw actors for plays, dancers and musicians for performance groups, athletes for sports teams. They could also, in a variety of ways, take on their own four identities.

Here, briefly, are several plans:

Content-Focused Schools. Our sixteen hundred students could be divided into four houses, all with grades 9 through 12, of roughly four hundred students each. These smaller houses would share the school's overall educational mission, but each would approach that mission in a different way. For example, one school could build its program around the humanities, another around science and technology, the third around the performing arts, and the fourth around the environment. Another way to divide up the school could be by thematic approaches to a uniform curriculum—one school applying the theme of Exploration to the disciplines, another using Power and Powerlessness to organize instruction and content. In either case, the point is to give each "house" an identity through developing its own way to address the academic mission of the school. Furthermore, students should be entitled to choose the house they want to join, and be allowed as well to change houses when necessary.

Freshman/Sophomore Core Program. Two schools of four hundred each would be devoted to a freshman/sophomore core program of general education. Students would be assigned by lottery to each school, with attention paid to gender, ethnic, and socio-economic balance. After two years students would choose from as many as eight special-focus junior/senior programs such as performing arts, scientific, vocational, or outdoor orientation. None of these programs would have more than a hundred students in it.

Four Schools. We could simply have four schools located within the building, to which students are randomly assigned. Again, attention should be paid to insuring a representative gender, ethnic, and socioeconomic mix, with students having the ability to move between schools to find the best fit. In all schools the program would be the same, but each could develop its own approach based on differing teaching strategies, calendars, or curricular organization. As approaches became more different, more student choice could be introduced.

These are just examples, deliberately left vague because my aim is not to provide a grand design that a school should copy. What I've pointed out is that we not only should but indeed *can* have smaller schools, even with the large school buildings we inherited from the era of consolidation. If we are to really build community in our high schools, it is with the issue of overall size that we must begin. But even once we have controlled the overall numbers in a high school, the issue of size again rears its ugly head because of the way we organize the schedule. We turn now to that set of issues.*

Strategy Two:
Reduce the number of classes per day

At FHHS we began with the distinct advantage of being a small school. With just over four hundred students, we should have been able to create the personal connections with every student that would motivate them all to do well in high school. Yet we knew that was not the case. Many kids were getting a good education and did work closely with teachers, but too many others did not. When we took a good look at ourselves, we came up with dual reasons—each teacher had too many students per day, and too little time with any of them.

---

* While looking over this chapter one last time, I found the January 1997 issue of *Horace*, the publication of the Coalition of Essential Schools, on my desk. Its title, "Why Small Schools Are Essential," sums up the message of this chapter. You can find ordering information in the Appendix.

For some reason we insist that high school students should take every class every day. Because of that we end up with the fragmented daily schedule that we followed Sharon and Jake and Nina through in chapter 1. We also saw how this schedule overloaded good teachers like Leon, Donna, and Reba with too many students and too little time. But what if, rather than letting this assumption about how to use time stand unchallenged, we rethought the daily schedule? What if we scheduled for the sake of connecting with kids rather than putting in a required amount of time? Might there be a way to redistribute time so that teachers had fewer students per day and more contact with them? Could we, in effect, slow down the clock to make possible the close connections that community requires?

To do so would not be an easy proposition. We live during what can only be called an information explosion. And one reason we are so busy overwhelming kids with material during the school day is our acute sense that there is just too much to know. The topic of what is important to learn will come up again when we look at what we should teach in high school. But clearly if we were to change the way we used time in our school, we would also have to change the way we thought about what we taught. It wasn't an easy decision, but in the end we opted for doing a few things well rather than trying to do everything in a hurry. The commitment to smallness, to knowing our kids, seemed more valuable than a commitment to a textbook's notion of what kids should learn. We decided that less would be more: more contact with kids, more in-depth work on subject matter, more meaningful feedback to kids and their parents, and more time to really understand our students.

How much less? For us it ended up being less by one-half. We took our eight-period, forty-two-minute-class schedule to a four-period, eighty-minute-class day. Each course met for half the year (except for some higher level math classes and a few specialty classes which met all year). So students, beginning in the 1993–94 school year, were on a semesterized schedule with four courses the first semester and four new ones the second. Teachers found themselves now teaching three rather than seven classes, and working with fewer than 65 students daily, as opposed to the more than 140 they had the year before.

There is, however, nothing magic about four periods a day. As we were looking at ways to make our schedule more student-centered, we visited one high school that was on a three-period trimester system. Each class met for two hours for one-third of the year. Some classes went on meeting for two or three trimesters; others met for just one. We also studied schools where students have only two classes that meet for the entire year (taught by interdisciplinary teams, see below). In fact, there are a wide variety of ways to schedule high schools that do not rely on simply distributing 120 hours in equal amounts over 180 days.

Here, beginning with FHHS's, are a few of those ways.

Four-Period Semester System

Students take four classes daily for between eighty and ninety minutes. Teachers teach three courses per semester. Some periods may be split in half to accommodate short elective courses, while other courses may run all year to facilitate more in-depth exploration. Example:

Period	Semester 1	Semester 2
1	Course 1	Course 5
2	Course 2	Course 6
3	Course 3	Course 7
4	Courses 4 and 5	Course 8

Extended Alternate-Day Classes*

This year-long "extended schedule" at Gig Harbor High School near Tacoma, Washington, also includes a 30-minute period four times a week for advisory teams and/or sustained silent reading (SSR). Teachers have 100 minutes of planning time every other day, and an extra half hour at the end of the day Friday, when students are dismissed early. Some team-taught integrated courses might meet daily.

*This and the following schedule are taken from the November 1995 issue (vol. 12, no. 2) of *Horace*, the publication of the Coalition of Essential Schools, written by Kathleen Cushman. (See the Appendix for ordering information.)

Monday	Tuesday	Wednesday	Thursday	Friday
Class 1 105 min.	Class 2 105 min.	Class 1 105 min.	Class 2 105 min.	Class 1 105 min.
Advis. Team	SSR	Advis. Team	SSR	Break
Break	Break	Break	Break	Class 3 100 min.
Class 3 100 min.	Class 4 100 min.	Class 3 100 min.	Class 4 100 min.	
				Lunch, 30 m.
Lunch, 30 m.	Lunch, 30 m.	Lunch, 30 m.	Lunch, 30 m.	Class 5 100 min.
Class 5 100 min.	Class 6 100 min.	Class 5 100 min.	Class 6 100 min.	
				Team Plng.

Eight-Day Alternating-Length Rotation

Here we have an eight-day rotational schedule alternating long-block days and short-block days. Croton-Harmon High School in Croton-on-Hudson, New York, adopted this schedule as a first move toward longer blocks, to give teachers and students time to practice the skills and strategies of teaching and learning in longer periods. Each cycle accommodates a session of the Student-Faculty Congress, one advisory group meeting, a daily 35-minute "helping period," and a daily 40- or 45-minute lunch period.

TIME	Day A	Day B	Day C	Day D	Day E	Day F	Day G	Day H
8:13–8:55	1	2	1 8:13–9:35	2 8:13–9:35	3	4	3 8:13–9:25	4 8:13–9:25
8:58–9:38 9:41–10:21	2 3	3 4	3 9:41–11:01	4 9:41–11:01	4 1	1 2	1 9:30–10:40	2 9:30–10:40
10:24–11:04	4	1			2	3		
11:07–11:47 11&12 Lunch C, D	5	6	5	6	7	8	7	8
11:50–12:30 11&12 Lunch A, B, E, F	6	7	←11:07–12:27→	←11:07–12:27→	8	5	Lunch 12:00–12:45 Everyone	Lunch 12:00–12:45 Everyone
12:33–1:13 9&10 Lunch A, B, C, D, E, F	6	7	←11:53–1:13→	←11:53–1:13→	8	5		
1:16–1:56	7	8	7 1:19–2:39	8 1:19–2:39	5	6	5 12:50–2:00 Student- Faculty Congress	Seminars 12:50–1:24
1:59–2:39	8	5			6	7		6 1:29–2:39
2:39–3:15								

HELPING PERIOD

Six-Period/Four-Period Schedule

All six classes meet on Monday (to introduce the week's work) and on Friday (for tests or review). On Tuesday, Wednesday, and Thursday classes meet for extended periods of time, twice a week each. Teachers have an 80-minute planning period twice a week and a 50-minute planning period on Monday and Friday.

Monday (50 min. each)	Tuesday (80 min. each)	Wednesday (80 min. each)	Thursday (80 min. each)	Friday (50 min. each)
Course 1	Course 1	Course 5	Course 3	Course 1
Course 2	Course 2	Course 6	Course 4	Course 2
Course 3	Course 3	Course 1	Course 5	Course 3
Course 4	Course 4	Course 2	Course 6	Course 4
Course 5				Course 5
Course 6				Course 6

Trimester Schedule with Three Long Classes Daily

The year is divided into three trimesters of approximately sixty school days each. Students take three classes each trimester, classes being 120 minutes long. Some classes may run for more than one trimester, and some periods may be subdivided to provide for elective courses. Teachers have one hour of planning time daily and a second hour devoted to working in a lab assisting students. Example:

Period	Trimester 1	Trimester 2	Trimester 3
1	Course 1	Course 4	Course 4
2	Course 2	Course 5	Courses 7 and 8
3	Course 3	Course 6	Course 9

In each case the motivation behind the change in the use of time was single—find a way to put teachers in closer touch with their students. This did not require a legislative change that altered the Carnegie Unit equation of 120 class hours equaling one unit. Instead, it was just a new way of looking at the 120 hours. Instead of 40 minutes in every one of the 180 school days, 80 minutes daily over 90 days provides the same amount of class time—or 120 minutes spread over sixty days, or virtually any other combination. So while it would be a giant step in the right direction to drop altogether the Carnegie Unit requirement, it is not a necessary step to take before making the changes we need now.

Does a changed schedule work? In school after school the results are overwhelming. Attendance rates and grades go up, discipline referrals go down, and students and staff alike report a more relaxed and comfortable learning environment. Regardless of whether or not we ever change what or how we teach (which we look at in chapter 4), just simply changing the way we organize our kids' day in high school can improve our schools. The simple reason for this is that changing the schedule releases the time necessary for teachers to build the community relationships necessary for learning to happen. The best way to see this is to stop in for a moment at one of Reba's science classes in our four-period schedule.

It's biology, second period. Reba is walking from group to group as they finish up a frog dissection. So far today each team has pinned down a sample, made the first cut, and are now labeling each organ on the guide sheet they were given. Class is only half over, no one is rushing, and it looks like everyone will finish the first activity today. Reba has already been around the room once and has questioned almost every student about his or her work. She now pauses at the chalkboard and surveys the room with a smile.

In the back of the room Carlos calls out for her help. His team have discovered something unusual with their frog.

"Ms. Theiss, what is this?" he asks, visibly pulling away from his sample.

"Oh, great! Hey, everyone come and look at this." Quickly, Reba unpins the frog and hoists it into the air, dripping formaldehyde. "See this mass right here? This, my friends, is a fellow traveler along for a free ride. You might also know it as a parasite. Any guesses as to what this little bugger is called?"

"Ugly."

"Brain, size small."

"Worms."

"Good, what type?"

"Fishing?"

Laughter all around.

"No more guesses? OK, they are called roundworms. Now, bonus points to any team discovering and correctly naming a parasite in their sample. Back to work."

The teams amble back to their samples and, with renewed energy, continue their attack on the anatomy of their frog. Reba begins circulating again, looking over a few shoulders, laughing with one team over the thought of discovering a new parasite, carefully making notes on the work of each group.

In a forty- or fifty-minute class this moment would have been lost. Rushed just to get the class through the basics, taking time to dig into an unusual find like the roundworm would not have been possible. The kids might not have even noticed the parasite in the rush to get every organ found and cataloged. But with twice the time, the pace in Reba's classes has slowed so there is time to inquire, discuss, discover, and reflect. Time to find a parasite and tell a joke or two. Time to build the relationship between teacher and learner that connects kids to school.

Strategy Three:
Pair up teams of teachers with teams of kids

High school creates a social dynamic unlike that in any other setting. Each day young people are under the direction of seven to eight different adults. While in general the rules of decorum from class to class may be the same, each of these teachers has a different personality, style, tolerance level for different types of behavior, and sense of humor. Students are expected to rapidly adapt to such differing personalities every time a bell rings to change class. As far as I know, it is an experience that no one else in our society must undergo.

This social dynamic is another way in which the current structure of high school prevents students from building close connections with the school and its teachers. It is not just that we expect young people to cover too much material in the day. We also structure school so that transient relationships between teacher and students are the norm. If you are not a teacher, it might be hard for you to imagine how one adult can build a personal relationship with twenty-five to thirty-five students each class period. If you are a teacher, you know that it simply is not possible.

Earlier I argued that learning is a very personal experience, heavily dependent upon the teacher-student relationship. Probably you can recall the time a teacher knew you well enough to find that one special way of "hooking" you on literature or history. Or the math teacher who knew when to push and when to accept a little less than the best you could do. Or the science teacher who linked physics to your performance on the athletic field, and the Spanish teacher who helped you learn to order in Spanish for that big date at the Mexican restaurant on prom night. Every young person should have an experience like this. To really connect our children, *all* our children, with the mission of the school means connecting them personally with adults who are their partners in learning.

Such connections cannot be built in our high schools as they are. Most certainly they do happen for some students. More than a few—because they are outgoing, obviously needy, or just simply fun to be with—find the attention they need from a teacher. Kids like William and Beverly often enjoy these close relationships because they are involved in so many activities. Clifton is found by teachers because his need is so great. But many students are lost in our high schools.

This is not the way our teachers would want it. Virtually all of us went into teaching because we liked kids. We enjoyed working with them and we hoped that maybe, just maybe, we could help change their lives. Reality set in too quickly. Confronted with two or three dozen different personalities for forty-five minutes a shot, we quickly found that, as is so often heard in the faculty lounge, "you can't reach them all."

A similar thing happens to students. Virtually all high school students I've met would like to get along with their teachers and do well in class. But quickly the reality of the high school social dynamic sets in, and students find teachers too overwhelmed with paperwork—not just grading homework and exams but all the record keeping and management tasks that the large numbers of students in their classrooms demand—to be really concerned with each of their students as learners. In response students decide school is more about getting through than getting involved.

While some of this fragmentation is overcome by shrinking the size of our high schools and the number of classes kids take, we could do even more with yet another approach to connecting with kids. To build even closer connections with students we could decide to put teams of teachers with groups of the same kids over longer periods of time. That is, rather than having random scheduling where students just take each individual course from whoever is teaching it that period, we could opt for "cohort scheduling." In such a system a cohort of students would be assigned to a team of teachers that would work with these students over a set period of time.

There is a wide range of ways high schools could be changed in order to allow students to work with teams of teachers over time. In each case, the purpose is building connections, getting to know well how each student learns, when to push harder and when to back off, what generates interest and what turns each one off. Here are three methods that various schools have tried with success.

Two-Year Teams

At Central Park East Secondary School in New York City the faculty, working to build more connections with students, divided themselves into two-year teaching teams. Students would work with the same teachers in seventh and eighth grades, a new set in ninth and tenth, and a third team in eleventh and twelfth grades. Each team consisted of teachers in the core academic areas—science, math, social studies, and English—and a special education teacher. The students were equally split between the grade levels, for example half ninth and half tenth graders. This way only half of the students with each team turned over every year, tenth graders going to the next team, ninth graders staying, and a new group of eighth graders working in. The team was responsible for the entire academic program for their students, including the integration of the arts, languages, and other areas into the curriculum.*

---

* I described the work of Central Park East in *Schools That Work*. Of course the firsthand source of information on Central Park East is Meier's *The Power of Their Ideas*.

Each team is made up of teachers in all four core areas, math, English, science, and social studies and one special educator. They have the students for half the day all year and decide how to divide up the academic time between them. Students stay with a team for two years, with half of the students moving up a team each year.

7th/8th Grade	Team A {	half 7th Graders half 8th Graders	Team B {	half 7th Graders half 8th Graders

half of each team's students move up each year

9th/10th Grade	Team C {	half 9th Graders half 10th Graders	Team D {	half 9th Graders half 10th Graders

half of each team's students move up each year

11th/12th Grade	Team E {	half 11th Graders half 12th Graders	Team F {	half 11th Graders half 12th Graders

Three-Year Teams

In one rural school, teaching teams are formed for each entering class, and they progress with their students for three years. The students they pick up as sophomores (the year they start at the school) stay with the team until graduation. The team members not only provide classes for the students but also meet weekly to discuss the kids on the team. In their three years they will get to know their kids quite well. They will watch them grow, see how they progress as learners, and organize an instructional program that makes sense for these kids, at this time, in this place. And when the students reach graduation, they have an entire team of teachers helping them find jobs or gain entrance to college. (Then the team, again made up of faculty from every core academic area, will rotate back and pick up a new group of sophomores.) As in the two-year teaming, the team shares the students for half the day and have a weekly conference time to discuss the students and the curriculum.

	Year 1	Year 2	Year 3	Year 4
Team A	Sophomores→	Juniors→	Seniors	Sophomores
Team B	Juniors→	Seniors	Sophomores→	Juniors
Team C	Seniors	Sophomores→	Juniors→	Seniors

(Arrows indicate teachers and students moving together. Teachers "loop" back to pick up sophomores after graduation of seniors.)

To put it in diagrammatic form:

	Team A	Team B	Team C
Year 1	Sophomores ↓	Juniors ↓	Seniors
Year 2	Juniors ↓	Seniors	Sophomores ↓
Year 3	Seniors	Sophomores ↓	Juniors ↓
Year 4	Sophomores ↓	Juniors ↓	Seniors
etc.			

(Arrows indicate teachers and students moving together.)

One-Year Core Teams

Yet another approach is core academic teams at each grade level. For example, one team of teachers at the freshman level will be responsible for all the freshmen throughout their first year. With a shared conference time, the team can meet to discuss the class as a whole, reviewing both individual and group progress, and finding places where the curriculum can overlap and be taught cooperatively. At the end of the year the team can meet to discuss how students should move on in their high school career, and provide the sophomore team with information about skill levels, individual student strengths, and material covered.

The one-year core team, rather than moving on with students, stays in place. However, instead of having four or five teachers teach Freshman English, for example, one teacher teaches all the sections, and the same is done in math, science, and social studies. This means only four teachers, not a dozen or more, keeping track of the entire class's progress.

Teaming teachers with groups of kids over time will require that we rethink the use of time yet again. No longer can we slice up a school day into small autonomous pieces that randomly fall together. Instead we will need to set aside large chunks of time that teachers use with their kids as they think best. This means that a week before a solar eclipse there might not be much U.S. History going on, while the entire team studies the physics and astronomy involved in setting up a school observatory for the event. Likewise, around early November the team's work might be centered on the elections (the math teacher organizing a fairly sophisticated polling study built around statistics and extrapolation), while the birthdays of various authors are cause for all-day readathons and period costume.

The benefit from such a scheduling change is the connection between teachers and students. With a teaching team we move away from the dynamic of just one teacher with a roomful of kids, and every student with multiple instructors. Now we have a situation where several adults work together to get to know a limited number of students, and where young people spend time with a group of teachers they view as real people, who are there to help them learn, not as the idealized (or demonized) entity called "teacher."

Strategy Four:
Provide each student with an adult point of contact

Every high school has a guidance counselor. This is the person whom students are to see about both academic and personal concerns. On one day in February I made a point of watching everything the guidance counselor in our high school did. What I saw included mailing transcripts to colleges, filling out college recommendations, checking class rankings for summer job opportunities, working with a student to keep her in school, registering and scheduling two new students, setting up four college visitations, interceding in an argument between two boys, talking with four students who were failing courses, calling six parents about student progress, and meeting with a teacher and student who were having trouble getting along in class—and that was all before lunch. It was also on a day that she did not have to administer any standardized tests, change any grades in the computer, process any financial aid applications, or attend a special education staffing.

Like most schools our size, we have one guidance counselor. One person responsible for knowing more than four hundred kids well—about the average in any school, regardless of size. Knowing them well enough to guess when they are really troubled and when they just want to get out of class. Being able to write, usually within twenty-four hours, a judiciously worded recommendation for a scholarship or college entrance. Being able to keep track of every student's standardized test scores, GPA, class rank, and current schedule.

What this means is that most guidance counselors have become primarily record keepers. The counselor function, by necessity and not choice, falls by the wayside in the crush of maintaining stacks of student records. Just at the time when students need more guidance than ever, the traditional source of that support is being swallowed up in a bureaucratic quagmire. As it has been put by one wag, high school guidance counseling is "either crisis or college."

In reality, there is no way for one guidance counselor to really know four hundred or more kids. The old notion of the guidance office as handling all student services never did work well. And as the needs of our children grow for even closer connections with adults in a more and more confusing world, it simply becomes more apparent how unsuitable this arrangement is.

The way to overcome this and create one more link with our kids is through a system where every adult in the school takes on the role of mentor for a small group of students.

The most common term for such an arrangement is "advisory." In this system every teacher, counselor, administrator, librarian, perhaps even a secretary or janitor, meets on a regular basis with a small number of students. Unlike the traditional homerooms that many of us remember, the advisory is not just a place to report for roll call and hear the morning announcements. It is, instead, the key point of contact for each child and his or her family with the school.

In one suburban school in New England, it is impossible to reach any of the faculty or administration for the first fifteen minutes of the day. Every staff member is meeting with an advisory group—twelve students, all in the same grade, with whom that advisor meets for all four years of their high school career. During this time the advisor checks on their academic progress, plans outings, reads school bulletins, and is simply there for the students. And all during the day, if a student has an academic or behavioral problem, the advisor is always consulted. He or she is the person who knows this particular group of kids best.

In another school, advisories meet for an hour every day. The classes each consist of fifteen ninth-and-tenth- or eleventh-and-twelfth-graders. For two years these kids meet with the same advisor, some days for study hall, others for the health curriculum each advisor teaches, some days for the career planning program carried on in advisory, and still others for a conversation about school rules, study habits, or just life in general. The advisor collects information on all advisees in the group, and it is with the advisor that parents meet for parent-teacher conferences.

At yet another school, an advisory system was conceived to ease the transition to high school for ninth graders. Each advisory is made up of students from all four grades. Seniors lead the daily sessions, sharing announcements and helping younger students understand the overall workings of the school. With the same teacher for four years, when advisees become seniors they are like junior colleagues in the room.

While different in virtually every school, the advisory has several constant features. First, it is small by design, with every able adult in the school taking an advisory group. Second, its main mission is to make sure every student has a well-developed personal relationship with at least one adult in the school. Third, time for building this connection is built into the daily school schedule. In these ways advisory is much more than the traditional high school concept of "homeroom." Homerooms seldom meet for more than five minutes, with their major function being to take attendance. Students are usually assigned alphabetically, there is no set curriculum, and the kids change homeroom yearly. Homerooms use up time rather than making use of time.

Again we confront the need to examine how we use time. To get to know young people well means taking the time to find out who they are. Unfortunately, as time spent in advisory does not yield a credit or grade, things like advisory do not always find their way into the school schedule. But if our priority is connection and not just credit, it would seem easy enough to make space for it, and if we keep it small enough, we should be able to use it quite effectively. While we were designing the advisory project at FHHS, one teacher envisioned it this way:

> Advisory gives kids a chance to start the day by getting organized, chatting with friends and/or teachers (some of

them have had some pretty stressful evenings or weekends), go over their assignments, plan their day, collect materials they will need, etc. They could be sent to get admit slips or to the counselor if necessary if the day is starting out badly. I personally would like my own [Special Education] kids in Advisory because they of all people need to start the day in a relaxed and optimistic fashion and be provided an opportunity to collect their supplies and their minds. . . .

I would also be interested in keeping the students' "Career Portfolios" or whatever we're going to call their plans for high school and beyond in my classroom and periodically reviewing them with each student. I think we could also provide speakers, such as the guidance counselor, nurse, principal, [vocational school] representative, etc., to go over some of the things they should be thinking about in terms of graduation. Perhaps even each department could have a representative go to homerooms and tell about their classes when registration time comes around. Each advisory teacher could also have a schedule of each student and periodically check on his/her progress in those classes. This would also be a possible time to call home if needed (kind of early for some, I suppose!). We also could do discussions on topics related to jobs and schools.

I think it would also be fun to offer some kind of a breakfast occasionally—even juice or doughnuts or granola bars, as many kids just drink a pop for breakfast. Those who were energetic could cook. Maybe we could ask for a few more small refrigerators and electric skillets for the building? Above all, it's a place to make sure no kid falls through the cracks.

Strategy Five:
Provide unstructured time for teacher–student relationships

Because we start our day so early, lunchtime comes early at FHHS. At 10:45 the lunch bell rings, but rather than making a mad dash to the cafeteria, our students head in virtually every direction. While a fair number do line up for the day's fare, others head to the library to study, the computer room or typing room to finish a paper, the gym to shoot baskets, and half a dozen other places to spend all or part of their sixty-minute lunchtime. But perhaps one of the best things that happens during this time is the casual conversation between teachers and students.

When we decided to change our schedule, we knew we had to do something with lunchtime. Universally disliked by teachers and students, it was thirty minutes of kids crowded into a cafeteria and teachers patrolling while they ate. Students had nothing to do but sit, and the teachers' role was to enforce their idleness. Sometimes a privileged few students were allowed to go to see a teacher or stop in the library. Most of the kids just killed time until the bell rang.

Borrowing the idea from Independence High School in Columbus, Ohio, we decided to provide all students with an hour for lunch. During this time teachers would offer tutoring, supervise an intramural program, keep computer and science labs open, open up the library and shop and art rooms, and just generally be present. We weren't sure how it would work; in fact, it was the part of what we were going to do that gave us the greatest pause. We were betting that if we treated our students like adults, they would respond in kind. Indeed, they have.

Lunchtime at our school has gone from being a time of control to a time of communication. It is the time kids can casually converse with their friends, an important time in a school whose attendance area covers 190 square miles and six telephone exchanges. It is a time when kids can get help with their academic work and can use school resources, such as computers, that they do not have at home. It is a time when, outside the structure of the classroom, kids can talk to teachers—and that may be the most important function of lunch at FHHS.

"Learning is spread all over the day," is the way Reba Theiss put it to me. "Kids just stop in at lunch and we talk about questions they have related to science. It may not be something I am teaching, it's just a question that they have. Now they have a chance to stop in and talk about it."

Connecting with kids means communication with them. One of the great pleasures of FHHS is to walk around at lunch and see three kids chatting with the secretary, half a dozen hanging around the counselor's office, four or five in the wood shop quizzing the Industrial Technology teacher about the jobs he's held. At the other end of the building one of our English and special education teachers moves from computer to computer helping kids work out bugs, the science teachers hold court over the strumming of a guitar, and the home economics teacher joins in a game of Magic. Up and down the halls and the school grounds teachers walk, talking with students, sharing stories, finding out what is going on in their lives.

Some kids have always had this experience—the ones who can stay after school or the ones we see in the band or on a sports team. What is important about our lunchtime is that it opens up the possibility of connecting with an adult, in an unstructured way, to every student.

Creating an unstructured lunch is not the only way a high school can do this. Scheduling coffee or snack breaks as part of the day would work; scheduling the final half hour of school as a self-selected study hall could do it; opening school twenty minutes before the school day is scheduled to start might help. Regardless of the approach, the strategy is simply to give kids and teachers a chance to talk together without the added pressure of grades.

It may seem somewhat contradictory to argue for schools scheduling unstructured time, after my earlier arguments for making every minute of the school day count. Sometimes the best use of time, however, is to let it find its own structure. With our longer lunchtime, we've moved many of the things that had previously disrupted classes—club meetings, tutoring, outside speakers—into the opening created by lunch. We've also found a way for teachers to connect with kids without forcing the connection. Because of these things, the time we spend in classrooms is much more effective.

For the third or fourth time a teacher had stopped in my office to talk about Evan. Evan was new in our school, a little timid, but always anxious to please his teachers. It was clear that he wanted to learn and wanted to fit in. I remembered how once, after I had been to visit a classroom, Evan showed up with the coffee cup that I had left behind, pointing out that he had stopped by the cafeteria and washed it for me on the way.

The teachers all liked him, but there was an issue they wanted to bring to my attention. It seemed that other students were unwilling to work with Evan because he had a hygiene problem. The fact of the matter was that he gave off a less than pleasant odor, and classmates refused to sit near him when this happened. We resolved to find out what the problem really was. Indeed, as Evan confided to a teacher, he knew he smelled bad. The problem was his clothes. His shoes were worn, soiled beyond hope of cleaning. Besides, what cleaning did go on was with water heated on the stove, as the family had no hot water heater.

Within a day of identifying the problem, the FHHS staff had come up with new socks and shoes, clothes, access to the school's washer and dryer and showers, and a plan to keep track of Evan's and his family's needs. We put his mother in touch with agencies that worked to secure new housing, job training, and emergency assistance for the family. A hot water heater was provided by an agency outside the school and installed. Christmas arrived on time, courtesy of a staff fund-raiser, and Evan's school needs (paper, pencils, etc.) always seem to show up in his locker.

Still, as hard as we have tried, we have not totally turned around Evan's life. His family have yet to relocate to a more suitable home, and his mom is still searching for a job. It is unlikely that the schools will ever be able to solve the types of problems that Evan's family faces. But our efforts did make one important difference: Since his teachers "adopted" him, his work in class is better, he takes part in more school activities, and he is talking about going to college.

In a large school, Evan would have been lost. Just one more needy case among hundreds. Even in our small school, I believe we might have missed Evan's needs. As he passed from teacher to teacher throughout the day with no real point of contact with the school, we might never have noticed what was happening to him. But in the restructured school where we now work, with teachers having more time with fewer students and Evan having daily contact with an advisor, it was easier for the FHHS community to come to his aid.

Having done so, and having found a way to connect with him so that he is anxious to learn from us, we now turn to what and how we teach.

CHAPTER FOUR

High School Communities That Help Kids Think

"But I don't need chemistry."

For the fourth time in as many days, Leslie was in my office. She was late again for her chemistry class, this time so late that the teacher actually left the class to go to find her. She was deposited in my office after the chemistry teacher had devoted the first fifteen minutes of class to scouring the building.

Leslie was not doing well in chemistry, felt that she could not succeed in this course and had basically just given up. I was trying to talk her into giving it one more shot.

"Well, you never know. You might choose a field, say medicine, that's going to require chemistry. Or a college that requires two years of lab science." I was sounding less than convincing.

"Look, Doc, the bottom line is that I'll never use chemistry and that I can get into college without it. Really, who do you know that has memorized the periodic table? Have you?"

She had me on that one.

"I like Ms. Theiss and all, so don't get me wrong. I just don't think it is worth my time to sit in a class that I don't need or want and get an F."

"Then tell me what you want to do." I figured that the other choices might just be worse than staying in chemistry.

"Well, I talked to my supervisor at Kroger. He said that if I could get there earlier in the day, he would be happy to use me. I'm having a hard time making my car payments and I could use the hours. Besides, I already have the credits I need to graduate, so I won't miss anything. So just let me go to work." I should have known that Leslie had come in with a plan.

Leslie went back to chemistry. She did little for the rest of the year, frequently producing notes from home dismissing her for a doctor's appointment so she would leave before chemistry class. She failed the course, deliberately. The next fall she enrolled in college, declaring business as her major and planning to take geology to fulfill the one lab-science requirement.

Leslie is not unlike millions of high school students who are unsure *why* they are studying the subjects they are. As we saw in the first chapter, the high school day is fragmented into small parts, with one topic following the next with no rhyme or reason. But even within each class the subject to be studied often seems to have little connection with students' lives. Equations are solved, chemical formulas written, novels reviewed, dates memorized, boards cut, and so on, with little explanation as to why students are doing these things. For high school to really impact upon the hearts and minds of our kids, how and what we teach will have to make sense to them now, not in some far-off imagined future.

Our current approach to high school graduation as just a collection of credits does little to engage students' minds. Can it be surprising that the five-thousand-hour high school experience is best remembered by our children as a time for basketball, dating, and learning to drive, when the academic mission offers so little to inspire or engage them? Coupled with a close relationship with their teachers, rethinking the work kids do in school would make it more likely that high school could make a difference in these kids' lives.

High school should be, most fundamentally, about the work of students. The quality of papers they write, the clearness of the explanations they offer, the persuasiveness of their speeches, the precision of their drawings, the creativity of their art, the skill of their play, and the integrity of their character should be our primary concerns. Unfortunately, because of the way we structure our high schools, our attention is too often drawn elsewhere. This shows up most clearly in what we teach and how we teach it.

Start with what we teach. We should begin, not with lists of courses and objectives, but with actual examples of the type of work we want our students to do. Next we should look carefully at the type of work students *can* produce upon entering high school. Only then, knowing what we want them to do and how we want them to do it, would we be able to set forth a curriculum for students to follow. The "stuff" we want to teach would be whatever is needed to get kids from where they are to where we want them to be. In fact, what we teach in high school is seldom based upon who our students are or what specifically we want them to be able to do when they finish school. Instead, we base what we teach on how many Carnegie Units are needed for graduation, what the textbooks have in them, and what certification the adults who teach in the school hold.

Most high schools do it this way: First, we read the state guidelines for how many credits or Carnegie Units per subject area students need to graduate. Then we simply spread courses throughout the high school experience so that kids will have an opportunity to gather enough credits for graduation. For example, if students are required to have one unit each of U.S. Government, U.S. History, and geography, a school would just require that each freshman take U.S. Government, each sophomore U.S. History, each junior geography. The problem with this way of looking at credits is that it is almost impossible to understand the Civil War, for example, without understanding the geography that caused our nation to develop regional economies or how the federal government responded to claims of states' rights. But cultural and political geography are saved for the geography class, and only the government teachers are allowed to discuss federalism. And what about the powerful understandings kids can come to through reading the literature of a period? Take *Uncle Tom's Cabin*, for example. But that's to be saved for the English credit.

Adhering to the Carnegie Unit scheme of organizing the curriculum—the "what" we teach—forces high schools into an artificial fragmentation of knowledge. It breaks apart the natural connections that should be made in order to deepen and broaden our students' understanding of the world around them. Besides, so organizing content often makes it bland and sterile, with little of interest for the young mind. All of this, interest, connection, understanding, is forsaken in order to parcel out content in 120-hour blocks of time.

Once the units are parceled out, it's time to fill them up with content. For the most part, the content in any course comes from the textbook assigned to the course. A quick scan through almost any of them will convince you that high school textbooks are not written with the work of students in mind. Instead, the goal of textbook publishers is not to offend too many folks, so the books will be adopted in the largest number of schools. Much concern has been voiced about how this leads to controversial issues being left out of texts. Perhaps just as important is how, out of fear of offending anyone by an act of omission, textbooks try to cover everything. As we expand what we know in virtually every field, textbooks merely get longer, with no attempt made to separate the wheat from the chaff. The clearest examples of this in my own work have occurred in our recent searches for new science and history textbooks. After hearing publishers' representatives glowingly describe how their books have been updated to include all the newest discoveries and latest events of historical significance, I would ask just one question: What was taken out to make room for the new material? Nothing, was the invariable reply; we simply added more. More to be covered, of course, in the same amount of time. The goal is coverage, the plan is that students will "get through" the book.

The cost of getting through the book is never having enough time to really work well on any one part of the material. At the end of every textbook chapter, be it in science, math, social studies, English, French, health, whatever, will be a set of student exercises. For the most part these exercises are checks of reading comprehension. Students have to define a few terms, work some problems, jot down some dates. Today kids carry out these exercises the same way you and I did when we were in school. Having been assigned the chapter and the first five questions at the end, they open up to the questions first, see what they need to know, quickly scan the reading for the answers, jot them down, and then put aside the text so they can read, watch TV, or do something else more interesting. Teachers, in a hurry to cover the book so kids will be ready for next year's math or science or English course, know these assignments do nothing to help kids learn. In fact, they know that kids would really work at the material if they were all assigned the "enrichment" exercises that are hidden in the Teacher's Manual. As they rush on past them, they tell themselves that maybe when they do the next chapter they can get to some of that material. But for now, well, there just isn't time.

Once the courses and texts are set, the next step is to staff them. This is where the high school schedule is constructed. Staying with our social studies example, if all freshmen are required to take U.S. Government, the scheduler simply divides the number of freshmen by the approximate class size the school can afford and then passes out that many class sections to the appropriately certified teachers. So, for example, if there are three hundred freshmen and the class-size target is twenty-five, then twelve sections of freshman U.S. Government are assigned to the certified teachers.

Of course, it is never that easy.

The first problem usually occurs with available staff. In our example, what happens if there are only two teachers with U.S. Government teaching certification and one of them also has to teach another course? The usual solution is to increase student numbers in the classes so that fewer sections are offered. But by closing out just two sections, the others now jump from twenty-five students to thirty. On the other hand, let's say the economics course the school offers enrolls only ten students. If we were to close that course and reassign the teacher to U.S. Government, our twelve classes could become thirteen, each with only twenty-three students. But we can't, because the teacher who teaches economics doesn't have U.S. Government certification. (This also shows up across disciplines, as when an English teacher has only seven students in Speech but cannot be moved to U.S. Government because of certification limits.)

An even more perplexing situation arises when the offered courses do not even reflect what our students need, while certification requirements prevent us from meeting that need. Perhaps a larger than usual group of incoming freshmen are having problems with reading, problems the school knows will limit their success in U.S. Government. And we may have several staff members who have, on their own, developed an expertise at teaching reading. While we know it would be in our students' best interests to provide them with a course to help with their reading, unless these staff are so certified, it cannot be done.

In all these ways *what* we teach seems to tell students that it isn't really their work that we are interested in. Rather, we want them to spend enough hours, covering enough material in the areas in which adults are experts, to collect the necessary credits for graduation. Whether or not they do anything of note is not really the issue. Especially when we combine *what* they are taught with *how* they are taught.

Ernest Boyer, former president of the Carnegie Foundation for the Advancement of Teaching, once said that secondary schools are places where "children go to watch adults work." Wandering up and down most school hallways, it is easy to see what he means. In classroom after classroom the mode of instruction can be depressingly the same: one teacher standing in front of thirty or so adolescents, talking. The talk sounds surrealistically similar from classroom to classroom as well—the teacher summarizes and simplifies the material, provides a few examples or stories, and ends up presenting the class with a neat little package that leaves scant, if any, room for questions or interpretation.

Of course, as long as the focus in high schools stays on the work of adults, this "talking head" style of instruction will stay the norm. The task of high school teaching is too often perceived as the task of "teaching algebra" or "teaching art" as opposed to "teaching seventeen-year-olds." I first noticed this as a college professor when I had both elementary and secondary education majors in my classes. When I would ask what they were going to teach, the elementary majors always referred to children: they were going to teach "six-year-olds" or "preschoolers" or "sixth graders." Secondary majors gave a very different answer: they were going to teach "math" or "psychology" or "industrial technology." This choice of words revealed an unfortunate bias. The focus for secondary majors was more often on the stuff to be taught and the work of the teacher, where for elementary majors the focus was on how to help kids learn.

High school teachers are not to blame for this state of affairs. Their college preparation for teaching has most of them spending more time in classes related to their discipline (English, math, French, etc.) than in courses studying how kids learn. State requirements for high schools are based on material covered (the Carnegie Unit yet again) rather than what students do. High school curriculum is virtually dictated by college entrance requirements which ask for schools to provide a listing of courses taken, not student skills achieved.

The outcome of this orientation is precisely what Boyer described. For most of their five thousand hours in high school, young people watch teachers try to entertain them.

It is a difficult job. Teachers first study their material carefully, choosing what to cover more thoroughly, what to skip over, what to leave out all together. Then they go to work designing ways to literally "perform" the material through lectures, films, overheads, worksheets, and readings so as to somehow interest students in material that they as teachers love but that they know many of their students do not care about. The performance itself goes on daily while the audience sits and takes notes. The teacher is both performer and critic, trying not only to entertain but also to judge if the audience is learning anything.

What about the audience, the kids? For the most part they are just that, an audience. Moving from room to room, they sit and watch performer after performer attempt to explain the world outside the school walls to them. While the teacher's activity may vary from day to day, the work of kids does not. Whether they are watching a film, hearing a lecture, or reading a text, their role can be described from classroom to classroom with amazing accuracy: sit in a private desk, take notes, memorize material for the next test.

This orientation to how we teach in high school leads to the strange situation where the bulk of the actual work of school is carried out by the teacher. Rather than being partners holding equal responsibility for what is learned in school, students are seen as empty vessels for teachers to fill with knowledge. So teachers plan, organize, carry out, and evaluate instruction; students watch, and guess what to memorize for the test. An amazing situation in a place where the work of kids should be of prime concern.

The final way in which high schools seem not to focus on student work is how students are evaluated. Perhaps the most common refrain in any high school classroom is "Will this be on the test?" Students know, all too well, that the test, not what they learn or what they can do, is all that really matters in school. The answers they scribble down on their notebook paper in response to the teacher's question, the multiple choice they make when trying not to be fooled, the T or F bubble they fill in after mentally flipping a coin—these are the only indicators used to judge their success in school. When marked and added together, the points earned will yield the grade that shows up on a report card, judging them to know an A's or a C's worth of American History, English Literature, or General Math One.

The entire method of evaluating what our high school students have learned is quite unique to the school setting itself. Nowhere else in our society will one's worth or abilities be measured by a paper-and-pencil test of short-term memory. Instead, we base judgments of competence on actual performance. Those aspiring to be medical doctors do residencies to see if they can do medicine; mechanics actually repair things and, on the basis of their work, hold a job or earn our business; farmers are paid for the crops they deliver, not for how many pages they can write on soil conditions. But in school most kids never produce anything "real," instead spewing back memorized facts to prove that they have learned.

My older son was taking yet another battery of standardized tests during his seventh-grade year. He was relating to me how easy they seemed and how quickly he was getting through them. Being somewhat worried that his cavalier attitude toward the tests might hurt his performance, I asked him why he thought they were so simple. "Dad," he replied, "the right answer is always there, you just have to pick it out."

Indeed, our evaluation of students is based too much upon their ability to sniff out the right answer from a list, too little on their really being able to do anything.

As with how we teach, the way we evaluate high school students puts most of the burden of work on teachers. They choose what to include on the test or assignment, prepare the test, administer it, and spend hours grading it and recording the results. Students, on the other hand, spend most of their time trying to get teachers to direct them to what should be memorized (or "crammed") the night before the test and then preparing mnemonic tricks to help them hold the needed information in their short-term memory. We all know what the result of this scenario is. If you doubt it, see which of your friends would be willing to stake their current job or income on once again passing their high school final examinations.

High school students know that all that really counts in school is their final grades. They also know that they earn those grades through an ability to quickly memorize facts, dates, formulas, and lists. They work relatively hard at this task of rote memorization. Since we know that students will work at what we evaluate, our next place on which to focus, in generating better student work in school, is the type of work we use to evaluate student learning.

The fallout in our high schools, from how we currently decide what we teach and how we teach and how we know what kids have learned, is a lack of focus on what school should really be about—high-quality student work. The message sent to kids is that *what* they learn is not nearly as important as the *credit* they earn. This is never clearer to me than when I sit in with our guidance counselor on sessions with students, and sometimes parents, who want to change courses. The vast majority of these requests are from kids wanting to find the easiest way to accumulate the credits we require. Here are just a few examples from the most recent school year:

Ralph and his mother have come in wanting to have him released from the last half hour of school each day so he can make it to his new job. In order to get to work on time, he will need to leave his fourth-period English class at 2:00 P.M. rather than the normal 2:30 dismissal. The answer is no. But I offer to call the employer to see if we can't help change Ralph's work schedule. At this point Ralph objects, saying it is only part of the class each day. "Besides," he finishes with a flourish, "I already have four English credits, so I don't need this course anyway."

Kelsey stops in two days before the school year starts. "Doc, you gotta change my schedule and get me outta English Eleven." As we talk about it, I find out that her request isn't based on any schedule conflict or other pressing need. Bottom line seems to be that she just doesn't want to put forth the effort she knows this demanding course will require. After I go through what will be taught in the class and how it will help her get ready for college, one of her goals, she reluctantly agrees that maybe she should stay in the class. Always one to get in the last word, she delivers a parting shot: "I thought I already had my junior English because I took Creative Writing last year. Now that it doesn't count, I think that was a real waste of my time."

Seth's request is to take his required U.S. Government course through correspondence. He isn't going to be allowed to, as we always insist that students take courses inside the school when they are available. Not good enough for Seth. Yes, he could schedule the course, but it wouldn't be "convenient" for him (especially since he wants to be in another course with his girlfriend when he is scheduled into Government). Patiently the teacher and I explain the drawbacks of correspondence courses, the lack of contact with a teacher, the rote memorization approach, the delay in getting feedback on his work. We are, most particularly, concerned about the quality of the experience. Seth's reply: "I don't care about the quality, I just want the credit."

In the complaints of Ralph, Kelsey, and Seth ran a theme commonly heard in every high school—how do I get enough credits to get out of here? Their complaints give a new meaning to the words of John Dewey, penned at the beginning of the century:

> What avail is it to win prescribed amounts of information about geography and history, to win the ability to read and write, if in the process the individual loses his own soul; loses his appreciation of things worthwhile, of values to which these things are relative; if he loses the desire to apply what he has learned. . . .

These students aren't concerned about what they learn or how to use it, because the way they are treated makes high school just something to endure. Since so little of what most high schools do is focused on the actual work of students, students themselves pay attention to what seems to matter more than their work—which is this gathering of credits. Ask a group of students how many credits they have and how many they need to graduate, and you will get quick and precise answers. Ask those same students what they need to know or be able to do to graduate, and you will probably stun them into silence.

Teachers certainly do not want it to be this way. As Donna, in a recent faculty discussion, put it: "Our kids need to know why things are the way they are, so they can think carefully about how they act as citizens. But," she added, pointing to the U.S. History textbook, "I'm not sure they get much out of that that really helps."

Another staff member, Sean, caught it best:

"I knew I was doing something wrong when I left school every day tired, worn out, and loaded down with grading to do, while our kids walked out full of energy and without a single book in their hands. They should work at least as hard at this as I do. After all, it's their education, not mine. When I figured this out, I started changing the way I teach and asking students to do more than sit, listen, and be entertained."

The traditional high school curriculum and teaching methods and testing strategies clearly reflect, as does the size of high schools, our institutional mind-set when it comes to teaching teenagers. Institutions are not concerned with the needs, interests, or abilities of individuals except as they serve the mission of the institution. Having a mission that is not dependent upon individuals, a large bureaucratic organization finds it makes little sense to tailor its work to the needs of its employees or even its clients. People are required to conform to the standards, goals, and procedures of the organization. So it is with our high schools. Every year we start at the same beginning, cover the same material, administer the same tests. Standardization is the watchword from coast to coast, as kids in Maine read the same textbooks as those in Alaska, kids in Texas take the same tests as those in Montana, and Michigan teenagers watch the same videos as those in southern California. In fact, if you didn't look out the classroom window (if there is one), you wouldn't know if you were in a classroom in Athens, Ohio, or Athens, Georgia, or Athens, Pennsylvania. This sameness is an amazing phenomenon for a system of public schools that claims to be under local control in more than 14,400 school districts.

An approach to teaching and learning that begins with community need not be devoid of standards, but it cannot begin with standardization. Communities begin with individuals. The individuals must share a commitment to a standard that they themselves have set, one that is based on the needs, abilities, and interests of the community's members. In a school this would translate to teaching and learning practices in which the goals for the learners were clear and shared in advance with students; where the curriculum certainly reflected shared national norms but augmented those norms with a distinctly local flavor; and where the evaluation of what young people learned would be based on their actual use of the material at hand. Building a school community requires that we begin with the kids, culture, and context at hand in planning the experiences our children have in their classrooms.

Changing the way we teach, rethinking what we teach, finding new ways to know what our kids know—these are the next steps, after altering size and time, in making the five thousand hours of high school a more meaningful community experience for kids. We need to ask what we expect students to be able to do as a result of their high school years. How do kids see what they do in school as related to the world around them? Do kids see what we do with them in school as connected, as making a logical whole picture of the world? Are the standards we set to judge the quality of students' work challenging, or do they encourage kids to just "get by"? Questions like these should guide our attempts to refocus our attention in high school away from the mindless pursuit of credits and toward generating quality work by every student.

The point is not just to "raise standards." Rather, in conjunction with putting young people in closer touch with adults, we need to make sure the work they do in school is both meaningful and challenging. After getting the issues of time and size right, we now turn to how we fill up the time. It is only when we rethink schools from the viewpoint of the kids' work, what it is they can *do* as a result of their five thousand hours invested in high school, that we will create school environments that work for kids.

Strategy One: Begin with what we want our graduates to do, and plan the curriculum backward from there

One of the best ways to rethink the high school experience is to begin at the end. For the most part, high school programs are put together in the same way as a building is constructed. First comes a foundation, then the walls, then a roof, finally the interior. Similarly, in planning a school program, the curriculum designers start with the ninth-grade program, then tenth, and so on to a finished picture. The problem with this approach is that it overlooks the first and most fundamental step in any construction project, the blueprint.

Every builder begins at the end. The architect's drawing presents us with a view of the finished product. It is to that end that the work is carried out. (Another example occurred as I was working on a draft of this book. With Christmas drawing near, I had several gifts for my sons that required assembly. While putting them together, I found myself looking at the picture of the completed toy as often as I glanced at the directions.) Can we imagine ever building a home, a car, or a simple bookshelf without some final product in mind? This is seemingly what we do in designing a school curriculum. Relying on some general statements about the school's mission, we design a school program with only the vaguest idea of what students should be able to actually do as a result of the four years spent in high school.

To students this translates into a concern with earning only enough credits to graduate. For students like Leslie it means that when a course seems irrelevant, it is either to be dropped or simply failed. Why work at something if it is not going to have an effect on your life? Not every student sees it that way. Some press on through their math, science, or English courses not always quite sure why they are doing it but anxious to make grades good enough to get them into college.

A more meaningful high school experience would begin with what we hope our kids can be when they leave school. Joe McDonald, senior researcher at the Coalition of Essential Schools, calls this "building a platform." A platform upon which every graduate can stand and say "I can do this." A platform which also serves as a place from which the faculty can survey the school program and decide how well it serves the school's clients, its students.

To really be meaningful to students, any school platform has to be built around what kids can "do." Most school programs are built around notions of what kids should "know." Lists of facts to be memorized predominate instruction, and tests ask students to choose the right answer, not to demonstrate the right reasoning. But much of this material makes little sense to students. When they do not see how it is used, what they might do with it, or why it matters, they are unlikely to commit to learning it.

Consider the two following statements:

1. Students will be able to recite the first ten amendments ("the Bill of Rights") to the Constitution of the United States. (Taken from a state curriculum guide.)
2. Students will compile a log of articles from this week's newspaper that demonstrate the use of the Bill of Rights. (Taken from the lesson plans of an FHHS social studies teacher.)

We all know what happens with the first approach. We memorize the material, jot it down on a test, and promptly forget it. The second approach requires us to do something, to be able to use what we know, to be able to show that we know it. More important, it shows us that what we know does matter.

So what is it we want our kids to be able to do? I have read volumes on the need for our kids to be productive, live good lives, practice safe sex, and vote. All of it seems to come down to one thing: We would like our children to become good neighbors. The bottom line is that the young people who populate our high schools today will, tomorrow, become our neighbors. They will buy houses next door, run our cities and towns, vote on tax levies and presidents, and watch over us in our old age. Our streets will be no safer than they make them, our schools no better, our products no more reliable.

While I make no claim to speaking for all schools, I believe that a high school platform could best be constructed around the three planks that we have adopted in the FHHS Mission Statement: Active citizens, lifelong learners, flexible in occupational choices.

The first plank, the most fundamental reason for having public schools, is the development of active democratic citizens. Since Thomas Jefferson first proposed free public education, the primary goal has been to engender in citizens the habits of heart and mind that make democracy possible. Too often we are tempted to overlook this function of public education. In the rush to get kids ready to take jobs or enroll in college we build a curriculum that responds only to a list of recommended courses for college entry or for entry-level jobs. Certainly this is part of our task—but *only* part. We should not allow the vocational side of schooling to overwhelm the citizenship side. In fact, given that the only constant for many of us is our status as citizens (most of us change jobs several times as well as changing residence), perhaps the civic, democratic mission of school is its most important task. Regardless, it is clearly a primary task and should be treated as such.

If we take this democratic task seriously, what would kids be able to do when they leave high school. This was the charge that our staff, students, and parents took on at a school-wide retreat. We came up with the following *working* list. While we did agree that it was not complete, we all were confident that we would be very pleased if our students could do the following:

> Work with other people in solving a problem
> Demonstrate an understanding of how our government works
> Act responsibly in allocating one's own time and resources
> Know how to take a position and advocate its adoption by others
> Speak and write effectively in order to persuade others
> Listen carefully, filtering propaganda
> Know how to vote, and do it
> Research issues and politicians
> See the "big picture"
> Take leadership roles
> Act on one's own rights and responsibilities
> Be able to organize
> Have a good "crap detector"
> Be able to pick one's battles

If all of our graduates could do these things, we would have much more faith in the future of democracy.

The second plank on the platform is to make our kids into lifelong learners. One of the reasons we try so hard to stuff facts into our students' heads is that we think they will just stop learning when they leave school. An alternative way to think about it is that what we are doing in high school is preparing kids to learn for the rest of their lives. It's not so much *what* they learn that sticks with them, it's the *ability* to learn that makes all the difference. Here's another list that we developed, partial of course, of what a lifelong learner can do:

> Use various libraries
> Use computers
> Use various resources: books, movies, plays, and newspapers

Develop hobbies and interests
Organize oneself
Communicate/express ideas
Take advantage of further educational opportunities
Be open-minded
Keep abreast of current events, globally
Be a risk taker
Think logically
Function in various environments
Use common sense
Read various materials for comprehension

Again, an ambitious list. Admitting the fact that most of what we know as adults we learned *after* high school makes us realize how vital, if ambitious, helping kids gain these skills is. Perhaps the most important thing we learn in school should be how to keep learning. In a world where information keeps growing, it may be more what you can find out than what you know that counts.

The third plank on the platform is to help our kids be flexible in their career choices. The task today is not just getting a job. It's being able to adapt to changing jobs and finding ways to productively contribute to any employment circumstances. We cannot prepare our kids to do a particular job. The job market fluctuates so rapidly that we do not know what our children will be doing. Instead we can make them ready to move through a changing labor market with skills and traits like these:

Confidence in one's own abilities
Awareness of available opportunities
Self-motivation
Resilience; the ability to keep trying
Computer literacy
Ability to learn new skills
Persistence
Adaptability
Interests in a variety of areas
Good level of comfort with technology

The curriculum we offer students should aim at outcomes such as these. I do not want to map out an entire high school curriculum here, because I believe that each school community is best able to design its own program. But one example will help illustrate what such an approach to a high school academic experience entails.

Virtually everyone would agree that to fulfill the role of citizen, learner, or worker we all need to be able to clearly present our thoughts orally. Too often this is reduced to the ability to give a speech, a requirement met in a speech course and left at that. A more meaningful approach would be to require students to speak publicly about their ideas, thoughts, and work throughout their high school years. The platform standard would be, as noted above, the ability to speak persuasively. Every part of the curriculum would prepare students to reach this platform. They would have to recite works from memory in literature classes, explain a lab procedure in science, demonstrate a statistical analysis in math, take and defend a position on a current or historical event, and explain the working of an electrical circuit in shop. In effect, every teacher in every area becomes a teacher of public speaking. The entire curriculum "owns" this vital skill, and young people learn this and other skills in the context of what they are studying.

What happens in this approach is that the educational experience is built around students developing skills, not amassing facts. Teachers are first generalists, responsible for a network of skills that students are to acquire. They use their specialty, be it history, English, science, art, or music, as a tool to help students build these skills—and these skills, not academic disciplines, become the organizing principles for the curriculum.

This in no way reduces the value of content, the stuff of the curriculum. To the contrary, it increases the value of the content with which students deal.

Currently we present students with literally thousands of facts, statistics, rules, and terms daily. How are students to know which of these is more valuable, which generates the greatest understanding, which to pay the closest attention to? They aren't. Assigning the same value to everything, nothing is very memorable.

When, on the other hand, content plays a role in helping students attain a skill, it gains meaning for them and connects them with the academic mission of the school. Students who need to know the chemical properties of oxygen atoms in order to complete their research on water pollution find a context for the periodic table. Having to give a speech in which one defends the right of hunters to own guns requires students to know the Constitutional and legal history of the Second Amendment, not just its number. Needing to do something with what we know means we know it better and will retain it longer. Focusing on what students can do, not just what they know, creates a connection between kids and content.

Once we have constructed this platform, this core of skills and knowledge that we want students to gain in their five thousand high school hours, we then need to present it to students. To do this means making these goals more concrete, turning what they are to learn into actions that kids know they can do. What it takes to demonstrate what they have learned should be clearly set out for students, and we should begin by replacing credits for graduation with exhibitions of mastery.

Strategy Two:
Base graduation from high school not on credits earned but on demonstrated proficiency

When Leslie complains to me that her chemistry class "doesn't matter," what she means is that she does not need that credit to graduate. Unfortunately, she's right. As we have seen, our high school graduation standards are such that students do not need to do well in the work they are asked to do. By providing only minimal effort in about three-fifths of their classes, young people can earn a high school diploma.

As long as credits are the key to graduation, we will have young people choosing to fail courses they do not "need" to graduate. This is not the way to help our students do their best work. It isn't that kids don't want to do work of which they are proud. It is that we simply don't ask them to show us what they really can do. What if we substituted actual performance for mere credits? Why not tell students that while earning credits is part of the key to graduation, just as important is their actual ability to do the things outlined in the school platform? Would this make the time students spend in every class more valuable? Could they then see each and every class as helping them gain the skills that receiving a diploma requires? Would we see them do better work in response to this challenge?

The Coalition of Essential Schools, a national restructuring effort led by Ted Sizer, made this way of thinking about graduation the sixth of their Common Principles (all ten can be found in the Appendix):

> Students entering secondary school studies are those who can show competence in language and elementary mathematics. Students of traditional high school age but not yet at appropriate levels of competence to enter secondary school studies will be provided intensive remedial work to assist them quickly to meet these standards. **The diploma should be awarded upon a successful final demonstration of mastery** for graduation—an "Exhibition." This Exhibition by the student of his or her grasp of the central skills and knowledge of the school's program may be jointly administered by the faculty and by higher authorities. As the diploma is awarded when earned, the school's program proceeds with no strict age grading and with no system of "credits earned" by "time spent" in class. This emphasis is on the students' demonstration that they can do important things.

Many schools are utilizing this approach to the awarding of high school diplomas, known as graduation by exhibition. Simply put, graduation by exhibition requires that students in some way demonstrate their mastery of the required skills for a high school diploma. The notion of an "exhibition" is taken from the arts. It is an opportunity for the student to display what (s)he has learned, to show to the faculty that (s)he can do those things that are expected of a graduate.

Perhaps one of the most extensive graduation-by-exhibition plans has been developed by the faculty at Central Park East Secondary School in New York City. For graduation, students are required to present a portfolio of their work covering fourteen areas. Each of these areas must be completed, with major presentations required in seven of the fourteen.

Here is CPESS's own outline of the plan:

The Fourteen Portfolio Areas:
An Overview for Students and Parents

The primary responsibility of the Senior Institute students is to complete the fourteen portfolio requirements listed below.

These portfolios reflect cumulative knowledge and skill in each area as well as the specific CPESS habits of mind and work. Students will present the work in all fourteen portfolio areas to their Graduation Committee for review and acceptance. They will meet for a full review of their seven chosen "majors" to present, discuss, and defend their work. There are, therefore, two stages to keep in mind: (1) preparation of the portfolio materials in collaboration with the advisor and others, and (2) presentation and defense of the materials. In some cases, portfolio work will need to be expanded, modified, and re-presented for final approval. Students may also choose to present work a second time to earn a higher assessment.

It is important to remember that a majority of the work done in connection with a portfolio can and should be the outcome of the courses, seminars, internships, and independent study that a student has engaged in during the normal course of his or her Senior Institute year. In addition, some of the material may be an outgrowth of work initiated in Division I or II or, where appropriate (e.g., the Language Other Than English portfolio), work completed prior to entering the Senior Institute.

Portfolios include work in fourteen areas: seven "majors" and seven "minors." There is no one way to complete these requirements, no one way to present them. People are different, and the individual portfolio will reflect these differences. The term "portfolio" covers all the ways in which a student exhibits his or her knowledge, understanding, and skill. CPESS recommends interdisciplinary studies wherever possible, so work completed to meet one requirement may be used to fulfill other requirements as well.

While the final review is based on individual accomplishment, almost all portfolio requirements can be based on work done in collaboration with others, including group presentations. Such collaborative work is encouraged, since it often enables a student to engage in a much more complex and interesting project.

Quality and depth of understanding, good use of CPESS's five habits of mind, and the capacity to present competent and convincing evidence of mastery as relevant to each particular field are the major criteria used by the Graduation Committee; however, portfolio work must reflect a concern for both substance and style. For example, written work must be submitted in clear, grammatical English that reflects the expected proficiency level of a high school graduate in spelling, grammar, and legibility. Errors should be eliminated before the portfolio is presented to the committee. Written work must generally be submitted in typewritten form. The same care in preparation and presentation applies to all other forms of work. Portfolio work should represent a student's best effort. The same holds true for the manner of presentation.

Different characteristics are more or less relevant at each portfolio area. Each academic discipline, for example, has developed its own "scoring grid" to help students and Graduation Committee members focus objectively on the appropriate criteria. Over time, the criteria for acceptable performance will be more fully developed through both the creation of new scoring grids and the compilation of past student work that demonstrates accepted levels of skill. Students are expected to become familiar with the criteria by which they are measured (both the scoring grids and former student work).

At Graduation Committee meetings, students should be prepared to discuss not only the content of the portfolio but their computer knowledge and growth in particular fields of work.

The following are the fourteen Portfolio areas:

1. Postgraduate Plan
2. Science/Technology*
3. Mathematics*
4. History and Social Studies*
5. Literature*

6. Autobiography
7. School and Community Service and Internship
8. Ethics and Social Issues
9. Fine Arts/Aesthetics
10. Practical Skills
11. Media
12. Geography
13. Language Other Than English/Dual Language Proficiency
14. Physical Challenge

One of the above portfolio topics or items will be separately assessed as a final Senior Project. Each student is required to make a major presentation in seven of the fourteen areas described above. These include the four starred portfolios, and at least three others chosen in cooperation with the advisor.

Grades of Distinguished, SatPlus, Sat, or MinSat will be used to grade work as a whole. In the seven "minor" portfolios, a student will be graded pass/fail. Passing will be upon recommendation of the advisor and approval of the full Graduation Committee. The student may, however, request a grade from the advisor (Distinguished, SatPlus, etc). In this case, the student must provide the committee with sufficient time to review all relevant materials and to discuss the recommended grade at a meeting of the committee. Such a grade would be subject to approval by the entire committee.

This portfolio is developed by students over a two-year period with the help of their faculty advisors. When weaknesses emerge in any one area, students take additional courses or tutoring in order to help them hone their skills. School time is arranged around experiences that help students prepare for their exhibitions; every course at CPESS is thus connected to graduation.

There are many other approaches to a required exhibition for graduation: a senior English thesis or paper, a final senior project in any field, a senior seminar, a senior presentation, portfolios in any subject. To be meaningful each must be connected to the skills we claim we want to see in our graduates.

At FHHS we are exploring an approach that would combine a senior project, portfolios, and course credits for graduation. Working backward from our list of desired skills presented earlier, we are trying to put together a graduation standard that would require students to demonstrate that they have mastered these skills. One piece would be a core set of courses for every student, within which the basic competencies are acquired. From these courses students would move on to assembling in the junior and senior year "passports" in areas such as Life Skills and Career Exploration, Academic Accomplishments, and Citizenship. As a capstone experience, a Senior Project would encourage each student to take a topic about which (s)he is passionate and explore it in detail, writing a research paper and carrying out an action component in the last semester of school.

The Senior Project: A Capstone Experience

Drawn from FHHS students and their colleagues around the country, here's a sampling from A to Z of what a senior project could be:

Agriculture: One young farmer-to-be spent his senior year studying soybean cultivation in order to make his family's farm more profitable. His final exhibition was a plan for making the transition from corn to beans, complete with recommended variety, marketing targets, and financing.

Beethoven: A young woman's study of the life and works of Ludwig van Beethoven culminated in a lecture and a recital of Beethoven's *Moonlight Sonata.*

Dragons: A literary exploration of the use of dragons in fantasy and myth, comparing the Eastern and Western uses of this beast, led to a final paper and presentation accompanied by slides and photos of dragons through the eyes of writers and illustrators.

Education: Interested in a career in special education, one young woman undertook a study of how well her country was serving the needs of special populations. Interviewing teachers, students, parents, and school officials, as well as observing classrooms, she produced a report for the county superintendent.

Hemp: The uses of industrial hemp, its historic ups and downs, and the current legal status of hemp was the topic of a young woman whose parents were involved in the hemp industry. Her congressman now has her recommendations on how hemp could help area small farmers.

Landscaping: Two young men spent part of the first half of their senior year with a landscape design firm. The second half of the year they designed, financed, and put into place a plan for the grounds of their school complete with a drystone wall.

Pediatrics: When she was a child, no one thought she would make it through school, owing to a series of mysterious ailments. But several doctors never gave up, finally diagnosing her epilepsy, and now her senior project is on the role pediatrics play in preventing the spread of childhood diseases.

Quail: Restoring quail to the region's habitat was the goal of another senior's project. After carefully researching the requisite ground cover, weather conditions, and hatchery processes, he obtained a grant to start the process on a nearby farm.

Ropes: On five acres of previously unused school property there is now a "ropes" course utilized in all physical education classes as well as by area youth groups—a senior project that will be visible for a long, long time.

Streams: Even though it didn't please several area industries, a report on the quality of stream ecosystems in the school district was compiled by a senior with an interest in biology. The township and city trustees each have a copy.

Underground Railroad: Missing from the textbooks used by students in her school was a reference to the important role her community played in the Underground Railroad. So this senior undertook a research project that yielded a set of maps for use by her teachers in showing exactly how escaped slaves made their way through the area.

Video: What better way to help the school understand the costs and benefits of the senior project than by making it into a movie? So this senior filmed the experiences of his compeers and provided the school with a documentary record.

Women: They were there during the Civil War, weren't they?

Again, noting something missing from her high school textbooks, this senior put together an essay on the contributions made by women during this time period, with an annotated bibliography for student use.

Zydeco: What is it, anyway? Simply one of the many forms of indigenous American music that was included in this senior's audio portfolio of American sounds.

Looking over these examples, we can see several common themes:

1. Interest and Choice: The students *chose* their topics based on their own interests. These were things that had the power to hold their attention even through the rough spots.
2. Research: All the projects required students to go beyond what they already knew. They had to bring to bear all the tools they had learned throughout their schooling in order to find new information.
3. Product: Something was actually produced by the student. This was not just a research paper, this was something kids actually did.
4. Audience: All of these involved students in preparing something for an audience beyond the teacher. Because so many eyes would see this, students knew it had to be good.

These types of changes require that the school rewire the way it uses time. As discussed in the prior chapter, time has to be used in flexible ways, especially if, as in this case, students are to have the time to carry out major pieces of work and faculty are to guide them. Second semester of senior year might find a student with nothing on the afternoon schedule but Senior Project. During this time the student is allowed to come and go from school to accomplish the work at hand. For those whom this "freedom" gives pause, it is important to remember that within four months most seniors will go from high school, where they have little control over their time, to real life, where they have total control. Perhaps a little practice at time management while they are still around would be useful.

Additionally, we could use such changed approaches to graduation to be more clear with students about why they are learning the things we try to teach. How often in our own schooling experience have we heard the phrase: "Because someday you'll need to know it." This is the stock answer when students ask "Why do we have to learn this?" I believe students are entitled to a much more honest answer than that. An answer that is carefully thought out and that clearly reflects the graduation requirements of the school. An answer that they are given before they even ask the question.

What might that answer look like? On the first day of high school we could hand every freshman a booklet simply titled *Graduation Standards.*

The first part of our booklet should outline the school platform, pointing out how the skills we want students to develop in high school will help them in life after high school. If public speaking is required of everyone and calculus only of those going into engineering, let's say that up front. If we believe all citizens should recognize a spurious scientific claim when they hear one, and that we all need to know how to type because of the growing presence of computers, we should say that as well. If the fine arts can enhance our ability to learn and to enjoy the world around us, while writing a research paper is a skill used only in college, let's say that too. The school should begin by being honest with its students about why we want them to know or to be able to do whatever it is we require.

Part two of our booklet will tell how we want our students to demonstrate that they have gained the skills and understandings that we require for graduation. For a portfolio, the booklet will say what that portfolio should have in it and how it will be judged and presented. For a final project, the criteria and some examples of acceptable work will be set forth. Our entering freshmen must be told as clearly as possible what it will take to graduate and how they can show off their accomplishments.

Finally, in our booklet freshmen will read about how the adults in the school will help them reach the graduation standards: How the courses they are required to pass will help them develop the skills and find the information we want them to know. How extracurricular activities can complement classroom experiences in developing necessary skills. What the guidance counselor or principal can help with. What resources there are in the library, gym, classrooms, and community that they can use to become a graduate.

Given all this information, students begin the journey to becoming a high school graduate. As they work toward the skills they need, the dynamic in the school changes. The learners become more responsible for developing as graduates. They are given the task of caring for their own development. They cannot assume that passing or failing classes is all that counts. Rather, they need to attend to how they are developing the skills that they will need in the world after high school. They need to be reflective about their own development as learners.

The role of the faculty changes similarly. What we teach now has to meet new criteria. It is not enough to say it is in the book, or required, when asked to justify what we teach. The more relevant question now is how it helps our kids reach the goals we have set for them. In this scenario no course is an elective. Every one is necessary for students to develop the habits of heart and mind we want in our grads, our future neighbors. Looked at in this way, how we teach is as important as what we teach, and it is the next topic we explore.

Strategy Three:
Shift roles to student-as-worker, teacher-as-coach

If we are to teach young people to become reflective and responsible learners, we have to make the act of teaching consistent with that agenda. To that end we must overturn Boyer's quip about kids watching while teachers work. We must make high schools places where adults and students work together.

The Coalition of Essential Schools put this most eloquently in their Common Principle number five:

> **The governing practical metaphor of the school should be student-as-worker** rather than the more familiar metaphor of teacher-as-deliverer-of-instructional-services. Accordingly, a prominent pedagogy will be coaching, to provoke students to learn how to learn and thus to teach themselves.

Most important in this approach to teaching is that students learn to learn for themselves. While most of us live well past the age of sixty-eight, formal schooling for many of us ends at eighteen. Here comes some simple math again, this time adding up to fifty years of life in which the average American is not under the tutelage of any teacher. It is only reasonable to assume that most of what we learn in life will not be taught to us in school. But what we do learn in school can make the rest of our life's lessons all the more possible.

Helping young people learn for themselves involves teachers "teaching from behind." While students are actively involved in learning, the teacher, as a coach, makes suggestions and gives hints on how to proceed, critiques student efforts, pressing them on to better work, guides students' reflections on their work, and applauds successful completion of each task. There is no one right way to do this. All kids require a special touch at the right moment to reassure them that they really can learn for themselves. We are never sure what will throw that switch with a particular kid. But it is only by putting students in situations where they actually do something, where they are allowed to see for themselves how things work or fit together, that they not only learn but learn to learn. Just as the best basketball coach doesn't teach her charges "about" basketball but rather how to "play" basketball, the teacher/coach teaches not "about" history, math, or chemistry but how to "do" history, math, or chemistry.

Walk with me through a high school full of teacher/coaches. This is the best way to sample the many ways coaching can happen. (For those of you who want more than just a visit, in the Appendix you'll find listed more complete works on each of these strategies.) Instead of monotonous droning on by talking heads in these classrooms, we'll find students busy at work on the lessons of the day.

First stop is a biology class. Good science teachers could always get students up "doing" science. Labs like the ones Reba Theiss carries out bring to life the often abstract concepts of the physical world. But today the students have pulled their chairs in a circle and are avidly engaged in a discussion of Stephen Jay Gould's essay *The Panda's Thumb,* which is about evolutionary theory. This is not just an ordinary shoot-the-breeze session. Guided by the format for "Socratic seminars" worked out by the Paideia Center at the University of North Carolina at Chapel Hill, the teacher carefully chooses the reading as a standard in its field that illuminates the topic at hand. The very process of the seminar is organized so that the teacher serves as moderator, carefully drawing each student in, keeping notes on how the discussion is moving, adding a thought-provoking question as the conversation moves on. As the time comes for class to end, students linger in the classroom asking the teacher for clarification of a particular point while other students continue the discussion on down the hall.

We'll visit an English class next, one where students are honing writing skills through writing children's books. A premium is placed on developing the story while not writing above the intended audience. This means every word must be carefully selected, no overwriting allowed. Walking in, we find students huddled over desks pulled around to create teams of four. Today they are involved in a cooperative learning process where they are analyzing award-winning children's books for descriptive writing. Each team member has a job, one keeping the discussion going, another taking notes for reporting back to the group, another keeping an eye on the time, the last preparing to speak to the class for the group. In this as in the biology class, the success of group work is not left to chance. The entire process has been organized by the teacher to insure that the students *all* understand what they are covering and are able to put it into their own words. As the class is going on, she moves from group to group, quizzing each student, making sure everyone is involved. Then the first group presentation begins. . . .

Taking leave of the English class, we walk to a U.S. History class and find . . . an empty room. Before long we track them down in the library, the entire class scattered around working on their characters for the current project on the Depression. As a class they are putting together a video to be used in future U.S. History classes, styled after Studs Terkel's book *Hard Times.* Based on interviews with local people who lived through the Depression and on library research, each student will take the part of an American and be interviewed for the video. One student is John Steinbeck telling why he wrote *The Grapes of Wrath,* another portrays Eleanor Roosevelt, another Eugene Debs, while one girl is struggling to find out more about those who worked in soup kitchens. The teacher moves from student to student, checking criteria sheets and deadlines, asking for an update from everyone. Clearly she has no time to talk to us, so we slip out of the library and head for the wood shop.

As with the science teachers, teachers in the areas known traditionally as "vocational" have always valued hands-on student work. In shops, kitchens, and greenhouses students have tried out the skills they are being taught. But today we find the class sitting at their drafting tables attentively following along as the teacher sets forth the steps in centering a drawing. When he finishes, the T-squares, rulers, pencils, and paper appear and the kids take their first stab at an overhead view of the pieces they will soon be building in the shop. There are times, even in the most active classes, when the teacher/coach sits the students down and lays out what is to be done next. Just as the athletic or drama coach explains how and why something must be done, the teacher/coach engages in lectures as necessary. But the relevance of the lecture is clear to the students, who see the information as necessary to complete the task at hand.

In each of these rooms the teacher and the students have been actively engaged in learning. The role of teacher as coach has been to select appropriate materials, plan classroom activities, present information, monitor students' progress, suggest resources, assist with student research, edit, review, critique, and compliment student work. It is the most difficult form of teaching, requiring much more than just well-organized lecture notes. But it is the most rewarding form of teaching as well, leading to deep engagement with students as active learners.

Students in these rooms work hard. Rather than sit passively and take notes, they learn what it means to learn. They are questioned and cajoled, they find new resources and stumble into dead ends, they write and rewrite, they put together and take apart, but most of all they use their minds all the time. Rather than just try to figure out whether or not what the teacher said will be on the test, they are busy working at finding out what fits where. They are challenged to have ideas, to make sense of new material, to think through what it means to know something.

Deborah Meier, former principal of Central Park East Secondary School, defines being well educated this way: "Getting into the habit of developing theories that can be articulated clearly and then checked out in a thoughtful way." This is what these teacher/coaches are about: helping young people use their minds to figure out how the world works. To do this means avoiding teaching-as-telling—putting the brakes on our natural instinct to fill kids up with every bit of knowledge we possess out of fear that they will stop learning after high school graduation. But it is hard to focus on how we learn to think when we are overwhelmed by what we are to think about. Such is the trap in which high schools are often caught. The drive to cover everything drives out the time to learn much of anything. Exploring that dilemma concludes this chapter.

Strategy Four:
Teach fewer things better: Less is more

On the first Sunday in May for the past few years my family, along with a host of friends, have launched our canoes in the Federal Creek at our town of Amesville. On our "Amesville to the Sea" annual outing we spend four to five hours paddling down the creek toward the Hocking River. How far we get depends upon the winter snow and spring rains, as they determine the flow of the creek.

Each year I find or see something new on our trip. One year it was the old abandoned coke furnaces outside the now vanished coal town of Utley, Ohio, furnaces from which were hauled the coke that burned bright in Chicago's steel mills and made the rapid expansion of the railroads possible. The best places to find morel mushrooms was the research project another year. Just this past year we floated under a blue heron rookery and watched as these great birds swooped in and out of nests certainly too flimsy to support them perched sixty or more feet above our heads. It is always a trip filled with surprises.

Alongside the Federal Creek runs State Route 329, which I take to school every morning. The trip that takes more than four hours by canoe takes me only ten minutes or so by automobile. And as I zip along I pass over the coke ovens (they literally bore under the road), under the heron nests, and right by the morels—never noticing any of them. My canoe and my car both take me along roughly the same route, but the consequences of each trip are drastically different.

The high school curriculum most of our children cover is similar to that drive in my car. I have stacked before me the textbooks that the average high school sophomore is expected to plow through in one year. In 180 days there are 750 pages of U.S. History, 900 of literature, 400 of Spanish, 830 of biology, 560 of geometry. Add in two or three elective courses—say, art and band with no text, and psychology with 600 pages—and we have a situation where sixteen-year-olds are expected to "cover" 4,040 pages of content a year. Or, allowing for a 180-day school year, nearly twenty-three pages a day. Cover it they will; teachers feeling pressure to get kids through the book will drive them daily through page after page, chapter after chapter, regardless of how well kids learn. But, what will they learn?

In chapter 1 we saw how Leon, Donna, and Reba, faculty at FHHS, felt pressured by the schedule and the number of kids they were expected to teach daily. We followed students Sharon, Jake, and Nina as they raced from class to class just trying to stay one period ahead in their studies. Now layer over that the vast amount of material we expect teachers and students to cover. Is it any surprise that in this scenario teaching is reduced to telling and learning to memorizing facts for tests? And at the end of this process, after five thousand hours, what do we have to show for our efforts? Not many students would be willing to stake their diplomas on again being able to pass an American History exam or prove the Pythagorean Theorem—things that at one time, during their sophomore year, each of our kids could do, things that they probably did not remember very long after they passed in the test papers, because we carried them through all those things by car when we should have let them help us paddle past in canoes.*

Anyone who has seriously worked at making high school a better place for children to learn has had to confront the issue of coverage of content. It is not enough to change the daily schedule or graduation standards. What also must be altered is how we think

* I experienced in my own home the lack of depth that teachers are forced to face when Michael, my older son, was in sixth grade. I was working with him on his math, and we were dividing fractions. His strategy was to invert the second fraction and then multiply. When I asked him why he did this, he replied that he did not know, but his teacher had told him this would give him the correct answer. I later met with his teacher, who we knew was a good teacher and whom Michael said he enjoyed. I asked her why she had taken this approach, as it really seemed not to have helped the kids understand the principles behind dividing fractions. Her answer, filled with the frustration so many teachers experience: With an entire book to cover she only had a few days for division of fractions, and teaching kids to "invert and multiply" was the quickest approach.

about content. Rather than assume there is something magical about the textbooks we race our children through, we should reconsider what we teach in light of what we believe about learning.

Led by Ted Sizer's work with the Coalition of Essential Schools, senior high school restructuring in this country has begun to challenge the notion that coverage equals learning. Looking seriously at that equation inside our high schools, Sizer has argued that a better way of looking at learning is to forsake coverage in the name of understanding. To really connect with students' minds we have to take the time to dig into the content deeply, helping young people make sense of the world around them. The clearest way to put this is found in Common Principle number two from Sizer's Coalition of Essential Schools:

> The school's goals should be simple: that each student **master a limited number of essential skills and areas of knowledge.** While these skills and areas will, to varying degrees, reflect the traditional academic disciplines, the program's design should be shaped by the intellectual and imaginative powers and competencies that students need, rather than necessarily by "subjects" as conventionally defined. The aphorism "Less Is More" should dominate: curricular decisions should be guided by the aim of thorough student mastery and achievement rather than by an effort merely to cover content.

(Interestingly enough, this is a choice long ago made by educators in Japan, a country with which the U.S. is often unfavorably compared in terms of education. While Japan does indeed have longer school days and a longer year, students in Japan do not cover as much content as American students. The pace in Japanese schools is much slower, and the goal is that all students gain an understanding of the workings of disciplines, not just a cursory memorization of facts.)

One of the most noted researchers on teaching for understanding is Howard Gardner of Harvard University. His research has shown how in the sciences, mathematics, and the humanities even the most "educated" students seem unable to use what they learn in the classroom when confronted with real-world applications of their knowledge. In the classic example of this problem,

Gardner points out that students who have taken a physics course are no more likely to understand what forces are at work on a penny in midflight after being flipped than are students who have not taken physics. (The incorrect answer is the force of the thumb that flipped the coin in one direction and gravity in the other. In fact, the only force acting on the coin once it leaves your hand is gravity.)

The reason for this misunderstanding, and others like it, is that while students have memorized the right answers, they have not taken the time to learn them in context. Gardner points out similar misconceptions in mathematics, as students rigidly apply memorized algorithms while not understanding the process behind them. Teaching in the humanities and social sciences also falls short of leading students to understanding and instead seems to reinforce student preconceptions. Exposing students to long lists of facts and/or data leads them to believe that every statement about the human condition—be it from literature, history, or the social sciences—is either fact or nonfact. In reality, while facts exist, it is interpretation that provides insights. But students, unaccustomed to checking out multiple points of view as the rushed teacher just tries to get them through the facts in bold print, forgo interpretation and insight for memorization.

Gardner's point, and Sizer's, is that if high school is to have any effect on how well children use their minds, it will have to cover less in more depth. Students will have to have more concrete experiences with the generative principles in each field in order to continue to use them throughout their lives. We cannot expect, in the time we have, our children to cover everything and simultaneously to understand what they cover. An ironic illustration of this simple truth is that in our high school we use the same U.S. History textbook that I used when I was a high school student. The only difference in the text is that it now includes twenty-five more years of U.S. History including Nixon's fall, the end of the Vietnam War, the shifting of economic power to Japan, the Camp David accords, the Reagan presidency, the Iran/Contra affair, the breakup of the Soviet Union, and the Gulf War, just to name a few. Yet kids still have the same 180 days of school to cover the book that I did, and they still only get to the end of World War II.

If we were to teach for understanding, we could do it by giving students more extensive experiences with the material we teach over longer periods of time. For example, rather than give students one survey course in U.S. History, why not offer a four-year U.S. Studies program? For good measure, let's call it a humanities course and include the English requirement as well. Over four years students could focus on particular time periods, studying the effects of physical geography on human geography, reading the literature of the period (including autobiographies), researching selected events or personages, linking what happened nationally with local and world history.

Here is an outline of such a program.

The American Experience

This four-year course combines history, English, government, and literature in a way that will help students use our past to understand our present. Each year students will study a theme tied to a particular time period in American history. We will use that theme to understand the American experience and what makes someone an American. To dig into each theme, students will use standard historical resources along with autobiographies, novels, and essays.

Freshman Year

THEME: Who Is an American?

TIME PERIOD: Prehistory (early Indian migrations) to the late 1800s.

FOCUS: The people who populated America, their dreams, hopes, struggles, and triumphs. Particular attention paid to African-Americans and Native Americans and whether or not they were allowed to "be Americans."

ESSENTIAL QUESTION: Who is an American, and why?

Sophomore Year

THEME: Building a World Power

TIME PERIOD: Industrialization to the Depression

FOCUS: A particular focus on Americans as nation builders. Also, how nation building began to raise issues related to poverty and social class.

ESSENTIAL QUESTION: What are the domestic and international responsibilities of the nation?

Junior Year

THEME: America and the World

TIME PERIOD: World War II to 1980

FOCUS: The nation's involvement in issues around the world as well as turmoil within the country. Focus on how economic growth and contraction affected social policy.

ESSENTIAL QUESTION: Can the American Dream be exported?

Senior Year

THEME: Power, Powerlessness, and American Government

TIME PERIOD: 1980 to the present

FOCUS: The current issues of the day from foreign policy to welfare reform. Particular focus on who decides and how they obtained the power to decide.

ESSENTIAL QUESTION: Who has power in America?

Science and math are logical multiyear partners as well. The manipulation of variables in algebra is a fundamental tool of scientific experimentation, as are statistics and probability. Rather than race students through a course on everything you need to know about biology or algebra in one year, why not a two-year science/math investigation? Begin with the basic tools of each area and then offer students a variety of options for their own scientific exploration in which they must utilize both the mathematical and analytic skills seen as central to scientific thinking.

Two teachers at FHHS have begun building exactly such a program with our freshman math and science courses. At the start of the year they began with a unit on measurement in which students manipulated variables in working out density, volume, and mass problems. One such problem asked students to work out the volume of the school's greenhouse, then calculate the weight of the building in grams if it were solid gold. (Just for fun, one could work out the value of a solid gold greenhouse as well.) Combined lessons such as these continued through units on acceleration, biodiversity, chemistry, and a host of other topics.

Of course there is no need to limit our less-is-more thinking to what are often referred to as the core academic courses. We could spread physical education and health courses out and have students utilize what they learn in other fields and in extracurricular programs to develop personal plans for healthy living. The arts and languages could become tools for adding dimensions to students' understanding of literature or history. Regardless of how it is done, the focus should be on doing a few things very well rather than everything at a surface level.

Imagine Leslie and her difficulties with science if we could build curriculum in this manner. Here's how I see her and Reba working together, based on the actual graduation platform used in one school.

"Ms. Theiss, I'm still not sure I understand how carbon was chosen as the key element for historical dating."

"Fine, no problem, let's look at it this way," Reba starts as she takes another approach to helping Leslie understand how carbon-14 deteriorates. It's a difficult explanation, but one that is crucial for Leslie as she is working on her final exhibition in science. She, like every other senior, has to demonstrate to the faculty that she can investigate a public claim that is based on scientific evidence and explain to a group of her peers whether or not it is reasonable.

The faculty at Leslie's high school had agreed that, in a world where consumers are bombarded with scientific claims, they wanted their grads to be able to separate the reasonable from the misleading. Thus, every student must present one such claim and his or her research on it to laypeople—fellow students— convincing them how they should respond to the claim. During their senior year all students took a science class totally devoted to researching this issue. The teacher played the role of coach, guiding them as they explored the issue.

Leslie was one of the more ambitious students, researching a recent public disagreement between two university biologists on the legitimacy of recent fossil finds. Other students were looking at advertising claims for medicines and weight loss programs, whether or not FDA tests on rats revealed genuine risk to humans, and the potential environmental impact of a proposed dump in the area.

Reba and Leslie finished, and Reba drifted off to help another student. Near the end of the class Leslie pulled out her daily lab log and jotted down what she had accomplished. She had found several more sources, one on a previous fossil hoax, and, more important, she had a much better grip on carbon dating. But perhaps the most significant entry in her journal was dated several weeks earlier. "I'm learning that science isn't just for scientists. It's for anyone that doesn't want to get fooled."

CHAPTER FIVE

Developing Responsible Citizens

One of the first students I met when I began work at Federal Hocking was a senior by the name of Janet. For two periods a day Janet presided over our outer office, answering the phone, greeting visitors, making copies for staff. While she could be headstrong, she was always cheerful and pleasant to everyone she met.

Each day I would learn a bit more about Janet through our casual conversations. She was planning to go into nursing after she graduated from a nearby technical college. She had married her steady boyfriend of six years the summer before her senior year—by her own choice, she was anxious to assert. Her husband, a fine young man whom I met later, held a good job: good enough that they were buying their own home, had two cars, and were even planning a vacation for the coming summer.

It struck me again and again how much responsibility Janet handled so well. At home she managed all the family finances, paying bills, budgeting the income, filling out the income tax forms. There was also upkeep on the cars, the maintenance of the house, and the hundreds of other little chores that Janet and her husband, like every married couple, faced daily. She did all of that while doing well enough in her high school classes to gain admission to nursing school. On top of all this, unknown to us at school, she and her husband decided to conceive a child, and Janet spent the last three months of the school year carrying on a responsible pregnancy complete with doctor visits, vitamins, and preparing a baby's room.

Janet has since had her child, her marriage is still strong, and she is almost finished with her nursing education. We could, and should, claim her as a successful FHHS graduate. But in the back of my head lies one event that involved Janet that has always bothered me, not only about her high school education but about the high school experience of every student.

It was a Thursday afternoon and I was strolling the halls, taking a break from finishing a report. Down the hall came Janet, with the resigned grin/grimace on her face that would show up whenever she ran into something she saw as absurd. Without even waiting for my greeting, she stuffed a small yellow piece of paper in my hand, said, "You'd think I wouldn't need this," and continued on down the hall. After she had passed, I unfolded the paper to find it was a hall pass, with time, date, teacher's signature, and "bathroom" checked in the appropriate box. More than any other example I could ever think of, this demonstrates why our high schools fail at one of our most important tasks, helping young people become responsible adults.

Janet's teacher was just doing his job. The rules of the school were clear—students are not to be in the hall without a pass. But how absurd it was that a young woman who could manage a family and home outside of school was not deemed responsible enough in school to decide when it would be appropriate to use the toilet. In this and dozens of other ways we have perversely organized our high schools to prevent young people from becoming responsible adults. This means we have not finished rethinking our high schools just by changing how we connect with students and what and how we teach them. We also need to rethink how they are treated on a daily basis and whether or not that experience will help them learn civic responsibility.

We learn socially responsible behavior the way we learn everything else, through practice. Unfortunately, the way we set up our high schools gives students very few opportunities to actually practice responsible behavior. Faced with large numbers of teenagers and very few adults, our main concern in high school is control. Students are provided handbooks that are full of rules about what they cannot do. Choosing to behave responsibly is reduced to merely following the rules. Not that schools shouldn't have rules, but rule following is perhaps the most limited way in which we display responsibility. More significant ways include being accountable for one's own actions, choosing to make a contribution, making wise decisions that take into account how decisions affect others, and making productive use of one's own time. In multiple yet subtle ways high schools almost seem to work against the development of these forms of responsible behavior.

Perhaps the clearest example of this is in how we monitor students' academic progress. Every high school keeps reams of paper on students' progress. Test scores, grades, reports, attendance records, teacher comments, papers of all colors, sizes, and textures fill file drawers, tracking each student's life in school. Students themselves, on the other hand, don't even have to keep the notes they took in classes from one year to the next. Ask a high school senior to pull out a paper she completed in her freshman English class and compare it with what she is doing now, and you will likely be greeted with a blank stare. While she may, and I emphasize may, be able to compare grades from one year to the next, it is almost certain she will not be able to compare what she has learned in any systematic way.

Now ask the same senior this question: "How has your time improved in the one-mile run (or score in band competition, average yards per carry on the football field, earned run average, kills per game in volleyball) since your freshman year?" Make sure you have plenty of time to sit and listen while time improvements are detailed with explanations linking them to new training camps, etc. Kids *can* and do take responsibility for tracking their progress. So if we want to teach responsibility, we might begin by considering how to make young people responsible for tracking their academic progress.

We tend to be more responsible when things depend upon our actions. In a conversation with a parent I was asked, "What do kids at our school have to take care of?" This father went on to talk about how his children had never been as responsible as when they had to take care of their own pets. They knew, he felt, that they were being depended upon, and that fostered in his kids a sense of responsibility. His question sticks with me today, four years later, when I think about how to help kids become more responsible.

There is very little in our high schools that kids have to take care of. The basic facility is provided, they are fed and picked up after. Someone else sees that the building is kept in working order. Perhaps even more important, kids know school will go on with or without them; whether or not they are there seems not to matter in the case of most students. With so little depending upon them, they are hard pressed to understand why they should be responsible. Again, we learn from experience; we become responsible when we need to be.

Another example of how we often fail to teach responsibility is in the use of time. Clearly most high school students know that they do not have to be responsible with how they use their time. Seldom are they unaccompanied, as schools are obsessed with watching students' every move via teacher patrols or surveillance cameras. In fact, kids spend more time trying to figure out how to get away with breaking the rules than how to manage their own behavior. Why bother? Someone else is keeping track of how they should behave. Besides, with every minute scheduled, there's no time left in the school day to be responsible for.

Perhaps the most unfortunate demonstration of how we fail to help high school students become responsible for their own time is seen in colleges and universities. Every year thousands of academically able students "flunk out" in their very first year on campus. The reason is not a lack of skills or knowledge. Instead, it is that after years of schooling where they were never responsible for how they used their time, in college our kids find themselves completely left to their own devices. No one gets them out of bed, makes them go to class, tells them when to eat or study. With little or no practice at making such decisions, it is all too easy to make the wrong ones—staying up too late, sleeping in too long, waiting to cram for a test until the last minute—irresponsible yet unsurprising choices that lead to many students arriving back home before their first year of college is over.

But what about student government? Don't we at least teach responsible behavior, even responsible democratic behavior, through having a student government? Perhaps in some schools the student government is one place where students learn responsible behavior through exercising it. But in most high schools this is not the case. Elections are, as most students will tell you, popularity contests (not much different from running for the presidency of the United States) in which the winners have little if anything to do. Sometimes they are given the job of organizing homecoming, but beyond that, what? In most high schools student government breeds more cynicism than activism, as the agenda is a steady round of fund-raising, boosterism, and organizing dances.

To add insult to injury, the amount of responsibility we grant students doesn't change no matter how long a student is in high school. Take Janet, for example. As a senior she could go to lunch a couple minutes early, work in the office instead of sit in study hall, and have a chance at becoming homecoming queen. Aside from that, not much distinguished her senior year from her freshman year in terms of the responsibilities she was asked to take on. Certainly eighteen- and nineteen-year-olds should be expected to act more responsibly and be given more responsibility for their actions than thirteen- and fourteen-year-olds. But such is not the case in our high schools today.

If we are serious about young people becoming responsible adults, we have to give them places to practice responsibility. Certainly they will fail at it from time to time—that is why we hire teachers, to help kids learn from their mistakes. But they cannot learn what it means to be an adult, to take responsible action, if they aren't given the chance to practice. High school is a great place to engage in such practice.

Our inability to provide students with the opportunity to practice responsibility is yet another way an institutional sensibility dominates our thinking about high school. Institutions are preoccupied with control, especially centralized control. Power is vested in a few individuals and exercised from the top down, rules and regulations are uniformly applied, and seldom is anyone outside of the central bureaucracy asked to assist in decision making. Some of this is due to size, as large institutions require uniform and often rapid responses to numerous issues daily. But even in small institutional settings the same behavior is observed, as the notion of sharing power in an organization is often perceived as weakness.

Schools that behave as institutions demonstrate this same fear of power sharing. Principals hold the power to make most decisions, as well as the only set of master keys to the building. Every student infraction of the rules is dealt with in the same manner so that consistency is maintained (even if justice is overridden in the process). While teachers may share some authority through a site-based management committee, the single largest group of the school's population, students, have little or no voice.

Communities see power in a different manner. In sharing power, through engaging all members in as many decisions as possible, communities see strength. Through reacting to every individual event as just that—an occurrence in its own right, not a repeat in a category of events to be dealt with in the same way—justice is more likely to be achieved while consistency is forgone. The strength in a community lies not in its rules or bureaucracy. Rather, communities draw their strength from their ability to provide every member with a connection to the community by sharing power widely. So it is in schools that work to be communities. By engaging students in sharing power, they build the connections with young people that are necessary if our students are to do their very best-quality work.

We now turn to how we can help our kids develop a greater sense of responsibility through building school communities where power is shared.

Strategy One: Let kids keep the books

The most important thing in school is the work of students. However, as we have seen time and time again, the most important thing to students is the number of credits they earn. So what happens if, as suggested in the previous chapter, we stop graduating students on the basis of credits earned and substitute portfolios, exhibitions, and other demonstrations of what they have learned? Such a strategy gives us the opportunity to help students learn responsibility through monitoring and chronicling their own achievements; each student should be the holder of his or her own permanent life.

We could begin this new movement toward responsible behavior the day students walk in as freshmen. Having laid out for parents and teachers a clear set of expectations for what students will be able to do upon graduation, we should set forth these expectations for the students. And what better time to do this than when they are starting high school? The first thing we can put in students' hands is a clear road map to graduation—a road map not only to follow but on which to chart their own progress.

Currently kids just count credits. Buried somewhere in the student handbook they are given on the first day of school is a statement that reads somewhat like this:

GRADUATION: To graduate from X High School, students must earn the following credits:

English	4
Math	3
Social Studies	3
Science	2
Health	$\frac{1}{2}$
Physical Education	$\frac{1}{2}$
Additional credits	7

From then on, the one thing that kids always know is how many credits they have. Not what they've learned, not how they have changed, sometimes not even what grades they have earned, but what credits they have amassed.

We know the downside of this—throughout this book we have seen examples of how credit counting gets in the way of learning. But there is a positive message in this as well. Kids *will* remember *exactly* what it takes to graduate. Lesson: Tell kids what they have to do.

Imagine if we substituted an entire manual for that paragraph in the student handbook—an "owner's manual" for all students to consult through an entire high school career, one in which they could note accomplishments, keep track of requirements met, and identify for themselves their own educational needs and ways to meet them, as outlined in chapter 4. Here's a different look at what we could tell our students about what is expected of them.*

---

* Much of the following student's "owner's manual" comes from the work of parents, students, and staff at FHHS. As we have not yet adopted such a package at our school, I have taken some liberties with their work to illustrate this point.

Graduation Requirement

Welcome to "X" High School. Over the next four years we will work with you to help you gain academic skills, explore various careers, develop into an active citizen, and learn to manage your daily affairs. In each of these areas you will be expected to learn various skills. In every class you take your teachers will focus on some part of these skills. Your job will be not only to learn these skills but also to keep portfolios where you keep track of what you have learned. Here are the four portfolios you will keep:

The Academic Portfolio

In your academic portfolio you will keep track of what you have learned in the subject areas of English, math, science, and social studies. You will also keep track of your work in areas of interest to you, such as music, art, industrial technology, or agriculture. Additionally, in this portfolio you will record how you are doing in your library skills, ability to type, and proficiency with a computer.

The Careers Portfolio

When you graduate from high school, it will be time to find a job or go on to college. To help you prepare for this, you will be developing a careers portfolio. In this you will have a resume, sample job and college applications, an autobiography where you detail your strengths and interests, and a record of careers you have explored. You will also keep track of your experiences with mock interviews, your internship, and field trips you go on to colleges, technical schools, and various places of employment.

The Citizenship Portfolio

When you turn eighteen in our nation, you become a full-fledged citizen. This is one of our most cherished rights and responsibilities in the United States of America. To help you be prepared to exercise these rights and to carry out these responsibilities, you will be assisted in putting together a citizenship portfolio. Here you will keep track of how well you can find information about and take a position on an issue of public concern. You will also record your attendance at local government meetings, how well you can analyze news articles, and what you have learned about how our government works. You might even record the date you register to vote.

The Life-After-High-School Portfolio

For many of you, when you leave high school you will also be leaving home. This means you'll need to be ready to do all sorts of things: keep track of your own finances, balance a checkbook, file income taxes, rent or buy a house, and hundreds of other small and large tasks. In the life-after-high-school portfolio you will monitor your growth to becoming able to handle your own affairs. When you are finished with it you'll have samples of how you can keep track of the day-to-day jobs we all perform as adults.

These are the things you will learn at our high school over the next four years. In all of your classes you will be given the experiences and opportunities to complete your portfolios. In the pages that follow you will find a more detailed explanation of each portfolio and the ways you will keep track of your learning. Your advisory teacher will go over these with you and will be available throughout your high school career for advice on your work. But remember, it is your responsibility to keep track of your education—an education that will serve you for a lifetime.

Following this overview, each area would be presented in more detail for students. They would be given checklists to keep and instructions on where to store their work, and shown how the courses they take are tied to the portfolios they are compiling. On a regular basis their advisory periods would be devoted to working through their portfolios and examining their progress. These would become their permanent files, which would follow them into the world after high school.

Let's look at the careers portfolio in some detail, just to see what students would be expected to track. This would be a particularly interesting one at many high schools, because at the end of their sophomore year in some states students may transfer from the comprehensive high where they began their high school career to regional vocational schools. The careers portfolio could be designed to help students make the often difficult choice between staying at their "home" school or transferring to the vocational school. (A similar argument could be made in districts where students transfer to "specialty" high schools for their final two years.)

The first piece of the portfolio that students would use would be a cover sheet that identifies the experiences and work students should complete. Each of these would be linked to a course or courses, so that kids would know when they can expect to complete it. Behind the cover sheet, perhaps in a looseleaf notebook, would then be placed the completed work that has been entered in the portfolio. Here's what it could look like:

CAREERS PORTFOLIO

Phase One

By the time you finish your sophomore year you should have completed the following activities. Check each one off as you complete it and keep any necessary records in your careers notebook.

____ date	____ (teacher's init'ls)	☐ 1. Development of a career exploration plan, which should include
____	____	☐ a) A record of all field trips, visits, speakers, etc. that you have been involved with during your freshman and sophomore years
____	____	☐ b) An essay on how you make your decision either to attend vocational school or to stay at our school for your junior and senior years
____	____	☐ c) Steps you intend to carry out over the next two years in your career exploration
____	____	☐ 2. First version of your autobiography (to be updated senior year)
____	____	☐ 3. First version of your resume (to be updated senior year)
____	____	☐ 4. Demonstrations of the following skills
____	____	☐ a) Composing and typing a letter of inquiry for college or a job

____   ____   ☐   b) Public speaking, in a presentation on a career you are exploring

____   ____   ☐   c) Using the phone appropriately to secure information or an appointment

Phase Two

By the time you finish the first semester of your senior year you should have completed the following activities. Check each one off as you complete it and keep any necessary records in your careers notebook.

____   ____   ☐   1. Completion of the career exploration plan
date   (teacher's   developed in your sophomore year,
        init'ls)   including

____   ____   ☐   a) Evidence of steps you have taken to decide what to do after high school: college or job applications filled out, visits made to colleges or job sites, internship experiences, tests taken, etc.

____   ____   ☐   b) An essay on your current career choice, how you came to this choice, and your future goals

____   ____   ☐   2. Final version of your autobiography

____   ____   ☐   3. Final version of your resume, including a cover letter and at least three letters of recommendation

____   ____   ☐   4. Demonstration of the following skills

____   ____   ☐   a) Personal interviewing

____   ____   ☐   b) Public speaking

This approach to having students, with the assistance of teachers, keep track of their progress in school not only makes students more aware of what they are learning, it also encourages them to keep track of their work and in so doing be more responsible for what they learn. The "Why do I have to do this?" question becomes replaced by "When should I get this done?" And students who wait for the guidance counselor to track them down to let them know what courses they still need for graduation might be replaced by students who know that learning is not a passive process of being taught but rather an active endeavor that involves being in control of one's own future.

Strategy Two:
Have every student do something significant

We are only as responsible as the task at hand forces us to be. When we know things will happen without us, as when students know high school will go on with or without their presence, we are less likely to behave in a responsible manner. However, when we know something depends on our behavior solely, when it is up to us to make a difference, then we are more likely to step up to the challenge. We see this in high schools every day with our marching bands, athletic teams, debate and mock trial teams, and various clubs and organizations. Students, without whom these activities would not occur, take on adultlike responsibilities willingly. Replicating this experience in the academic arena would be yet another way to teach responsibility during a student's five thousand high school hours.

The best way to do this is actually outside the school. One of the errors we make is thinking the school walls delimit the arena within which kids learn. In fact, within the walls of the high school are only a few of the resources and experiences we can use to educate our kids. Outside the school walls are some of our best, but often most underutilized, educational resources. Primary among them are the real life experiences kids can have under the tutelage of adults.

We discovered this resource quite by accident at FHHS. During the 1992–93 school year, before we changed our academic schedule, we had several students with simply too much free time on their hands. I had noticed two of them, Bonnie and Lynn, showing up for several periods during the day to help in the office. When I asked them why they were not in class, they said they didn't have class then but instead had three study halls daily. Rather than sit and waste time, they thought we could use the help in the office. Indeed we could, but that didn't seem to me the best way for them to be spending their time.

It was a Wednesday afternoon when I had a chance to talk to the girls about why they were working in the office. We were sitting at one of the cement tables outside the cafeteria, sharing cans of soda as a small reward for their good help. Both of these young women talked about having finished most of their required courses and not wanting to sign up for another physical education class or something they knew would not challenge them. So they had ended up in study halls and from there found their way to the front office.

As our conversation progressed to plans for after graduation, I was pleased to learn that both girls had high hopes for the future. Bonnie hoped to follow several relatives into the medical profession by becoming a nurse. Lynn was intrigued by the field of interior design, an interest spurred by her late arrival in an introductory drafting course during her senior year. Both girls also faced one major obstacle to realizing their dreams: the funds it would take to go on to college.

When I returned to the office I did two things. First, I fished out both girls' schedules to see if it would be possible to get all of their required courses scheduled in the morning. As luck would have it, it was. The second step was to see if someone in our area was willing to take our kids on, letting them learn some valuable hands-on lessons.

I was pleasantly surprised by the positive response I received from the local hospital, indicating that for years they had tried to get high school volunteers during the day. It took only two calls and one visit and Bonnie was on the job.

For Lynn it was a bit more difficult. Interior design is not exactly a booming profession in our area. But my wife reminded me that one of our neighbors was employed as a consultant at a museum design firm located just outside our town. I explained my idea to him, and three days later he called to say, "Let's just go ahead and give it a try."

In this rather haphazard and accidental way the Federal Hocking High School Internship Program was begun.

For both girls the experience was a tremendous success. Bonnie spent every afternoon of her senior year at the hospital. She started out as an errand-runner and by the time she graduated was doing everything from filing X-rays to feeding patients. Lynn spent her first weeks answering phones, but the staff soon recognized her skill and desire to learn and had her sorting paint samples, making suggestions on lighting, and attending regular planning meetings. Before long she had her own desk and was presented with a Christmas "bonus" check (all interns are unpaid), a tradition that continues today.*

Lest one get the impression that the program was instantly a success, it's important to note that we were tripped up by several unforeseen obstacles. We had to find ways to get our students to their internships when their own transportation broke down and to finance the clothing required for students who couldn't afford it. We also learned a valuable lesson from a notable early failure. In a last-ditch attempt to prevent one young man from dropping out, we created an internship within the school, having him do independent research on historical materials for our social studies classes. We hoped his interest in Native Americans would propel him to work harder in all of his classes. We were wrong. The reason: he wasn't assigned a task to do *with* an adult, but simply worked alone on something we did not have to have to make our curriculum work. We needed to keep reminding ourselves to have kids take responsibility for something, something that adults normally do and that other people depend upon them for.

Since this limited start the internship program has grown to include virtually every senior and a significant number of juniors. Even though we are a rural school located fifteen miles from the nearest town of any size, we are able to place students in an ever expanding range of sites. We've had students work in physical therapy clinics and accounting and law offices, ride with university police, rock babies to sleep in maternity wards, help design the Negro Baseball League Hall of Fame, test soils for local farmers, assist in kindergarten classrooms, design book covers and flower gardens, teach mentally handicapped adults and

* While throughout this book I have used pseudonyms, I do want to change that here and mention by name the pioneers in our internship program. Thanks go to O'Bleness Hospital in Athens, Ohio, and Volunteer Coordinator Wanda Llewellyn for providing our first internship site. Thanks also to Andy Merriell at Gerard Hilferty and Associates Inc. for listening to our half-baked ideas and to company owner Gerard Hilferty, who took a chance on high school kids. Both of these organizations continue to this day to take on students and make a difference in their lives.

children, write advertising copy, perform surgery on dogs and cats, watch surgery on humans, counsel mental health patients, help build houses, and on and on. We've even found places within the school for assistant athletic directors, lab and teaching assistants, recycling coordinators, and administrative assistants to coordinate visits to our school and outreach to other schools. There is a very good chance that any time you run into a young person doing volunteer work in our neck of the woods, you will also see a Federal Hocking Lancers book bag, hat, or jacket.

Unlike many of the recent "community service" requirements that are added on to the school day, our internship program goes on during school. For each period students are out on internships (having a four-period day makes it easier for students to leave) they earn a class credit and grade. But it takes more than just showing up to earn the grade. Interns keep journals, write papers, and, as a concluding activity, make public presentations complete with displays about their experiences. The best of these presentations are repeated at our annual Internship Banquet.

Most of our students sign up for the internship program thinking that it is about jobs, that it will give them a way to try out a career or make connections while in high school. For many of them this does happen—they find things they are good at and would enjoy doing. Conversely, sometimes they find out that they really are not cut out for the demands of the field they thought they would be entering. No matter what they begin by thinking, they end up just where we knew they would—with an experience that teaches them just how much responsibility they can handle.

In virtually every final presentation, internship kids talk about what it meant to have someone else depending upon them. "I knew that I couldn't put off preparing for the presentation at my internship, like I do sometimes at school. There was a meeting coming up that if I wasn't ready for it wouldn't happen." "Every day people come to therapy who depend on me being there. I never stay home just because I don't feel well." "When you know those kids are counting on you, well, you just try harder." But their actions speak even louder than words. For example, there was the young woman who, during the winter of 1993 when the weather was so bad only emergency vehicles were allowed on the roads for days at a time, made her way to her internship at the hospital and spent three days as one of the few staff at the maternity ward. Or the intern I found busy at the copy machine on the Martin Luther King Jr. Day holiday getting materials ready for class the next day. Or the young woman who, long after the school year was over, was still meeting during the summer with one of the mental health clients she had been counseling.

High school will always play a social and socializing function. It's where all the other kids are, a place to meet friends, show off for members of the opposite sex, try out new identities and ways of demonstrating that you are an individual. Because of this, kids find plenty of reasons to be irresponsible, and perhaps we should make sure there is always space for this in high school, as we remember that kids should have the chance to be kids. But pushing down the walls of the school shows them how well they can take on responsibility, what they can do when given a chance. While still being kids, they can also be adults, and it's always a pleasure to see them in both roles.

Strategy Three: Give kids more control over their time

Remember the irony of Janet's life in high school? Married and responsible for managing every moment of her life outside of school, she had very little control of the time spent inside school. Fortunately for Janet, her day after school was such that she learned how to make good use of her time. Unfortunately, many students never learn this. This shows up clearly when we see how many kids flunk out of college within their first year or are unable to meet the demands of their first job. The reason most often cited for both failures is the inability of young people to manage their time so they can get things done. Having spent more than a decade as a college professor, I have seen firsthand how student after student falls by the wayside, unable to find enough time to prepare an assignment or study for a test but spending two hours dawdling over lunch or three hours a night watching television. In real life we are each responsible for how we spend our time and for planning to meet deadlines that are often far in the future. Yet very little about high school prepares kids to take such responsibility, as a student's days are tightly controlled and deadlines closely monitored.

High schools have always struggled with issues of control of students. Part of the reason is that we take too much responsibility for students' behavior. No principal wants to hear that his or her high school's students drive too fast, smoke too much, or are rude in shopping areas. So we do all we can during the school day to make sure every student behaves in a way of which we can be proud. But as I have slowly come to realize, we cannot be responsible for every bad habit that kids come to school with. While we can and should prohibit self-destructive and disrespectful behaviors on the part of our students, we cannot and should not accept responsibility for starting students on these same behaviors. Parents who allow their children to drive recklessly, stores that sell cigarettes to minors, adults who model bad manners are the ones responsible for some of the worst teenage behaviors.

Because schools take too much responsibility for student behaviors, they seldom give kids the chance to manage their own time. Fearful that kids will choose inappropriate behaviors for which the school will be blamed, we choose instead to tightly control kids while they are under our supervision. The problem with this strategy is that, while it does control students, it does not allow them to learn to manage their own lives. Then suddenly they graduate and, with the exception of those who opt for the military, they find themselves in charge of their own lives as they have never been before.

What high schools could provide is a place to try out being responsible for one's own behavior, where failure could be a learning experience. We tend to be too afraid of failure in schools, wanting everything to be perfect and students to perform flawlessly. But if they did so, they wouldn't need schools or teachers. Instead, schools should be places where kids can fail with the minimum amount of fear or penalty. In failure we can see where the next lesson should be taught. To help kids learn responsibility for their own time and behavior means giving them the space to be responsible for these things with the full awareness that they will fail and that we will have to teach them how.

One way of doing this is creating spaces in the school day

where students are responsible for their own time. Earlier I talked about the FHHS lunch program. One of the strengths I discussed was the way this "slack time" gave students a choice to connect with the school community. Another strength is that it gives students a block of time during the school day for which they must be responsible. Initially, students are not told where they must be or what they must do. Instead, our kids choose to either use or sometimes waste this time. There are plenty of ways to use the time wisely, with computers, typewriters, and the library available. There are also recreational opportunities, with the gym and outdoor facilities open. But the choice to use the time to their fullest advantage, and the opportunity to squander that same time, is left up to students until they prove that they need more direct instruction in being responsible. Students who fall behind in classwork or demonstrate unacceptable behaviors are assigned to study halls or detention during lunch to catch up or to rethink how they conduct themselves. The important point is that we begin by assuming responsibility and only pull back when kids show they have yet to learn it.

Of course, as with most things, lunch period sometimes looks much better on paper than it does it practice. At the beginning of the 1995–96 school year we noticed way too many kids wandering the halls and disturbing other kids who were trying to study. It seemed time to remind the kids that the freedom they had at lunch carried with it a certain amount of responsibility— responsibility that they were not displaying. Meetings were called and held with each class, where I pointed out to them that what they had could be lost if they didn't rise to the occasion. The issue was not only taking responsibility for their own behavior but sharing responsibility for the behavior of all students. We scaled lunch privileges back somewhat, restricting for a while the students' freedom of movement and where they could eat.

These restrictions were soon lifted as students took control of the situation. In fact, for our seniors (who were the only group of students not to be restricted), this experience generated wonderfully responsible behavior. Within two days we observed them coaching younger students on acceptable behavior and taking charge of supervising several areas.

Out of this breakdown of the lunch program came a powerful teaching moment. Our students were able to see that they could keep or lose something they valued on the basis of their behavior. They learned what responsible behavior is, how to exercise it, and that it pays off in the long run. This one experience was worth more than any lecture or textbook could teach.

Inside the daily course work students carry on, there are ways to provide students more opportunities to demonstrate responsibility as well. Some things are simple to do. For example, at FHHS we allow students research time at the local university library, where they can spend part of their day using a resource stocked well beyond the capabilities of *any* high school library and with a minimum of teacher supervision. Frequently entire classes will disappear into the stacks and periodical rooms searching out documents or books to help with their schoolwork. Teachers also attempt to assign large projects due at various times during the term, for which students have to plan their time and organize their resources. These require that students develop timelines and deadlines to make sure they are getting their work done on time.

A more complex approach to the same agenda is developing a major final piece of work for students to conduct during their senior year. When students take on the Senior Project, it might involve being dismissed from attending school an entire semester in order to devote their time to the project. The type of effort demanded by such a Senior Project will require students to organize their time, secure necessary resources, seek out adult advice, and coordinate the activities of others. In other words, they spend part of their senior year practicing what they will have to do daily as adults.

These are but a few ways to help students "join up" with the adult world through exercising self-responsibility. There are probably many others. However we do it, we know students will learn to be responsible for their own time only if we give them time to be responsible. As with most lessons in life, experience is the best teacher.

Strategy Four: Give students decision-making power

One of the things I remember best about my own high school experience is how few decisions as students we really had the chance to make. Even though I served as a class officer, it seemed we were not asked our opinions about very much. We did get to choose the location and band for the prom, and the theme (within limits) for homecoming. Beyond that there wasn't much over which we had control.

While we had so little to decide in high school, in the world beyond school we were enfranchised adults. Before graduation from high school I had turned eighteen and registered for the draft and to vote. Not only could I be sent to Vietnam, I could vote for the president who was sending us off to war. On the other hand, while in school, I didn't even get to help decide where graduation would be. Once again we come face to face with one of the great ironies of high school—meant to prepare responsible citizens, it never gives kids the experiences needed to make that happen. When young people leave high school, they leave as fully enfranchised citizens. While they are in high school, they have no idea what that means.

The point here is not to put more burdens on students than they need. Students still need time to be kids, and they shouldn't try to take on the weight of complete citizenship in school. A vast number of school decisions, from when custodial shifts are scheduled to the dates for standardized testing, really do not need their attention. But there is so much more students can and should be involved in concerning school governance, and much better ways to involve them in the process.

At FHHS we've worked to include students in as much of the decision making about the school as possible. It began when we were first looking at restructuring. Students engaged in the same discussions as did faculty (see chapter 6) to figure out how to improve our school. When we visited other schools to see what we could learn, students went along. When we held meetings to explore our options, students were a part of the discussions at every step. And when we voted to go ahead and change our schedule, our classes, and our program, students joined in at our faculty meeting.

Because of the excellent work our students did in this process, we have worked to find even more ways to give them a say in decision making. The first place they became involved is in the hiring of staff. How well I remember being hired for my first teaching job. For some reason my resume had risen to the top of the pile and I was summoned to meet with the principal. After an hour or so the principal made a quick call to the assistant superintendent, assured him I was their man, and arranged my second interview of the day. Having assured the assistant superintendent that I would be happy to coach a few sports, I was sent back to the school to pick up my books for my new job. While I was clearly the beneficiary of this process, it seemed to me then, as it does now, a very poor way to choose a faculty member.

We have changed the hiring process at FHHS to put the authority to hire in the hands of those who will spend the most time with teachers—their teaching colleagues and students. One team of teachers and one of students interview all applicants and observe them teaching a sample lesson in our school (each interview takes a full day). Afterward nearly all the applicants stop to talk to me about the student team. They remark on how well prepared they were and the quality of the questions they asked. As one candidate put it, "It's the most thorough and honest interview I've ever been through. They don't just want to know what you think, they want to know what you'll do."

It is when we've finished interviewing all the candidates that the students really show their abilities. Alone, they sort through the interviews, compare notes, and talk about the strengths of each candidate. Then they gather with the teachers who interviewed, and they discuss each candidate in a meeting over which I preside. Sometimes it takes just a few minutes, other positions have taken several days, but in the end a consensus is usually worked out, and more than once the kids have convinced the staff to change their minds.* When I watch the teachers that we have hired teach, I am reminded of the wisdom of giving students a voice.

Again and again it proves true: the more opportunities we give our students to be full-fledged citizens of our school, the more they amaze us with their ability to take on responsibilities. No one would have ever imagined, for example, that turning over *all* student affairs to our Student Delegation (which is what we call our student government) would actually make them run better. Like every principal, I am deluged with requests to run fund-

---

* To show how deeply ingrained our lack of respect for students is, I should note here that on several occasions candidates for positions at FHHS have refused to submit to a student interview. "Why would you want to let students interview a teacher?" one applicant asked. Needless to say, she was not invited to interview at all.

raisers, have dances, schedule club meetings, and organize dozens of other student events. And just like every other principal, I forget to sign the appropriate form once in a while or am accused of favoritism when I have to decide between two student groups that want to hold a dance on the same day. Not being a very quick learner, I took a year or two to realize that I shouldn't be the one to make these decisions. Why not have students handle student affairs, let them act on the democratic principle that those most affected by a decision should be the ones to make it?

Today our student activities run like clockwork. All student events, from dances and fund-raisers to club meetings, have to first be approved by the Student Delegation. Forms and requests are submitted to the group, which meets during advisory for the first fifteen minutes of every day. The Delegation, with representatives from every class and most clubs, uses criteria of equity (making sure everyone gets a chance) and consistency (with the school's mission) to decide what goes on. Even when adults come in wanting to sponsor some school-based activity, they too, to their frequent amazement, are sent to the Student Delegation to make their request. And, thinking they will see a principal they can bribe with a few trinkets such as wall calendars and desk clocks, fund-raising "experts" have more than once left the building disappointed that they couldn't get past our kids.

Our interns who work in the school also learn an important lesson in democracy. For example, if you were to call FHHS and request information on our program or a desire to visit the school, you would be turned over to the student intern who handles those requests. When you get a call asking if you are available to officiate a softball game or if you can reschedule a track meet, it is probably from the intern who serves as assistant athletic director. If by chance you realize you are speaking to a student (most people do not) and attempt to go "over their head" to get to the person in charge, you'll find out that the student intern is indeed in charge and the intern's decision is the school's decision. These young people handle the details and carry on just as if they were members of the staff, which for the most part they are. What they learn in addition to everything else in their internship is the importance of personal over positional authority.

Central to democratic community is personal authority. While authority based on one's position in a bureaucracy exists everywhere, it is seldom seen as genuinely legitimate. It is ceded to just because "she's the boss" or "he does my evaluations" or "you can't fight city hall." But compliance with such authority is always grudgingly given, doing just enough to get by until payday. (We often see this in schools as well, when students question the daily routine or the content being taught and the response is "Because I said so and I'm the teacher." Or principal.)

In democratic communities we willingly cede to authority of a personal nature. For example, in my town we don't choose the fire chief, mayor, or city council members based on the number of college degrees they have or certificates on their wall. Rather, we willingly put these people in positions of authority because, through their own commitment and hard work, they've earned it. We know from face-to-face contact and daily experience that these people can be trusted with our welfare.

It is the same with the interns in our school. Not holding college degrees or certification, they can still do the job. They enjoy newfound respect among their peers who willingly comply with their requests and directives. Authority, they are finding out, shouldn't come from who you know or what hoops you've jumped through. Instead it comes from how well you do your job and how responsible you are in carrying out your mandate.

Student government, involvement in the curriculum, hiring staff, and school internships are just some examples of how young people can see the theory of democracy translated into practice. And the practice of democratic citizenship is about balancing rights and responsibility. High schools are places where future citizens can try out authority and delegation. By providing such places, we provide perhaps our most important public service—making democracy possible.

As I mentioned above, in the fall of 1995 I had to hold meetings with each of our classes to discuss their behavior at lunch. Most interesting of all the meetings was the session I had with our seniors. They were not part of the problem, and I wanted to let them know that. I also felt they were part of the solution: that by displaying responsible behavior they could lead other students to do the same.

We sat in a circle and I looked around at the group of students who were freshmen when I became principal. I was surprised by how mature they had become, how concerned they were during our discussion with the behavior of some of the younger students. Looking around, I could think of a way in which virtually every one of them had assumed some responsibility for improving our school. This, I thought, would be their biggest test. Could they, without reverting to coercion or force, find some way to turn around the inappropriate behavior of the underclassmen?

They passed with flying colors. Within two days most of the issues of concern were solved and the seniors were serving as surrogate staff members all over the building. It started with a more positive sense of their own leadership—they were not only adhering to our shared norms but also talking with pride about their school. From there they began to generally encourage other students to make sure the building was clean and to use the facilities with respect. Finally, they took it upon themselves to directly deal with several students who were still not getting the message. Asking to use my office, seniors met with small groups of unruly freshmen. No threats or intimidation ensued; it was more like an instructional setting where the younger students were asked to think through the consequences of their behavior for themselves and the rest of the student body.

I would like to say that our seniors solved all of our problems, but that isn't true. Besides, it isn't all their responsibility anyway. We still see troubled kids acting inappropriately for a wide variety of reasons. But we see less of it every day. Not because we purchased some high-priced responsibility training program or sent our kids to hear yet another motivational speaker. No, all we did was provide a genuine experience with responsible behavior, stand ready to help when mistakes were made, and step in to instruct whenever we could.

One mother of a senior relayed to me her daughter's comments as we were working on our lunch issues.

"Andrea was so upset," she began, "she just couldn't get over how irresponsible some of the younger students are. She told me, 'Mom, you wouldn't believe what they are doing. They don't know how good our school is and what they have. . . . It's really up to us [the senior class] to show them how to act responsibly.' You know, George," she finished, "there really is hope for them, isn't there?"

CHAPTER SIX

From the Schools We Have
To the Schools Our Kids Deserve

On Thursdays during the school year the staff and students of Federal Hocking High School host visitors from around the state and nation who come to see the changes we have made in our school as a model of what they might do. Colleagues from as far away as North Carolina and as close as Athens County come to see what we are trying to do in transforming ourselves from institution to community. Each visit is arranged and hosted by one of our students, whoever is working that semester as my intern. Our guests begin in my office, being oriented by their student host to the building and our program, meeting the office staff, and hearing an overview of our program from our head teacher. Then they are offered a tour of the building before landing in a classroom for the rest of the morning.

At midday they gather in the Work and Family Life room, to be served lunch by our FHA/HERO club.* Teachers drift in to answer questions and talk about life in our school. Students sit in as well, telling our guests with unnerving honesty what they do and don't like about what we are trying to do. I stop by for coffee, but everyone is usually too busy to even notice my presence. During the second half of lunch hour the visitors wander

* Work and Family Life is the program that was once known as Home Economics. The new title reflects an orientation to helping students explore career options and maintain healthy family relations. FHA historically was the abbreviation for Future Homemakers of America. Today the initials refer not to any name but to a club devoted to community service.

around, seeing what students are up to during this unstructured time.

Just for fun we try and make sure to walk these folks through the halls of our school after lunch. Because our kids are so good about taking care of the place, I like to challenge our visitors to count how many pieces of trash they can find. After they finish complimenting us on how good it looks, they head for the classrooms again, anxious to see what they can learn.

Around 1:30 or so they drift back to my office for a final discussion or just to bid us farewell. The usual pleasantries are exchanged, final questions are answered, and then the "yes, but's" begin. Not always, but frequently enough, the "yes, but" is the closing ritual for a visit to FHHS. This is when I am told by parents, teachers, administrators, even students why what we do won't work in their school. Confiding that they would love to attend or work in our school (I have more than a couple of resumes in my desk from visitors), they find multiple reasons why it just isn't possible to make similar sweeping changes in their school. Here are just a few examples of the "yes, but's" that we hear:

"I don't think the teachers at our school would be willing to try this," from a parent.

"It won't work with the kids we have," from (believe it or not) a student.

"Our administrator wants more control over things than you have. He'd never go for this," from a teacher.

"I'm not sure this will work given EMIS (our statewide student data system) requirements," from a principal.

"Our community is too conservative for a change like yours," from parents, administrators, teachers, and students.

As our guests leave the rocking chairs in my office, I usually stay put, allowing their student guide to see them to the door so they can ask their last-minute questions without the principal listening in. I also try to imagine what is so very different about their high school that they cannot try to better organize themselves in order to help children learn. All of our visitors are treated to one caveat: We are not perfect, we still have much to learn, and it would be a mistake for any other school to put in place exactly what we are doing in ours. Even with the assurance that every good school is different from every other good school, so many of our visitors leave unsure of whether anything can change back home.

While I think we are a very good school, I have never thought that we are necessarily any better than anyone else. We face the same problem of limited resources that many schools do, and our staff is not the product of any specialized training. Our kids are no different from other kids, our parents like all parents wanting a good education for their children, our community no less or more supportive than others. While I know other high schools face specialized problems that we do not (such as gang violence, racial tension, overcrowding), we have our own set of specialized challenges with which to deal (lack of employment, high poverty rate, a geographically large district—190-plus square miles—forced together in a still unpopular state-mandated consolidation). Like most high schools, we are simply good people committed to giving our kids the best possible high school experience. So why, I wonder, do other schools seem to think that what we've done is impossible for them?

When members of the FHHS staff gather to talk about precisely this issue, four recurring themes emerge. The first is *tradition*—the notion that we have always organized high schools the way they are now, so why change them. It is easier just to continue with the status quo than to rethink what we are doing. The second is lack of *vision*. One of the points that our visitors seem to miss is that we did not set out initially to simply change our daily schedule. We began instead with a vision of the school we would like to be, and we have gone on to make the changes needed to reach that vision. The third is the paucity of good *models*. Since we so seldom see high schools that are any different from the ones we grew up with or know today, we imagine that we cannot change our schools without risking chaos. The fourth is *bureaucracy*. The legion of state and federal rules, the numerous clauses in the various negotiated contracts with employees, the special categories into which we must put students for funding purposes, all seem to overwhelm even the best-intended reforms.

Our is not the only school that has overcome these obstacles to change. Honesty requires me to tell you that many of our visitors have now perhaps "passed" us in the new ways they are reaching their students and that we are busy trying to learn from them. I know that many people reading this book have thought "yes, but" themselves as I have tried to present workable strategies for building community in each high school. For them the following strategies for overcoming resistance to change are offered.

Strategy One: Remind folks the good old days maybe weren't so good

Very few parents, students, or educators would be willing to argue that high schools as they are work well for all kids. No doubt, as we have seen, some kids do well at the tasks the high school sets them. Yet even for those students, the way in which we operate a high school limits the many ways they might use their minds. Certainly, for many other students, the high school experience is at best just a good time, while at worst it is a waste of time.

Yet we hold on to the current structure of our high schools because that's just the way they are. The traditional high school structure is a shared experience that virtually every one of us has been through. With some minor variations, we all remember high schools where we earned credits in separate courses by listening to lectures and taking tests. Never mind that none of us would be willing to stake our current job or previously earned high school diploma on once again passing those high school final exams. The point is not that we remember what we learned, it is that we survived the experience.

Tradition has prevented us from seeing the average American high school for what it is: the product of a different era, an eighty-year-old antique. Can you imagine driving to work in a vehicle eighty years old? How about using eighty-year-old appliances to prepare meals or clean clothes? Eighty-year-old medical practices to remove your infected appendix? While we may romanticize about the good old days, very few of us want to live in them.

But our kids and teachers have to. While we try to disguise it with a few computers, different elective courses, and media centers (rather than libraries), the basic contours of the high school are the same as they were eighty years ago. As I said earlier, if we were able to use time travel to bring residents of a town in the early twentieth century to that same town today, there would be little that they would recognize—except for the local high school.

Imagining that the structure of high school is simply a given, many people hold to the notion that just a few alterations will keep the system running. It is true that for decades high schools were able to hold students' attention even though they offered a setting that did not connect kids to the school community. This was possible because young people had so few other choices. Either they attended high school or they were working on the farm or in a factory. Leisure was not a factor. The diversions we take for granted—television, video and computer games, and automobiles, to name a few—were simply not available. School was a ticket out of hard labor, and kids would tolerate almost anything to get that ticket punched. Today high school prevents kids from playing. So we should not be surprised when old structures and methods fail to hold kids. Actually, what should be surprising is that, faced with this new reality, we still seem unwilling to let our schools catch up with the times.

We stay with traditional ways of organizing our high schools because we think things just aren't that bad. Of course, we view high school from an adult perspective. We reminisce about our glory days, and glibly say kids complain just to complain. While there are plenty of signs that our high schools are struggling to reach our children, we take those signs only to indicate that some fine tuning is needed (more time, tests, and texts) and not that something is fundamentally wrong. Perhaps we do not see it as it is because of our perspective—because we don't see or experience high school like a kid.

My friend Marilyn Hohmann, formerly principal at Fairdale High in Louisville, Kentucky, devised the best scheme I have ever heard of for reorienting our point of view and seeing high school for what it really is. Frustrated at frequently hearing there was no need to rethink Fairdale's structure and program, she decided the best way to expose the limits of the current program was to have the staff experience it—as students. Eight teachers were recruited and assigned, at random, to shadow a student, going to every class, doing whatever the student was assigned to do.

At this time Fairdale was on the standard eight-period-a-day schedule. By third period, according to Hohmann, the dropouts began. One by one they slipped into her office, looking as guilty as a kid cutting class, and asking not to have to continue the exercise. Each had some excuse: other work to do, the need to get to an appointment, always something more pressing than attending class. By the end of lunch half of the teachers had begged off, and not one made it to the end of the day. Boredom, from the sheer repetitiveness of the day, and the difficulty of really engaging in something in small chunks of time had taken their toll. That was in just one day of facing what the students were facing for all 180 days of the school year.

Once they were confronted with the reality of what their students experienced daily, it did not take much prodding for the faculty of Fairdale to begin restructuring their high school. Today Fairdale is recognized as a leader in Kentucky in providing more ways for students to experience success. They have undertaken many of the changes recommended in this book, changing how they use time, what they teach, and how they connect with kids. It all began by questioning the status quo from the point of view of the students.

There are other, perhaps less dramatic, ways to help us rethink the day-to-day high school experience. One strategy that works well is to ask a group of adults to reflect, write about, and discuss questions such as these:

1. What are the conditions under which you learn best? It might help to think of something you have recently learned of which you are proud. How did you learn that? How does the way we organize our high school resemble those learning conditions?

2. How do you know when you really know something? Does the way we assess students in our high school tell us whether or not our kids have really learned something? Do we know what they can do or what they have done?

3. What are the most important things we could teach our kids? Do we demonstrate to them that we value these things? Is the school organized in such a way as to show kids clearly what we want them to learn?

4. If you were a student in our school, what would you like about our school? What things that are happening here would really turn you on and excite you? What things would make it hard for you to learn? What would really turn you off and make you unhappy in our school?

We tend to get so caught up in the day-to-day minutiae of school that we don't take the time to stand back and see what is really working. When we do, it often becomes very clear to us that our assumptions about how our high school is running are not true. The best way to see that is to put ourselves in the position of actually being a student. Short of that, I am suggesting we at least write, reflect, and discuss how we think we would do as a student in our school.

So often I have heard adults say: "It was good enough for me, it's good enough for kids today." "It," of course, refers to whatever facet of the high school we happen to be discussing, be it the schedule, curriculum, textbook, or teaching practice. What I am suggesting is that we not rely on our memories, gracefully tinted by the passing of time, when we suggest that our high schools are as good as they can be. Reliving that experience today, knowing what it takes to do well as a citizen, wage earner, and lifelong learner, might make us more willing to rethink our high schools. Few of us would be able to say, "It's good enough for me." Instead, we might find ourselves saying, "It isn't good enough for me, and I think our kids deserve more."

The next stumbling block to change is knowing what that "more" is. That takes us to the second strategy that will help us rethink what our high schools are: creating a vision.

Strategy Two: Imagine what we want our schools to be

"Thanks, we enjoyed the visit. The kids were great and I love your schedule." I was seeing another guest, this one a school principal, out the front doors after a visit to FHHS. "I'm going to make sure we put the Federal Hocking Plan into effect at our school next year."

As I watched her leave, I could not believe that I had failed, yet again, to get across one of the most important messages I share with every visitor: There is no magical Federal Hocking (or any other, for that matter) Plan that will transform a school.

Attempts just to put in place a quick-fix program, or shift around a schedule, or offer a few different courses, are certain to fail because they lack any sense of vision. Meaningful school change only happens when educators, community members, parents, and students themselves share a new vision of what their school could be. A lack of vision is, in my experience, one of the most intractable obstacles to high school change. Once we have gone beyond the agreement that we need to change, many people are stymied by the issue of how to change. Part of this is due to a lack of models for change, which is discussed in the next section of this chapter. But, before we can get to actual models, we need to know to what end we are making change. We know we do not like what we have. If we could have something else, why would we want that? Another way to put it might be: We are already working hard at being teachers/parents/administrators/ counselors in the school we have. Now you want us to put in even more time in trying to figure out a better way to run our school. Why should we do that? What will we gain from this effort?

This is where an honest and clear vision of the graduates and the high school we want to have plays a central part in efforts to restructure. A road map and an inspiration, it can make all the difference.

At FHHS we did not set out to change our school's schedule when we began rethinking our students' high school experience. Certainly this is one of our most notable changes and what most of our visitors come to see. But it was not what we set out to do when we undertook the process.

In fact, all of us, including me, had differing ideas about what we wanted to do in changing our school. What helped us decide what to change and how was a vision of what we wanted our kids to learn as a result of the changes we might make. We worked at this sense of vision with our staff before we began thinking about what changes to make. The first step was to ask ourselves one simple question: What would we like our kids to be like and be able to do as a result of their five thousand hours with us?

Behind this seemingly simple question were a whole host of issues that we had to think through, issues that in many schools never come to the surface. We decided not to debate how many credit hours to require, what texts to use, how many class periods there should be in a day, or who should teach what. These, we know, are questions that often turn into discussions of the work of adults. Too often the issues in high school are adult issues: what should be the teacher's "load" (number of courses taught), how can the teacher get to teach his or her specialty, what is the easiest way for the administration to put together a schedule, who gets to use the library, etc. When we focus on the adults in high school, we miss the opportunity to restructure our schools in ways that affect the daily experiences of kids.

At FHHS I was pleased that we were able to start with the kids. Key to everything that we, and any other good high school, have done is starting with a vision of the graduate we want to produce. That is what so many of our visitors miss. Assuming that they can just transplant "the Fed-Hock Plan" into their school, they miss the step that is crucial to their planning. They come to us knowing that they are dissatisfied with the way things are. Such dissatisfaction is the beginning, often the motivating force for change. But the next step is *not* to go find some new program that has gained a lot of media attention and try to transplant it into their school. The next step is to figure out what they want the outcome of their work as educators (and parents and community members) to be. It is only when they figure that out that they can put into place the high school program *their* students deserve.

Before we ever went to look at another school, before we read books together about high schools, before we created teams to research what we might do, we sat down together to determine what we should do. Much of what you read in chapters 3, 4, and 5 came from these discussions. Our quest began, as any such quest must, with list after list of characteristics we hoped our students would develop. Everyone was invited to add to the discussion and contribute from an individual point of view. Nothing was taken off the list, no one was denied the opportunity to add, and every idea was initially given an equal footing.

Having compiled our lists, we turned to the challenge of pulling together our ideas under some common themes. Recommendations were grouped and regrouped. We talked over coffee before school, fish sandwiches at lunch, and sodas after students departed. How could our list of student attributes be compiled so they could be briefly and directly stated? What was the FHHS graduate to be? Who did we want for our fellow citizen and voter, our coworker or employee, and our neighbor? Finally, we sent it all to a smaller committee with representatives from all the academic areas in our school and told them: Make sense of this. Indeed they did, and from them came the common goals we all share of helping our students become "active democratic citizens, lifelong learners, and flexible in their career choices."

As I've said, many schools skip this entire discussion, eager to race from dissatisfaction to action. Just as misguided are those schools who stop at this point. Having written something called a "school vision" or "mission statement," they seem to believe that saying they will do these things is the same as actually doing it. However, our vision of the graduate we hope for is incomplete without a vision of the school that will nurture and develop that graduate.

Anyone who has worked in a high school will be able to relate to the good-natured (and sometimes not so good-natured) cynicism that surrounds writing a school mission statement. For the most part this is an exercise undertaken to meet accreditation standards or to preface a grant application. Forgotten more quickly than it is written, the entire exercise is often seen as just one more waste of time. To alter this view requires that our vision of our graduates be tightly linked to our vision of our school. By tying together the ways in which we see the current high school structure failing to help our students to become the graduates we want them to be, we lay the groundwork for putting together a new high school program.

There are a variety of ways to build this schoolwide vision. All of them involve taking the time to talk with one another about how the high school—in what we teach, how we are organized, and how students are treated—reflects the vision we hold for our graduates. It is also crucial that in the process we recognize what we have already been doing well, not just what we have to change. Perhaps the best tool that I have found for facilitating such a discussion is the exercise we used at FHHS and have used with many other schools in developing a schoolwide change agenda. It consists of taking staff, students, and parents—first in small groups and then as a whole—through five questions concerning our vision for our graduates:

1. What do we do well at _____ High School?
2. What prevents us from doing more of what we already do well?

3. What do we not do well at _____ High School?
4. What prevents us from changing what we are not doing well?
5. What resources can we call upon to surmount the barriers we identified in questions 2 and 4?

Each of these questions plays a crucial part in developing a vision of the high school any community wants. It is worth taking some time to work through each of them in order to see what the process of building a schoolwide vision must include.

1. *What do we do well?* This initial question helps us see that, while restructuring our high school means a break from the past, it also means the break need not be total. Every school has a history. In that history are the triumphs of good teachers and administrators that have made a difference in students' lives. There are also good programs and experiences for students that we should build upon. In fact, while it may be too easy to take from this book the message that nothing works well in our high schools, we all know of successes. There are experiences like marching band and theater productions that give students a place to perform and belong. Small advanced classes in the sciences, arts, and humanities give some students a chance to dig deeply into content. In the vocational areas, classes are often scheduled over two class periods, allowing students to undertake extensive projects. For students who need special help, classes are smaller and a close bond is built with the teacher.

Seeing these things, knowing that it is possible in our high schools as they now are to have meaningful educational experiences, begins the process of building a schoolwide vision. There is security in taking from our own history, and dignity in realizing that we have tried, regardless of circumstance, to do well by our students. The question we are led to next is why every student does not share in these opportunities.

2. *What prevents us from doing more of what we already do well?* Indeed, why doesn't every child have the opportunities that those deemed "special" in some way have? Why isn't every program outstanding, every class engaging? What keeps us from doing for every student what we know works for a few?

The one not-so-hidden danger in pursuing this discussion is that it can lead to even more "yes, but's." Instead of focusing on how to do more of what we do well, we can fall prey to the trap of justifying our not having expanded our best efforts. The first "yes, but" will most likely be a lack of funds. Others will include a perceived lack of parent or student or administrative support. Unfortunately, there will always be naysayers who want to slow or stop the process.

One of the best tools for overcoming such objections is to limit the discussion to items the school itself controls. Schedules, class sizes, curriculum, teaching methods, materials, and dozens of other rules and roles in the high school are almost totally under the control of the staff. We should not be allowed to hide on this one. We can change a great deal about our schools *if* we choose to. Concern about support from parents and students also tends to evaporate if they are involved in the process of making change. Only money seems beyond our control, but even there the school has some ability to direct different uses of financial resources in the building.*

The way to overcome the "yes, but's" in this phase of the discussion is through an administrative tactic that the art teacher at FHHS taught me. He put it this way: "Don't ask the staff to be managers. Ask them to be salespersons, or idea people. They come up with the ideas, they're the closest to the kids, they know what will work. Tell them not to worry about the details, how to schedule it or pay for it, that's your job. They give you the ideas, you make them work." I must admit that I have had a few ideas of my own that I have thrown into the mix at our school. But I also know that when I can get the detail stuff out and away from our staff's thinking, then we come up with our best plans.

Getting through the "yes, but's" and exploring why we don't do more of what already works is the first part of identifying what needs to be changed. The structures, rules, and roles of high school that we so often take for granted are found, through this exercise, to be precisely the problems. By the time we have finished this part of our discussion we are halfway to a vision that we can act on.

3. *What are we not doing well?* This is a much harder question. It is important in this discussion to allow for different perceptions of the same experience. For example, while small "advanced"

---

* School funding is an issue to which we'll return in the Afterword.

courses may be a blessing for some students, they may force other students into large classes due to staffing problems. In fact, in looking at what a school does not do well, we often find almost an exact repeat of what *is* done well. That is, our concern may be that not all the students get what we know works.

At each school the list of what isn't going well will be different. The key thing is not to browbeat ourselves but to be honest about our work. We cannot find solutions for problems that we refuse to acknowledge. Besides, so often these problems relate not to who we are as teachers but to what the institution of high school has become. This part of the exercise is designed to look carefully at exactly that issue. What institutional structures do not work for our kids?

Our discussions at FHHS focused on time and size. We had a good teaching staff and kids we all enjoyed. The problem was that the structure of our school day did not let us spend enough time with each other. Lists we produced in this part of the exercise included items such as these: "Too many students for me to give them personal attention." "Not enough time in class to go into depth about the material." "Too many kids are disconnected from the school." While we all shared responsibility for these problems, we didn't spend time on blame. The overall way we organized our school was what prevented both teachers and students from doing their very best work. Now we were ready to look at what could be altered to improve the way we run school.

4. *What prevents us from changing what we are not doing well?* If the "yes, but's" were dealt with correctly in question 2, this can be one of the most important parts of the exercise. Here is where we can really get at what holds us back from being the school we should become. At this point we are most likely to point a cold, direct finger at the ways in which our high schools are organized that hinder us in our efforts to help kids. Taking these together with the items from question 2, we will have a laundry list of the things we need to restructure in our school.

Now the task of putting together a vision for our school becomes possible. It is simply a task of turning the negative statements that were generated in answer to questions 2 and 4 into positive statements. For example, in our work at FHHS (and I have seen this to be the case at other schools) our answers were quite similar for all groups—staff, students, and parents. In both cases one of the things that prevented us from doing what we knew would work was a lack of time to really work closely with students. Teachers felt rushed by the clock and unable to help kids dig into the material in our forty-two-minute-per-class-per-day schedule. Kids complained of never having enough time to get to all their work and of feeling that they were just a number to the teacher. Parents pointed out that they missed the experience they had in elementary school when one teacher knew their child's strengths and needs; they were concerned that their young ones were getting lost in the daily shuffle from class to class. We all agreed that we needed to slow down the clock and get to know one another better.

Turning that into a positive vision of what we wanted our school to be meant restating that limitation as a vision: We want a school where teachers have sufficient time with their students to insure that every child does quality work. Now we knew what we had to change to make our school a place where kids would become "active democratic citizens, lifelong learners, and flexible in their career choices."

5. *What resources do we need?* In effect, this question is the beginning of building a plan for change. Based upon the vision of the school community that has been generated in questions 2 and 4, the discussion should not be around what we can't do, but rather around what we want to do. We should all be encouraged to think out loud about what we might need to learn, read, see, hear, or experience in order to make the change necessary to put the school vision into place. Here is where grants are planned, trips suggested, committees organized, and resource lists compiled. This is where we put our words into actions—actions focused by our shared vision.

After completing these two tasks at Federal Hocking, one of the things we knew we needed was a model or models. In completing the above exercise, staff, parents, and students all came to the same conclusion: that we needed to deal with time and size first if we were to change our school. But how? Most of the staff and all of our students and parents had only experienced a traditional eight-period school day. We knew that before we could get to the changes in curriculum, teaching and learning, and graduation standards that we wanted, we had to change our schedule. In a sense, our vision depended upon it, but our experience limited what we could imagine. This lack of models is the next obstacle to change that schools in transition from institution to community must overcome.

Strategy Three:
Learn from the models around us

I remember well how hard it was in early December 1992 for all of us at FHHS to figure out what exactly we should do. We knew that our traditional schedule was not working. We also knew what we wanted for our kids upon graduation and that to get to that goal meant finding a way for teachers to spend more time with fewer students. What we were not sure of was how to go about it.

The lack of models, of actual examples of what changes in schools could look like, is the third obstacle to restructuring high schools. It almost stymied our work as we found ourselves both uncertain of what we could do and somewhat distrustful of purely theoretical recommendations. Even my own previous work in writing books about school change did not seem very helpful when confronted with having to recommend changes for our school. In a similar way, many schools get only as far as setting forth a vision, because they cannot really imagine that their dreams will ever come true.

It is the fear of this cruel hoax that stops many schools from even imagining that things could be different. "Why bother?" the reasoning goes. "If no one else is changing, they certainly won't let us be any different." It is also fear of the unknown that holds us back. "How do we know that anything other than what we are doing now will be any better?" is a question I've often heard. Finally, there is the fear of rejection of any change by the community each school serves. "I don't think people here will accept anything too radical" is often offered as a reason for resisting change.

A great deal of this fear is overcome when a model of what is possible for a high school is available. The temptation, however, is to look for recipes rather than models. As with our guest who wanted to put into place "the Federal Hocking Plan," there can be a tendency to want a set plan just to copy. But this ignores the fact that every good high school is different. Each has its own personality, often springing from its sense of place, and will have to restructure in ways that meet its own needs and not those of others.

Two examples from our own experience help illustrate this. First, our hour-long lunch period. As I pointed out, we put this in place because of our geography. With our students spread far and wide and their access to educational resources limited, we saw lunch as an opportunity to serve both our academic and our social mission. While we did indeed borrow this from a city school, I can imagine other urban or suburban schools forgoing a long lunch and instead using the time to, for example, enhance an arts program. Another example would be some of our courses that meet for the entire year, rather than one semester, in our eighty-minute periods. We felt our students were having too much difficulty with upper-level math and that a yearlong exposure would help. Again, I can easily imagine another excellent school program using yearlong courses in English for English-as-a-Second-Language students or in some other area—or perhaps having no yearlong courses at all.

Importing another school's program, following its recipe, if you will, fails to follow up on all the work that I have suggested should go on before making decisions about how to change. If every school is to follow just one recipe, why bother asking what needs to be fixed and how we would like it fixed? That is, after all, the beauty of a recipe. Once we've decided what we want, we just choose the right recipe and follow it. But schools are not cakes or cookies or meatloaves, they are places where we help kids learn. Which means that, while they may have similarities, they cannot be carbon copies of one another because that denies the differences in who our kids are and what our communities are like. (Of course, even recipes are often better when the cook takes liberties with them.)

While we don't need recipes, we do need good models to help us overcome our fears of school change. Knowing that other schools have restructured helps overcome the fear of being alone. Knowing that, in a place similar to ours, restructuring has led to success and has been worth the discomfort helps overcome the fear of failure. Knowing that other communities have embraced change and, if skeptical at first, have become supportive helps overcome the fear of rejection. Knowing these things cannot come from a book, a lecture, or a film. Such knowledge can only come from direct experience with a school or schools that have ventured beyond the status quo in how they are organized.

The very best tool we had at FHHS in restructuring our school was the models other schools provided us. Through visiting these schools, walking their halls, talking with teachers and students, we came away inspired and willing to take a chance on changing our own school. Our visits provided us with something that we never could have gained from reading an article or sitting through a workshop called "The High School of the 21st Century." They freed us to think in new ways about high school, to question the things we took for granted, to see that change can and does work. Visiting other high schools that had already restructured their programs helped us believe in our own ability to do the same. I cannot imagine any high school getting very far down the road of change without seeing other models of change in operation.

Step one in such a process is to find schools to visit. Initially it does not make much difference if the schools are much like yours. (We learned a great deal from Independence High in Columbus, Ohio, and Fairdale High in Louisville, both large schools serving an urban population.) What is important is that fundamental change be happening in the school you choose to visit. Be wary of schools with specialized programs for just a few students or a small group of teachers operating independently inside a larger school. Certainly they may be doing good work. The problem is that such programs can be too easily dismissed as potential models because they serve "special" students unlike the ones in your school or rely upon "special" teachers.

It is when you visit an entire school in the process of change that everyone leaves energized. There are several ways to find such schools. The first is to just ask. Contact your state department of education, a nearby university, the teachers association, or a professional organization and ask if they know of a school that has changed in ways you are considering. In Ohio, for example, there is a statewide Venture Capital program which has funded nearly three hundred schools to try and restructure along a wide variety of lines. All of these schools have plans and summaries of their work on file at the State Department of Education, and one could quickly find nearby schools to contact for a visit. In other states programs such as "charter schools," site-based management, or similar reforms are in place and information is readily available. If these sources prove fruitless, a call to organizations like the Coalition of Essential Schools or the Education Commission of the States will provide you with information on high schools in your area that are immersed in change. (Information on these and other groups is found in the Appendix.)

Once schools to visit are located, it is important to carefully choose a visitation team. Our own experience is that making change requires a very high level of trust. After all, we are dealing with an institution with a long-standing tradition which serves our most precious commodity, our children. This is about our kids and their futures.

Such trust will only come about if staff, administration, parents, and students are involved in the process of visiting other model schools. All too often we have visitors at FHHS who represent just one part of the school community. Sometimes it is just a principal, other times a team of teachers only. I can almost guarantee that whenever the team does not include teachers *and* administrators, little will change as a result of the visit. Usually this is because those who did not come are demonstrating by their absence that they have not really bought into the need for change. So, when whoever is visiting returns home, the teachers (for example) will deliver a glowing report only to be "yes, but'ed" into inaction by the administration, who did not bother to make the trip.

More important, I have noticed how few visitation teams include parents and students. This is a crucial mistake for several reasons. First, it tells parents and kids that we really are not interested in their opinions and input. Second, it generates mistrust as these groups are left wondering what it was they were not allowed to see on the visit, what it is that is being hidden. Third—and this is vital—we lose some of the most important perspectives on change and sometimes our greatest allies in the process.

Every visit we made to schools included parent and student representatives who were perhaps our best pairs of eyes and ears.

Away from the teachers and me, the kids were able to get the real lowdown on how the school we were visiting worked for students. Shadowing another student's day, they went to classes, took tests, ate lunch, and just talked to other kids. If you really want to know a school, you have to experience it as a student does. The same goes for parents. Most parents make judgments about the quality of the school based upon their own child's experience. During our visits, I watched our parents interview students again and again, finding out what the changes in the school meant to them, how they helped or hurt, and what worked well versus what still needed to be fixed.

Two things happen when everyone is included in a school visit. First, the base of support for restructuring and building school community is expanded. Not only do teachers and administrators fear change, parents and students are worried as well. While they know things can be better, there is security in staying where they are. These fears are often overcome when they see that change can mean very good things for students, as demonstrated not in the convincing words of advocates for change but in the daily school experiences of kids in a restructured school. Second, by including different groups in a visit, multiple ways of seeing the school are generated. We know that after such a visit we will hear about what works for students and parents as well as teachers and administrators. In fact, more than once, students on our visits convinced skeptical teachers and their principal that the managerial headaches that a particular change might cause were well outweighed by the benefit that students would reap. To actually take full advantage of such perspectives means not just visiting the model school but debriefing attentively to make sure we all learn from the experience.

All too often visitors to FHHS arrive late and leave early. I've also noticed that they have a tendency not to stay through an entire class period in any one room. No matter how hard we try to schedule a full day for our visitors, they often seem anxious to leave. Unfortunately, you really cannot learn what a school is doing if you do not immerse yourself in the entire life of the school. It is too easy to be fooled by a visit that lasts just a few hours, too easy to see only what works with ease and not the hours of effort and toil that went into making it all come together. You can only get behind the scenes and really see what is happening in the model you are studying if you arrive early and stay late.

To take full advantage of our time in the schools we visited, we would arrive the night before our scheduled visit. Our team spent time together, having dinner and talking about what we hoped we would learn. Sometimes we would meet with faculty or students from the school that evening, being oriented to what we would see. We might take in a ball game at the school or just hang around and talk with one another. By arriving the night before, we insured that we would be present for the start of the school day.

We tried to arrive before the students, so we could learn our way around the school. Among other things, we wanted to insure that we would see several entire classes and have free run of the building. The best visits were directed by students, which is how we run ours now. At the end of the day we had time to gather back together with staff and administration and have our questions answered in a leisurely manner without stealing minutes from other staff duties.

Spending an entire day (sometimes two or more) is the only way to really learn from the model schools that are available. For one thing, going through an entire day insures that what is seen is genuine. You never leave wondering if you were just shown the high spots; you know you've seen all there is in the school. For another, you have time to see up close the nature of the work kids are doing in the school. Throughout this book I have argued that the one thing that matters most in a high school is the quality of the work the students do. Observing their work takes times. It takes sitting next to a student as she completes a chemistry lab and questioning her about her findings, or listening in on a team's discussion of how they intend to present their work from an investigation of the causes of civil wars. You cannot just "drop in" and sample these activities. Instead you have to take time to develop trust and rapport so that students open up and share their work with you.

It is also important to debrief after any visit. Reminding yourself that the task is not to copy someone else's work, take time to talk about what everyone learned. With visitors at FHHS we try to force this discussion by telling them that my student intern or

I will meet with them at the end of the day in the principal's office. Then I make sure that we do not show up until twenty minutes or so after the appointed time. By the time we walk in, they don't even notice our presence.

The most important part of debriefing is to insure that everyone learns from the model. After a visit the focus should be on what can be taken from this model school and applied in your own setting. One effective question for guiding such a discussion is "What did we see this school do well that we could do even better?" Such an approach does three things. First, it avoids looking for faults in the model school, which can only encourage another set of "yes, but" comments. Second, it avoids criticism of your own school when you aren't comparing schools but instead are focusing on possibilities. Third, it directs attention to *adapting*, not copying, what works well in the model school.

After developing a vision and witnessing firsthand that change is possible, there is frequently one more obstacle to overcome. We turn now to the barriers, real and imagined, erected by the education bureaucracy in every state.

Strategy Four:
Do what is best for students first, worry about changing the rules later

Becoming a school administrator quite by accident has been for me a blessing. While I have stumbled around and been fairly ineffective in filling out state forms, filing reports on time, and making sure we run enough fire drills, I am learning with experience. These shortcomings are more than compensated by not having learned the built-in fear of bureaucratic rules that other school administrators seem to suffer from.

I first noticed this fear during a visit to our school a few years ago by a team of administrators from a nearby school system. After spending the day talking with kids and staff and being fairly impressed by our programs, they acted as if what we were doing simply couldn't be done. Forget about the fact that they had witnessed it firsthand. It just wasn't possible to change their schedule and offer the programs we offer, owing to state department regulations. The discussion was nothing short of fascinating.

"I don't think we can do this with the EMIS [Education Management Information System, a statewide student accounting system in Ohio] requirements," began the superintendent. "You can't make it accept this many different schedule types inside one school day."

"Well, it worked for us," I replied.

"Maybe, but I can't really see it working." He was clearly unconvinced.

"Besides, it's against the law to let students travel to other sites for classes," the high school principal commented on the internship program. "You have to cover them with liability insurance."

"That's not our experience—"

"Besides," she cut me off, "there is no teaching certificate for internships, so you can't offer it."

"No, that just means anybody can teach it" was my response. I continued, "In fact, there are many courses that, because of their nature, any certified person could teach."

"I doubt that," she said, dismissing my statement as naïveté.

"And how do you get away with nonteachers taking an advisory?" the assistant principal put in.

"We just list them in the schedule."

The superintendent rejoined the discussion. "I can't see that working at all. You know, I just don't think what you do here is possible in Ohio."

Later that day I took out a map to check my geography and, sure enough, Athens County has yet to secede from the great state of Ohio.

There is no doubt in my mind that there are genuine regulatory limits to what we can change in our high schools. Certification rules limit what teachers can teach, special education regulations require particular types of tests to enable us to get kids the help they need, and a myriad of rules from a variety of programs dictate everything from the number of fire drills we run to the fat content of the food we serve. Add to this literally volumes of labor laws, OSHA regulations, and student data reporting regulations, and the mountain of paperwork virtually guarantees that every high school could be found in violation of some rule or other.

My conversations with school administrators who visit our

school have led me to believe that many of them are so over-whelmed by current regulations that they hesitate to take on any changes in their schools for fear that they will generate even more paperwork. On the other hand, I am also convinced that many times the myth of regulatory limits is used as an excuse to prevent change. Like the administrative team I described above, they have no intention of changing the practices in their school. To insure that no change occurs, the opponents of change argue that change is, in essence, against the law.

Change is not illegal, and any such claim should be challenged. But change is indeed hard, and sometimes made harder for high schools by the morass of regulations they face. So while such regulatory limits should not be accepted as an excuse, they do have to be confronted. There are four ways that have worked for us.

First, be sure you know what the regulations really are. This I learned while filling in for a principal friend before I came to FHHS. At this middle school the staff were struggling with how to come up with a team-based schedule, given state mandates on how much time per day kids had to spend on each subject. The teacher who was dealing with the scheduling and I were working through this problem when one of us decided to look up what was actually required by the state. Lo and behold, students *did not* have to have a certain number of minutes per day in each subject. Rather, they only had to have a certain amount of time per week in each area, opening up all sorts of possibilities with the daily schedule. Within two days of this brief foray into researching state requirements a new team-based schedule was in place.

So the first route over the bureaucratic hurdles is straight through them by learning what they really are. In fact, you may discover that what you think the rules are just isn't true. Remember, just because we have been doing it one way does not mean that it is necessarily the correct way.

There are times, however, when the rules and regulations generated by either state or federal bureaucracies prevent schools from doing what is good for our students. When these are encountered, there are other ways to make changes.

The second approach to bureaucratic red tape is to find who can cut it. Virtually every rule has an exception, and someone who can grant that exception. Again, from personal experience

I've learned that any rule has someone who can waive it. When I wanted to become a principal, I did not have the appropriate certificate. Initially I was told that I could have a temporary certificate, but that I would have to take more than thirty hours of university course work to make the certificate official. (Some of the courses were courses I had taught while a college professor.) It took only one call from a friendly county superintendent to the correct state official and I am now the proud holder of an Ohio principal's certificate.

Similarly, at FHHS, when we have found that rules prevented us from doing what we needed to do, we have usually found someone in the state capital who can help out. It often takes more than one phone call, but by being persistent we can reach whoever has authority to remove a regulatory barrier. The point here is to never take no for an answer. Behind every regulation or form is an initial desire by some legislator or bureaucrat to solve a problem or insure a good educational program. When those regulations become a barrier to good programs, it often only takes convincing the proper person that change will more likely achieve the result desired.

That takes us to the third approach to dealing with regulatory limitations: Be ready to demonstrate student success when regulations are changed. Here is where we must remember that it is the work of kids, not adults, that high schools are about. Too often we complain about regulations that, even if changed, would not affect kids. In fact, many times we resist change because it would mean filling out even more forms or making more appeals to cut red tape. But this only approaches our "yes, but's" vis-à-vis bureaucracy from an adult point of view. When, alternatively, we are willing to approach needed regulatory changes from the point of view of students, we are more likely to get the charges we need.

The first question that has to be asked in confronting any bureaucratic barrier to change is: How will changing this rule lead to higher quality student work? The answer to this question suggests the types of evidence needed to convince anyone a change is needed. For example, when we needed a state waiver to offer our special math classes, we asked to try it for one year and then see what the results were. If it worked, the state agreed to continue our waiver; if not, we agreed to look somewhere else in solving our problem. By defining what would count as success in terms of actual student achievement, we were able to remove a state regulatory barrier to our work.

It has been my experience and the experience of our school that one of these first three approaches usually removes any bureaucratic barrier—real or perceived—from our way. On occasion, when we find that none of these tactics work we find a way to work around the barrier. But occasionally every good school, unable to wait for the slow wheels of bureaucracy to turn while its students have to tolerate a less than positive high school experience, has to break the rules in the name of student learning. For high schools in this position, the fourth approach— finding it easier to ask for forgiveness than permission—is all that is left.

When we began restructuring FHHS we knew we were going to be doing something to help our students. The problem was that we were making so many changes that we were not sure all of them would fit into all the various state regulations. After all we had done we felt that we could not just stop and wait for all the proper forms to be filled out. In fact, as I said earlier, as a new administrator I didn't even know what forms to use. With the support of our faculty, parents, and district administration we went ahead with the plan, knowing we would run afoul of one obscure rule after another—but also knowing it was the right thing for our students.

Frequently during that first year of change I found myself on the phone to one state official or another trying to explain what we were doing. I filled out the correct forms, sent in revised reports, met with the right people. In the end, almost all of our changes were granted official state blessing. For those that weren't, we found other ways to accomplish change while still obeying the rules. Happily we found that often the very people whose job it is to enforce the regulations felt limited by those same regulations themselves and were more than pleased to help us around them in the name of a better high school for our kids. It wasn't so hard to get forgiveness, we just had to know who to ask.

I believe that there is nothing but ourselves standing between the high schools we have now and the high schools our kids deserve. Again and again on the road to change the faculty at FHHS and other schools have had to confront themselves as the biggest barrier to change. Change is hard for us because it means moving beyond established patterns of behavior and taking on new ways of teaching or administering. It also means admitting that some of what we are doing may not have worked as well as we thought. But in the end it also brings us back to remembering that the main task of the high school is to help young people do the good work that will help them become productive and active members of our communities.

Because it is about kids, I believe that high school change should involve a certain amount of impetuousness. We tend to devote years to studying what to change and little if any time to actually making change. In the meantime, kids continue to go through our schools without the benefit of the programs we know we should run. Perhaps we delay action because we get to do high school over and over again. Perhaps it is because we fear change. Whatever the reason, while we do not act, kids continue to come and go. They won't get another chance at the five thousand hours we call high school. They should be entitled *now* to experiencing high school as we know it could be. For that reason, I believe Joe McDonald of the Coalition of Essential Schools is correct when he says that the motto for school reform should be "Ready, fire, aim." We should go ahead and change what is obviously not working, and during, not before, the change we should refine and improve upon what we are doing.

Our experience at FHHS has been that impetuousness is a virtue. After half a year of study we instituted a wide range of changes schoolwide. During the 1993–94 school year we were all first-year teachers, learning as we went along, supporting one another, refining what we were doing, planning for the future. Today we look back on that year with a certain amount of nostalgia. We know we are even better today, but it is the 1993–94 school year that we will always remember, because it was the year that together we took a chance on becoming the excellent high school we knew we could be. We will never experience anything quite so dramatic again. But we will continue to enjoy seeing the better effect we have on our kids at FHHS now and in the future.

CHAPTER SEVEN

Building a Community of Hope

We began this trip through the American high school by spending a day with three teachers at Federal Hocking High School: Reba Theiss, Leon Talbert, and Donna Bennett. Now, four years later, Reba, Leon, and Donna still grace the halls of FHHS. Because of their hard work, and that of their colleagues and of our parents and students, all three now work in a very different place from the one we visited back in chapter 1—a place that has tried to implement many of the changes I've suggested, some with more success than others. We're not a perfect school, but we are a different school, where kids experience more success and do better work and where teachers can better practice their craft.

Of course, as always, there is still much to do. It is one of the challenges and pleasures of working with kids that the job is never finished. There is always one more kid to figure out, one more topic to reconsider for inclusion in what we teach, more rewiring of the school for success for every child. As I put the finishing touches on these pages in the summer of 1997, the staff and community at FHHS are conducting summer workshops on using more seminars in our classes, more successfully using the advisory system, fitting in exhibitions with revised graduation standards, and finding a balance between the sense of "less is more" in content areas and increasing our students' exposure to more diverse experiences in areas such as the arts. It's an exciting and exhausting time all at once, and there is no telling where we will end up.

But just as a snapshot of our school five years ago revealed a great deal about high schools that needed to be changed, a retaking of that picture today can demonstrate why there is hope that we can restructure the five thousand high school hours to better connect with our students. That is what it has to be about, hope. Hope that motivates teachers to get up every day and go back to work trying to make a difference in kids' lives. Hope that makes parents sacrifice their own time to insure that their kids have the support they need to do well in school. Hope that causes all of us in our communities to make sure schools have the resources they need. And hope that is generated in all children through their school experiences that they can make a difference in the world.

In the years that have passed, the students we met in chapter 1 have all graduated. Jake finished his undistinguished high school career a father and unemployed. Maria and he were later married, and are now raising a child with no employment prospects between the two of them. Sharon has finished art school, having used out internship program to its fullest by working as an assistant curator at the local university's art museum and as assistant program director at the regional cultural arts center. She turned those experiences, with the help of her art teacher, into a portfolio that helped her gain admission to the school from which she just graduated. Nina left us last year and has completed her first year at the regional technical college. She's taking advantage of the college's free tuition program for area graduates and hopes to finish nursing school in another two years. Sharon still stops by whenever she is in town, and Nina shows up at the high school every so often to get help with her math.

As at any school, new students arrive to take the place of those who have moved on. This year's graduates were eighth graders when I began at FHHS. The class before them was the last group of kids to ever experience what high school was like before we began to restructure. Our new seniors, juniors, sophomores, and freshmen just think high schools have always had four periods daily where subject matter is taught together and where kids have long lunch periods and can leave school for internships and the like. Because they have lived through and helped with the changes we have undergone, we will follow three seniors through their day as well as one more student from each of the junior, sophomore, and freshmen classes. Watching these six young people and our three teachers go through a typical day at FHHS will show us the beginnings of a high school experience that makes hope possible.

Reba, Leon, and Donna still arrive early every morning. But unlike four years ago when early arrival was a matter of survival, today it's because they use the time to be involved in the overall life of the school. All three teachers have had their teaching loads cut by more than half. Where they had been teaching seven classes a day and averaging more than 160 kids daily, today they have three classes a day, fewer than 70 kids daily, and an eighty-minute planning period to help them find time for preparing lessons, contacting parents, making materials, and grading papers. Because of this change in their teaching load, while they still work every bit as hard as they always did, they can devote more time to each student and to the general welfare of the school community.

Donna is, as always, one of the first to arrive. Sometimes there are a few handouts to run off or materials to copy. But this morning she is meeting with Steven Musick, with whom she team-teaches a section of our sophomore U.S. History/U.S. Literature program known as American Studies Two. They have arranged to meet early to go over the unit they are finishing up on the Depression. Today the building will be filled with community members who lived during the Depression being interviewed by members of Donna and Steve's class. With the arrival of their guests just hours away there are still dozens of details to nail down, and this morning Donna and Steve are running through the final checklist.

Reba is puttering in the science room, setting out the materials for a first-period biology lab. This will be the first of three labs today, but her student intern will help her take down the biology lab and get ready for the Science Nine classes. With the extra minutes she has this morning she is checking with one of the other science teachers about materials needed for the Science Nine course. The other issue they are discussing is whether or not to convert the Science Nine class to a Natural History course to better capture the interest of students. Since so many of our students live on a farm, hunt, fish, hike, camp out, and just generally live in the out-of-doors, we may be able to connect science to that experience to help kids see some purpose in what we teach. No decisions are made, more questions are raised than answers given, and it's agreed that this decision will wait for another day.

Leon comes in followed by Alex, a student we will be following all day. In the past two years Alex has figured out that he thinks he wants to become a math teacher. As part of his investigation of that possibility he has signed up to intern this year with Leon, helping teach a freshman algebra course. I'm not at all surprised to see Alex here, as our senior interns often arrive early to prepare lessons or materials. In fact, it isn't unusual to see them in the building on the weekends and even on holidays, just like their teacher counterparts, getting ready for upcoming classes. This morning Leon and Alex are putting the finishing touches on Alex's first solo lesson for the class. Alex is visibly nervous, and Leon does a good job of being supportive, encouraging, and reflective all at the same time.

Meanwhile, five other students are beginning to make their way to the high school's front door. Mikki, a senior, drives to school with her younger sister. Mikki, as would be expected of someone who will graduate at or near the top of her class, is well rested and prepared for the day. Like every other student at FHHS, Mikki has only four classes a day, each long enough that she usually has very little work to take home. Last night she spent some time reviewing for a vocabulary quiz in journalism and finishing up note cards for her Senior Project paper. But she spent most of the evening on the phone interviewing people for an article in the local paper that she writes as part of her internship. Running every Thursday with her byline and photo, the column is a source of pride for the entire school.

Michele, a sophomore, and Romona, a freshman, share the much too early bus ride to school. Unlike their predecessors, their book bags are weighted down only by a couple of books and notebooks. Michele in her sophomore year is taking a math course, Ancient Cultures, and American Studies Two during the first semester. Most of her homework the previous evening was in math, as she prepared for an oral presentation she has to give on a problem solution. Romona had very little to do that evening: to help the transition to high school, the curriculum for freshmen is set up with three core courses and one elective each semester. We'll look at her schedule, and all the others, in more detail below. The important point here is that both Romona and Michele, not outstanding but good students, are coming to school not dreading an arrival without their homework but clearly prepared to face the day.

Lawrence, a senior, jumps in the car with several friends and immediately leans back trying to go to sleep. Last night he, like many students, stayed up a bit too late cheering on the Cleveland Indians in the league championship series. Up until this year he rode to school with his girlfriend, Carol. But this semester Carol, also a senior, doesn't come to school until lunch, spending the first half of her day at her internship at the hospital. Lawrence has not demonstrated in his first three years that he is very serious about school. While he's making much more of an effort this year, he's backsliding a bit now, having not yet finished his math assignment. But not to worry, he thinks as he drifts off, there will be time in advisory to finish it up.

Kent, a junior, drops his younger brother off at the middle school and turns east toward the high school. He takes the last curve before the high school driveway a bit too quickly, and his football gear slides off the seat and falls on the floor. Like Lawrence, Kent starts on both offense and defense on the football squad and so spends most of every afternoon at the school, seldom arriving home before eight. Adding the seven hours of the school day, the twenty-minute drive each way to and from school, and practice from 4:30 to 7:30, Kent's day, like most athletes', is almost eleven hours long. He sometimes wonders how athletes in other schools, with seven to eight subjects to prepare for daily, do it. It's enough for him to be ready for four, a task he accomplishes while making the honor roll every marking period.

Back in chapter 3 there was an outline of the current FHHS master schedule (along with several others). To really see how this schedule works for students and teachers, reproduced on the facing page are the schedules Reba, Leon, Donna, Alex, Mikki, Lawrence, Kent, Michele, and Romona will follow for both semesters. While changing the way we deal with time is, as I've said earlier, only one part of what we are trying to do, in high schools this is probably a necessary first step to any lasting change. As we follow Reba, Donna, Leon, and our six students through the day, referring to these schedules will help illustrate what is going on.

First Semester

Students	Academic Advisory 7:40–7:50	1st Period 7:55–9:15	2nd Period 9:20–10:40	Lunch 10:40–11:40	3rd Period 11:40–1:00	4th Period 1:05–2:30
Mikki (Sr.)		Pre-calculus	English 12		Internship	Internship
Lawrence (Sr.)		Pre-Calculus	English 12		Biology 2	Spanish 1
Alex (Sr.)		Internship	English 12		Advanced Spanish	College Career and
Kent (Jr.)		Biology 2	English 11		Algebra 1.5	Life Choices
Michele (Soph.)		Algebra 1 Keyboarding/	Ancient Cultures		American Studies 2 Algebra 1	Industrial
Romona (Fr.)		Nutrition	Science 9			Tech

Teachers		1st Period	2nd Period	Lunch	3rd Period	4th Period
				Math Tutoring		
Leon (Math)		Algebra 1	Algebra 1.5	Free	Planning	Algebra 2A
				Science Tutoring		
Reba (Science)		Biology 1	Science 9	Free	Science 9	Planning
Donna (Soc. Stud.)		Planning	Ancient Cultures	*Social Studies Tutoring* Free	American Studies 2	

Second Semester

Students	Academic Advisory	1st Period	2nd Period	Lunch	3rd Period	4th Period
Mikki (Sr.)		Advanced Spanish	Calculus		Journalism	Art/Band
Lawrence (Sr.)		Senior Projects	Algebra 2B		Spanish 2	Internship
Alex (Sr.)		Physics	Calculus		College	College
Kent (Jr.)		Chemistry	Geography		Geometry	Spanish 2
Michele (Soph.)		Resource Managmt/PE	Spanish 2		Biology 1	Current Events/ Band
Romona (Fr.)		Health/PE	American Studies 1		American Studies 1	Spanish 1/Art

Teachers		1st Period	2nd Period	Lunch	3rd Period	4th Period
				Math Tutoring		
Leon (Math)		Algebra 1	Geometry	Free	Planning	Algebra 2B
				Science Tutoring		
Reba (Science)		Physics	Science 9	Free	Science 9	Planning
Donna (Soc. Stud.)		Practical Law	Planning	*Library supervision* Free	American Studies 1	

At 7:40 the first bell of the day rings and Lawrence and his buddies just slip into academic advisory on time. Academic advisory is a compromise, arrived at after we've experimented with all sorts of ways to do it. Even this year all of the freshman advisors have been meeting to come up with ways to use their time better. One plan has been to develop a "student guide" to the school for kids. To put that together, each freshman advisory is discussing what freshmen wished they had been told when they came to high school. Sometimes we overlook the simplest things, as one freshman advisor finds out when an advisee suggests that "I would have liked a map of the school with room numbers so I wouldn't have had to ask the upperclassmen where to go on the first day of school." But the one thing we have all agreed is that, once you get a homeroom, you keep the kids for all four years of high school. So Lawrence and Mikki and Alex join their teachers and their groups of around fifteen others with whom they've spent this time together for the past three years and a bit.

Just the other day I was talking with Leon about the seniors he's worked with during those three-plus years. "When they were freshmen I could barely stand some of these kids. But they've grown up so nicely, and now one of the things I look forward to is the time we spend together at the start of the day. I'm really going to miss these kids when they graduate." I have the feeling that the kids feel the same way about him.

In the ten minutes of advisory all types of things go on. Today, seniors are filling out questionnaires about what they plan on doing next year. The guidance counselor and I will use these to schedule meetings with colleges, hold seminars on finding jobs, arrange for voter registration, and so on. Kent's advisory, like all junior sections, is hearing about the upcoming PSAT tests, while in Michele's advisory the sophomores are getting only the regular morning announcements and a little time to catch up on any homework. Kent, Michele, and every other student at FHHS know that their advisors will cajole, encourage, and remind them to turn in the forms and other materials that have been handed out. It's like having your mom at school with you, and the truth of it is that most kids like the gentle reminders.

Romona has a different advisory experience because she is a member of our Student Delegation. The Delegation is our student government, which meets every morning with me. We have worked hard to give students more control of issues that affect them in the school, from social events to the hiring of teachers. Today, Vicky takes her subcommittee on a school constitution to my office to review comments they have received on the first draft of the document. They are meeting with representatives from each advisory, going over each section, and receiving feedback and comments to guide their revisions. (The impetus to write a student constitution has been the realization that the power the students currently have is merely a grant from the staff that could be taken away by a different administration.) Other Student Delegation committees are meeting to schedule events (all club meetings, dances, fund-raisers, and the like are approved by the Student Delegation) and select the student interview team for a teaching position that we will be filling. Ten minutes is seldom enough time to get everything finished, so most of the committees agree to meet at lunch.

At 7:50 the bell rings dismissing students from advisory and sending them on to the first of their four classes. In the five minutes between classes they talk with friends, sort out books, organize papers, talk with teachers, and finally get to class. The academic day, as the kids see it, begins with the bell at 7:55 A.M. signaling the start of first period. However, the faculty and I know that every minute of the school day is devoted to teaching. Academic Advisory has already begun the effort. In those ten minutes before "real" school, teachers have worked with students catching up on homework, struggling with problems at home, talking about what college they might go to. It's part of the commitment that every good high school must make if we are to build a learning community that connects with every student. By creating advisories that keep track of students through all four years of high school, we can be more like elementary schools where one teacher knows every child well. In this way we make sure no student is anonymous, the worst thing that can happen to anyone.

First period finds Mikki in Journalism, where she's editor of the school paper. For the next eighty minutes she and her band of roving reporters will be all over the building, conducting interviews, taking pictures, and collecting materials for the next issue of the paper. They are not the only students out in the halls. Today is also the day that the Environmental Science class is making its weekly rounds, emptying the recycling containers in all the rooms and sorting the materials for our next recycling day. Through their efforts and that of the ecology club, Common Ground, we've saved the district hundreds of dollars in waste management fees by reducing the number of garbage pickups at all of our schools. Additionally, students are learning the economics of recycling, the nature of waste disposal, how materials are processed for reuse, and the issues the community faces in terms of waste reduction.

Throughout the day different classes will be out and around the school conducting activities similar to those of Journalism and Environmental Science. For those not familiar with daily life in high schools this probably seems like a small thing. In fact, one of the biggest barriers to overcome in connecting with kids is the issue of control. Out of fear of their misbehaving, we attempt to virtually "lock down" kids in schools. We believe we are controlling behavior by controlling movement, when we are only gaining momentary compliance. Witness how kids will contrive to take another five minutes on a hall pass whenever they can. Real control of behavior comes from fostering self-control, which is only developed when kids have the opportunity to take on real tasks and the freedom to do them. So now, unlike my first year at FHHS, when I stop students in the hall it isn't to check a pass, it's to talk about the articles they are researching, the number of pounds of aluminum we are selling this month, the samples they have just gathered down at the pond. In this way we are partners, not adversaries, a much more pleasant way to run a school.

Lawrence and Alex are both in math classes during first period. Lawrence is taking an advanced senior math and doing well. "I've got time to get this stuff, I hardly ever miss an assignment, Doc. Just got a little behind today," he replies as I ask him why he's sitting at a desk in the hall working during first period. His freshman year was a real struggle, as was his junior year. But this year he's on his way, next week meeting with college representatives and hunting down scholarships and loans.

Like most students, Lawrence appreciates the longer class periods. He remembers hearing about math from his older siblings, who never had enough time to get help in class. They would fret over it at the kitchen table, with Lawrence's parents unable to help much once they progressed past Algebra One. Now it seems he has plenty of time to get his work done in class. The period begins with a series of "bell ringers," problems that everyone starts on and that are usually taken from the ACT prep materials. After these are finished (they are done in all math classes), the work from yesterday is reviewed, new material is presented, and there is time for everyone in the class to work with the teacher to make sure they all understand the material.

It was only four years ago that there was so little demand for the Advanced Math class that we had to schedule it outside of the school day (over lunch, with six students enrolled). This year, Lawrence shares the class (now called Pre-Calculus) with 33 other seniors (one-half of the senior class). This increase in enrollment in upper-level math is a product both of the longer class periods and of stretching out the time we take to cover core concepts. The math faculty at FHHS saw our change to longer class periods as a chance to rethink the entire math program. Now freshmen begin with one semester of Algebra in which we cover about two-thirds of what usually makes up a freshman algebra course. This means teachers take more time to cover material in detail, knowing that a sophomore's schedule will call for one semester of Algebra 1.5 which will finish up and go well beyond the traditional algebra course. Second semester will find those same sophomores in Geometry. As juniors our kids will take Algebra 2A and 2B, stretching over two semesters. At this point they have completed their math requirement, but many go on to take Pre-Calculus and Statistics and Probability in their senior year. Lawrence, hoping to major in engineering in college, will be well prepared.

Alex is sharing teaching duties with Leon, as his internship has him teaching an Algebra One class. Together they are walking around the room and reviewing the previous day's assignment, making sure every student understands the concept from the day before. "There's time now to make sure the kids get it," Leon points out. No more collecting the homework, grading it that night, and finding out that the kids aren't getting it only when it's too late to do much about it.

"Of course, the new schedule means we move a lot slower in math." Leon is sharing his reflections with the mini–faculty meetings we have every other Friday. On these days we officially take the first forty minutes of each period and have a conversation about school with whoever is on planning period. So six to ten teachers, from all areas, join me to discuss curriculum, students, and school in general without the pressure of voting on something or running through the usual administrivia of faculty members. This time we are discussing one of the principles of the Coalition of Essential Schools to which we belong: Less Is More.

"We do cover less. You can't do two separate lessons in an eighty-minute period." Leon again. "So when we meet for just a semester, we're covering only about seventy percent of what we covered when we met all year. But the difference I've noticed is when students come into their second year of math. They remember more from the prior year, they seem to have a better understanding of the core principles, and so we move faster and in more depth."

Alex has his turn in front of class today. He's working through an approach to factoring polynomials. It's a lesson he and Leon worked on earlier, and our intern supervisor has stopped in to watch. I've deliberately chosen to stay away, even though I'd love to see Alex in action. One more adult in the room might add too much pressure.

I catch Alex between classes and ask him how it went.

"I was so nervous, Dr. Wood. I forgot some of the stuff I was going to do, and when the kids had questions I was afraid I would give them the wrong answer." But he loved the chance to try out teaching, something he wants to do for a career. "I just didn't realize how much responsibility there is."

Welcome to the adult world, Alex.

Second period finds Reba and Romona together in Science Nine. Science Nine is part of the freshman core program designed to give all entering freshmen the same high-quality, high-expectation program that will prepare them for any path they want to take later in school. If you take a minute to look back at Romona's schedule, you'll see the basic outlines of the program. Each freshman will learn how to type and will take core courses in math, science, and humanities (English/social studies combination), as well as physical education, health, nutrition, and two electives (including band, Spanish, art, industrial technology, and agriculture). Kids aren't ability-grouped in the program, the only distinction being that some students are ready for Algebra One while others start with Pre-Algebra.

We were not sure that students would have chosen, among all the things they might do, this rigorous core on their own. They are really not much different from us, after all—and who among

---

The FHHS Core/Elective Program

	Required Courses	Electives
Freshman Year	Algebra 1 or Pre-Algebra Science 9 American Studies Health Physical Education Keyboarding (Typing) Nutrition	May choose two to four Recommended: one fine arts
Sophomore Year	Algebra 1.5 Geometry American Studies Physical Education Biology	May choose two to four Recommended: foreign language

Junior Year	Algebra 2A
	English 11
		May choose six
		Recommended:
		  Algebra 2B
		  Biology 2 or Chemistry
		  Career and Life Choices
		  foreign language

Senior Year	English 12
	Senior Government
		May choose six
		Recommended:
		  Pre-Calculus
		  Physics
		  foreign language
		  internship

Required to graduate: 25 units.

us can say that at every turn we have chosen the most demanding plan of action? We all need guidance, and our core curriculum provides it for our students (as well as our staff, as it points out what is most important to teach). Believing that every student needs a core high school experience, we began our task of figuring out the core with our mission statement: to develop active democratic citizens, lifelong learners, and individuals flexible in their career choices. We took these goals to meetings of parents, community groups, employers, students, and staff, and came up with a list of things our students should know and be able to do, if they were to be the sort of neighbors we wanted. It was also a general consensus that younger students should have fewer choices while older ones had more. It was from these discussions that we arrived at the current Core/Elective Program reproduced on page 187.

Two of the keys to making the freshman program work are Science Nine and the Humanities program. Science Nine provides all students with an introduction to science regardless of whether or not they think they are going on to college. Today Reba is conducting a lab that has Romona and her friends preparing slides so they can see cells rather than just read about them. Using microscopes that have been begged, borrowed, or stolen (I can't remember which, but I know we didn't have the money to buy them) from a lab the university was closing, each lab team is carefully staining a sample and begging Reba to come see their slide. In the time allotted everyone finishes, cleans up, and starts to write a lab report. The stragglers will hang around for part of the lunch period to wrap up their work.

Next semester, taking a cue from the humanities staff (see below), the math and science staff will be working on team-taught projects that bring Algebra One and Science Nine together. This year is the first time we have been able to schedule our core freshman science course with the freshman math, so both teachers are finding their way. The first assignment is one on measurement that takes kids around the building to find the volume of a wide variety of structures and then asks such brain-benders as calculating the mass of our greenhouse filled with gold or our gym filled with water. It's one of many places students will see how math and science work together while they do labs in chemistry, physics, biology, and environmental science introducing every child to what it means to "do" science.

While Romona and colleagues are in Science Nine and a math class, the other half of the freshmen work with two teachers from the humanities department for half the day (two periods) in the American Studies One class. A combination of English and American History, American Studies One is the freshman component of our two-year humanities core. Designed to use the development of reading, writing, speaking, and research skills in understanding American history, the class covers several important periods from prehistoric settlement to westward expansion. As a sophomore, students will take the second half of the course, American Studies Two, which begins with the Industrial Revolution and ends with the events of today.

The American Studies program is one of the major curricular changes that the FHHS staff has undertaken. Taught by a team of teachers, the courses dig deeply into a series of major topics rather than merely surveying everything that occurred. The course is built around a sense of local history, with the context of our region serving as an organizing tool. For example, when studying the Civil War special attention is paid to our area as a major stop on the underground railroad and to the experiences of soldiers from our county as well as to the county's physical and cultural geography during this period.

Today students in American Studies One are doing research on the first settlers in Stewart, Amesville, Coolville, and Guysville, four communities our school serves. It will be the day that one member of the class stumbles upon the fact that Daniel Stewart, for whom the town is named, was the cultivator of the Rome Beauty apple (named after Rome Township, where Stewart is located). Similar "discoveries" of local cultural and historical highlights will continue to spark students' interest throughout the program as they read and write about a history that is theirs.

The teachers who share our freshmen all have fourth-period planning time together. They meet regularly, thinking about what skills they are trying to teach in all their subject matter areas. Additionally, as part of our efforts to help the staff develop their skills, teachers spend time on Tuesdays with Susan M. A former FHHS teacher, she is hired through a grant to work with teachers during the day on issues related to their teaching.

Then, every other Friday, they spend their planning period with all the other teachers who are not teaching that period in an internal conference in my office. These "planning period meetings" give faculty from all areas the chance to meet, talk through school issues, and share ideas about teaching and learning. Both these efforts replace the usual "in-service" program that teachers often suffer through, featuring some consultant who stops in for an hour, lectures, collects a hefty fee and leaves. Instead, faculty development at FHHS is an on-going part of a teacher's day at school. Because of this collaborative work on the part of the faculty, when Romona finishes her first year of high school she'll have a start on the habits of mind and social and academic skills that will make success both in high school and in the years following possible.

Meanwhile, back in Science Nine, Reba and her intern, Frankie, have to be almost everywhere at once. For most of our students it's the first time they've used a microscope, and they struggle with focus, magnification, and getting the right amount of reflective light. Lawrence, who has stopped by to use Reba's computer for his English Twelve project, chuckles softly to himself as he watches the seeming chaos. It was, he thinks, so long ago that he was one of them. Now he's a senior, independently putting the final touches on his Senior Paper.

During second period Lawrence, Mikki, and Alex all have English Twelve, where they are working on their Senior Papers. In fact, all of our seniors take English Twelve during either first, second, or third period. We have set up our schedule to accommodate most senior classes in the morning so that our upperclassmen can do their internships or attend college in the afternoon. The goal is to have every senior in some way begin the transition to the after-high-school world through an out-of-school experience. Mikki interns third and fourth period at a local newspaper, Lawrence will work as a middle school coach next semester, and Alex, as we have seen, teaches high school math and next semester will spend half the day taking courses at the university. All day long kids walk in and out of school, going to real work in real places, and in four years only one of them hasn't shown up where she was supposed to be. It's a record of which we are very proud.

During second period the seniors are to be found all over the building. They are either at a computer putting the final touches on the first draft of their paper or working with the teacher on some sticking point. Some of the seniors struggle with the Senior Paper. It requires that students choose a topic about which, as the teacher has put it, "they have a passion." For twelve weeks they immerse themselves in researching whatever it is they have chosen. We send them to the university library and out into the community to work with a sponsor. At the end of this process they will each have produced an extensive research paper, the ones of highest quality being presented at an evening ceremony.

"I've never done anything like this." Lawrence and the guidance counselor are talking about his paper while I listen in. "When Mr. Musick told us fifteen pages, I thought 'no way.' But my outline is thirteen pages and I don't know how to cut it down. I'm gonna have to cut somewhere, but where?" Lawrence, a kid who for years has been an average but not strong student, ends up pulling an A in what is widely considered by students the toughest course in the school. What's more, he has decided to carry his paper further second semester by taking the Senior Projects course. Here he will turn his paper on engineering into a project on an amphibious go-cart. The test launch is scheduled sometime in April.

Kent, our junior, is also in an English class second period. Believing that every student has the right to a high-quality education, we do not ability-group in our core subjects. Every student takes English Nine, Ten, Eleven, and Twelve. English Nine and Ten are part of the American Studies core. English Eleven focuses on World Literature and is one of Kent's favorite courses. Today he and two other students will spend most of the class working on a project about the literature of South Africa that includes reviews of books, stories, and poetry as well as an historical and cultural background.

The fact that we have only four class periods a day, each eighty minutes long, really pays off in a project like this. After the daily grammar lesson (a routine in all the English courses), Kent and company head to the library to gather more information on South African history. They have the time to consult numerous sources, compile their notes, draft an outline, and assign writing tasks long before the bell rings. (They also have plenty of space in the library, as there are no study halls at FHHS, meaning no kids sent from such places to the library just to kill time.)

After her first-period math class, Michele heads for Donna Bennett's second-period Ancient Cultures class. This class is one of our more popular elective courses. It's an area that Donna is devoted to, and she passes that love on to her students. In fact, two of our football players are doing their senior project on the Incas, which they learned of from Donna.

During her first-period planning time, after she made phone calls home to several parents who had inquired about their children's progress, Donna readied materials for today's Big Dig. The Ancient Cultures class, after studying what characterizes a culture, has been divided into teams, each assigned to develop its own culture. Having done that, they then create artifacts which they bury on the school grounds. Each team is assigned another team's site to unearth and to interpret. Today they begin excavations.

"Time. That's the only reason we can do this now." Donna and I are watching the kids dig. "I'm able to work with each group, watch them develop their artifacts, and talk with them about cultures and cultural studies, rather than just lecture all the time. I do still lecture, you know. But now that's just one way among many to get this material across to the kids. And now"—she waves to the two groups, hip deep in muddy clay, sorting out pottery shards and animal bones—"they're having so much fun they don't even know they are learning."

That the kids are learning is clear from the debriefing I sat in on last year after the Big Dig. Each student took a turn describing how culture relates to geography, technology, and/or science. In their own ways they were all trying to work out the interplay between man and nature that results in a culture, in a way of living on the earth. Adam summed it up: "Each culture makes sense to itself. That's what we are trying to understand. Why it makes sense to the people inside it. We can't judge them as right or wrong until we understand them. . . . I think that is what I've learned, understanding has to be first."

At 10:40 the lunch bell rings. For Leon, Reba, and Donna this signals the start of a tutoring session in their classrooms. Some students will just show up today because they are behind in their work or need someone to help with a difficult concept or idea. Other students, falling behind for whatever reason, are assigned by their teachers to come for help. Time is also devoted to those students who have yet to pass the Ninth Grade Proficiency Tests (discussed in chapter 2). But these aren't the only places where kids are getting one-on-one help with their work. Today Alex is taking over tutoring duties for another math teacher who is out sick. Down in the computer lab, as on computers all over the building, seniors are busily finishing up their Senior Paper drafts. Kids are busy at work in the art room, industrial technology shop, library, agriculture shop, and even my office, where a team of kids are busy planning a talk they are to give next week about our school.

For the majority of students, lunch means a social hour. The cafeteria is full of joking, talking, loud kids. The gym is home to half a dozen basketball games, with another two taking place on the outside courts. To an outsider there is no doubt it appears a bit chaotic; teenagers are, I'm afraid, by nature loud and boisterous. Parents who have had a group of their teenager's friends over for pizza know that an afternoon spent on an airport runway can do less damage to your ears. But if you look closely, you get a better idea of how it works.

For example, Lawrence and his girlfriend can be found sitting against the wall in the gym, catching up on the events of the morning while she was at her internship. Similar groups of both romantic and platonic friends can be found throughout the "open areas," the cafeteria, gym, and courtyard. While this may seem like a small thing, allowing kids time to spend with their friends helps with the school's agenda in a variety of ways. No longer do students try to arrange their schedules to have lunch with girlfriends or their buddies, they don't try to slip out of class to see someone or trade notes, and they don't feel like we are trying to keep them away from their friends.

Kent can be found over on the stage in the gym talking to Kevin Haines, the business teacher. Also Kent's wrestling coach, Kevin has taken the time to get to know Kent quite well and today they're talking about Kent's plans for college. Michele is in the guidance office, along with a group of about seven other kids who hang out there during lunch, eating M&M's and talking about school student romances or life in general. Romona is in the band room at a freshman class meeting. This meeting, like every student activity, has been scheduled through the Student Delegation and is voluntary for students who want to attend. Like all club and class meetings, these occur at lunch so they do not disrupt classes. Each and every one of our kids is busy at something. While it is noisy, it is productive.

Mikki is nowhere to be found at lunch. Immediately at the start of lunchtime she signs out and heads to her internship at the local newspaper, where she will spend the afternoon editing two weekend feature stories. Other days find her out with reporters, attending editorial meetings, or covering her own "beat," which includes community events in the school district.

With five minutes left in the lunch period, a warning bell rings and students begin heading back to class. Stops by lockers, visits to teachers or myself, stops at the drinking fountain, and before you know it the halls are clear and third period begins.

Leon is on the phone in the teachers' lounge along with Meredith, a senior who is my intern. We get a wide variety of requests for visits to our school or for teachers to present workshops for other teachers. It is Meredith's job to coordinate all of these, and more than once our visitors have been surprised when a student, not the principal, meets them at the door and begins their orientation session. Today Meredith is helping Leon with the details for attending a math conference next spring where members of our math staff and students (including Alex) will be presenting.

Reba has another section of Science Nine, where she is running the third lab of the day. It's hard to believe how recently she struggled just to do one lab a week. The cleanup from second period Science Nine and setup for this was directed by Frankie, her intern, during lunch. It's not just the longer periods that make the labs possible, it's the new roles students play as well.

Michele and Donna Bennett start third period along with about fifty other sophomores in Steve Musick's room. This is the all-afternoon humanities block, American Studies Two, that brings together U.S. History and American Literature. They started their work this year with a look at the great waves of immigration that came to our shores at the end of the 1800s (this is where American Studies One ends). Now they have moved on through industrialization and World War I to arrive at the Depression, with today's interviews of community members who lived through the era being the highlight of the unit.

Even with some fifty kids and teachers crammed into a room meant for thirty, the session goes well. Kids are meeting with their teams, the teachers go from group to group to supervise, students prepare interview questions and continue their practice. Several parents filter in and out too, helping with preparations for the interviews. It's not nearly as confusing as you might assume, since these two classes often meet together for library research, films, or other such activities. In just a few minutes our guests will arrive and the interviews that will be recorded and kept on file for future classes will begin.

Lawrence is in Biology Two for third period. It's a class he is struggling with, but passing. The first part of the class is a lecture on the life cycles of aquatic organisms in regional waterways. The second part of the class is what gets students involved in this topic, the planning for a canoe trip down the Hocking where they will put into action what they are learning in class. As with all our science classes, Biology Two is a heavily hands-on course, with kids putting into practice the concepts and skills found in the texts. Over the past three years this hands-on approach has pushed enrollment in science courses well past the breaking point, and we are looking for ways to add a teacher and more sections of advanced classes.

Kent is in math. It's an all-year math class, of which the first half finishes up Algebra One (we call it Intermediate Algebra) and the second half is Geometry. In math more than anywhere else, perhaps, we are seeing the payoff of taking more time to cover content in more depth. Kent is clearly pleased with the approach. Under our old system he would have taken Algebra his sophomore year and then either Geometry or Consumer Math as his final math class his junior year. Instead, he is headed toward what he hopes will be a career in engineering, as he has found late in his school career that he has a real flair for algebra and equations and enjoys the reasoning behind them. All too soon for him the bell rings signaling the end of third period.

Reba heads for my office at fourth period. She and most of the other teachers who teach in the freshman core are meeting to discuss particular students as well as some proposed changes to the core program. The schedule is structured as often as possible so that teachers who share students share a planning period. The goal is to facilitate the very sort of conversation that we'll have today, tying what we teach together with who our students are.

Leon's fourth-period class is Algebra Two. It's a bit larger than his Algebra One class, which is by design. We've made a deliberate attempt to lower numbers in our introductory courses, so that we build a more solid foundation under our younger students. Usually the upper-level, more advanced courses are smaller than introductory courses (also by far the norm in university life). But if you think about it, it's the novice, for whom everything is new and thus more difficult, who needs the most help and attention. The more advanced students are more likely to learn and thrive with less, albeit more advanced, help. To that end we've arranged class size to put the help where it is most needed.

Back in Donna's class the pace has quickened. Interviews are going on, and she and her partner are busy checking to make sure all the tape recorders are working. But several glitches have cropped up, as a couple of our guests had car trouble and could not get to school. The solution: a mother gathers up four kids and they are off down the road to do the interviews on site.

Alex checks out of school for fourth period and heads for his college statistics class. A new state law allows high school students to attend college at our expense, and Alex is getting a head start on his Math Education major. In just over two hours he'll return for football practice, having had to miss only one class in order to get to campus, attend class, and return.

Lawrence is in Spanish One. Since he decided late that college might be for him, he is just now getting around to taking a foreign language. In many schools it would hardly be worth the effort. One year of a language won't meet many entry requirements and certainly wouldn't help a student pass a language proficiency test. But Lawrence has scheduled Spanish One this semester and Spanish Two second semester, hoping to meet the requirements of several of the colleges he's interested in. I'm not sure he'll get there, but it's worth the try and great to see him making the effort.

Mikki always slips back to school for the last half hour, from 2:00 to 2:30, to practice with the marching band. Since she goes to her internship at the start of lunch, she's easily putting in the 160 minutes (equal to two class periods) that are required to earn two credits. So in order to accommodate the inevitable schedule conflicts, we're happy to have her come back and join band practice. Michele, our sophomore, does the same thing. Not today, given the interviews that are going on, but on most days she'll be excused from the last half hour of class to hit the marching field with the band. Because there is extensive class time to cover material, it's easy for kids and teachers to accommodate these arrangements. In this way the fewer periods, contrary to popular wisdom, accommodate more rather than less flexibility in student schedules.

Kent has a Career and Life Choices class fourth period. Broken into three parts, the class covers decision making, a career/college exploration, and a consumer education segment based on shopping for a car (as well as filling out a 1040EZ form). At the end of the course the students will have portfolios containing a resume, letters of reference, filled-out college and job applications, and other items of their own choice describing who they are. At a recent meeting of our advisory committee for the high school one participant mentioned that a local employer had said that our students were the only area students who had a resume when they came looking for work. "The course where they do that is such a valuable experience, why don't you require it for all kids?" he asked. Good question; we'd better work on that one as well.

Romona, along with all the other freshmen, is in her elective class fourth period. From the various choices she has taken Industrial Technology and is bent over her third try at a three-dimensional drawing. Next semester she'll take Spanish and Art, other freshmen having chosen Agricultural Science, Band, Environmental Science, or Information Technology as their elective.

The last period of the day for some students is split into two parts to accommodate a wider range of elective experiences for our freshmen and sophomores. This is the one time we go against our usual less-is-more philosophy (less coverage for more depth). Given the lack of resources for many families in our area, we try to give our kids a wide sampling of areas to expose them to the many possibilities the world has to offer. This is Romona's and her colleagues' chance to try out what high school has to offer, and for Romona, Industrial Technology has opened up a whole new world. In fact, she's stopped me several times in the hall to ask if she can take I.T. again next semester, willing to repeat the very same course again to help develop her interest in interior design.

At 2:30 the final bell rings to send everyone home. I try to be in front of the school as everyone leaves, ostensibly so that I can "manage" student departure. The real reason I'm there is to check in on the health of the building at the close of the school day. For the most part everyone leaves smiling, and not just because the school day is over. While not weighted down with them, most kids carry a book or two to work on overnight. As always, teachers carry work home as well, though now from three rather than seven classes, papers from 70 students rather than 160.

Work still goes on in the evening. But, as with the work in the classroom, while the quantity may go down, the quality goes up. Again and again essays have replaced short answers and in-depth projects are replacing book reports. The reason is simple: teachers have the time to deal with these more complex assignments when they have fewer students. Similarly, kids do better work when they have the time to attend to fewer tasks.

Of course, not everyone leaves at the sound of the bell. The freshman team is still meeting, having begun to figure out a new way to organize the freshman core. There are kids all over the building, working on computers, laying out the yearbook and school paper, practicing music and sports. And often there are presentations to prepare for the evening.

I've mentioned the time teachers and students transformed the cafeteria for the Roaring Twenties celebration. A stage was erected on one side of the room for both Bing Crosby to croon from and Einstein to lecture on relativity. A speakeasy was set up on the other side, for which there would be special passes and signals provided. Dinner was served as well, helping the kids earn the funds to pay for this production. Makeup and costumes were tried, retried, rejected, and redone. And by 7:00 P.M. the house lights went down and a group of "flappers" started us off with a rousing Charleston. A repeat performance of the dance closed the show two hours later, much to the delight of the parents, siblings, teachers, students, and community members who spent the time talking with characters from the twenties, watching stage productions, hearing lectures and poetry recitals, and just simply having a good time.

The Roaring Twenties show wasn't the only time we've put on an evening academic exhibition. Over the past few years we've held a Renaissance Fair, a Night in the Colonies, and other festivals. Twice a year we also have our Internship Exhibitions, where students present what they've accomplished to an audience of internship supervisors and parents. This year we will add our Senior Project exhibitions, an evening where all the Senior Projects will be displayed and the most outstanding projects will be presented by their authors. Events like these are celebrations of our kids' work and of our school's successes. They show what kids can do with five thousand well-spent hours.

By the time the final bell rings, a great deal of quality work has been done by students in our learning community. To be sure, we are always trying to find ways to make it better. As I write this we are working on a plan to develop a Community Research Center where local residents can conduct research on area issues, a plan to expand support for our students so they can all undertake internships regardless of personal resources, a peer mediation program, and more infusion of local culture, geography, history, and geology into the curriculum. But the seeds we have taken to date are already bearing fruit by such traditional measures as better student achievement, reduced discipline issues, more kids going to college.

And there is something much deeper that has changed in our school. While it is almost impossible to put a finger on it, I would say the most important change about our school is that we are a community. We have personalized the experiences of each student, put into place a curriculum that makes sense to kids, and allowed our students to take responsibility for much of what goes on in school. When I read the grand national reports about changing high schools, I seldom see these things mentioned. But when I watch the day-to-day lives of students and staff at Federal Hocking High School, I know that these are really the only things that matter.

Afterword

While working on this book I have had the opportunity to travel and speak to educators about high school change. Often questions have come up about issues that, while important, somehow did not fit with the stories that served as the basis for this book. Four key issues seem to come up again and again: money, school choice/charter schools, site-based management, and student achievement. I do not claim to be an expert on any of these, but I want to try and address them from the position of an actual school rather than the halls of Congress or the talk-radio airwaves.

Does Money Matter?

The changes in high schools that have been outlined in this book are not reliant upon schools receiving more funding. But when I am asked if money makes a difference, there is only one answer: Of course. While money may not be needed in order to make changes, it does make a difference.

More money does not guarantee that the restructuring needed in our high schools will occur. Most certainly, fewer funds make change more difficult if not impossible, as teachers' time is consumed by larger class sizes and the energy needed for reform is lost to making ends meet.* If additional money is

---

* In fact, as I write this, our district is struggling to make enough budget cuts to overcome a $300,000 projected deficit. Concerns with such cuts preoccupy faculty and staff throughout the district.

needed to make changes, it is often best spent as a one-time infusion of funds to provide for staff development, research, and public information. In fact, the changes at FHHS actually work to save our district money in several ways. For example, with semester-long courses such as American Studies we only need to purchase texts for the seventy or so students taking the course each semester rather than the one hundred forty texts needed if all students took the same course all year long. We also experience a savings in having fewer staff sick days, a direct result of staff feeling better about their work since the changes. And we have more teachers teaching class rather than wasting time monitoring students, as we have eliminated study halls. Change, therefore, can mean using resources more efficiently.

But when I hear grand pronouncements about how much we spend on schools and how no more money is needed, I can feel my blood pressure rise. I will leave the discussion of overall resources to those who know the subject better than I. In particular I want to recommend that anyone with any genuine concern about these issues read Jonathan Kozol's heartbreaking work *Savage Inequalities* (New York: Crown, 1991) and view the PBS special "Children in America's Schools" produced by South Carolina Educational Television and narrated by Bill Moyers. The PBS documentary was filmed near our school and reflects the disparity of school funding in Ohio (and many other states) which is the focus of a current Ohio Supreme Court case.

The message from these works is that we are pretty cheap when it comes to our children. The average annual expenditure per pupil nationwide in our public schools is $5,541, or $30.78 per day (assuming 180 days) or $4.40 per hour (a seven-hour day). We pay less per hour to have our kids taught in school than we do to have our hamburgers served at the neighborhood fast food restaurant.* Furthermore, we have allowed our physical structures to deteriorate to the point that by one estimate it will require $112 *billion* just to bring current buildings up to acceptable standards. We tell our children a great deal about

---

* Figures on per-pupil funding and other data in the chapter are taken from a special edition of *Education Week,* "Quality Counts: A Report Card on the Condition of Public Education in the 50 States" (Washington, D.C.: Editorial Projects in Education, January 22, 1997).

how much we value them based on how we provide services such as teachers, safe school buildings, and adequate books. Right now the message to a lot of kids is that they do not count for a whole lot.

National numbers are always liable to manipulation and interpretation. For me the issue of whether or not dollars matter comes down to my experience in our school. Bottom line—we spend at FHHS approximately $1,000 per student *less* than the average expenditure in Ohio. I often imagine what the additional $400,000 per year our high school would receive would purchase if we just had the state *average* funding to spend on our kids. More realistically, let's scale it down to $200,000 additional dollars. Here's a laundry list of a few essentials we could then provide our kids:

3 additional teachers—$90,000 (with fringe benefits)

1 additional guidance counselor—$40,000

Library acquisitions—$5,000 (to add to the paltry $1,500 we now have)

6 new computers each year—$24,000 (to supplement the 40 we now try to make serve our kids, many of them castoffs from businesses or universities)

Repairs to our building—$10,000 (better than the scant $800 per year we currently have for a twenty-seven-year-old building with more than 450 students and staff in it for ten hours a day)

New texts—$10,000 (for our first new texts in two years; our history books are more than ten years old)

And we would still have $21,000 a year left over to cover any emergencies—emergencies which today would simply shut down our school.

If we would simply commit ourselves to being as generous to our children as we are to our military, we could have higher-quality work from kids tomorrow. We need more money, not for more administrators, coordinators, or special programs. We need dollars devoted to having more adults available to work with kids and more up-to-date tools for kids to work with. These things will make a difference, and only money can buy them.

Choice, Charter Schools, and Equity

A reform effort that is getting plenty of attention is the movement to "school choice." Included in this effort is the creation of "charter schools." First, two quick definitions. "School choice" refers to programs where parents may choose the school their son or daughter attends regardless of where they live. In most school choice plans choice is limited to other public schools, and any state aid a school would receive follows the student to his or her new school. "Charter schools" are schools that parents may also choose instead of their neighborhood public school. The charter school concept adds more variety and flexibility, as such schools are freed from state and local regulations in order to design a program that is unique to that school. A "charter" is granted by the local school system, a university, or the state itself to run a school according to a plan submitted by the teachers or community members who want to start the school.

The thinking behind choice plans is that such freedom of attendance will force schools to improve. Students and their families are viewed as consumers who will "vote with their feet," leaving schools that do not perform well for those that do. Thus, schools are opened up to the effects of the marketplace as opposed to having monopoly control over student attendance.

Charter schools are similarly thought to work to improve schools by providing options for students. Freed from external bureaucratic meddling, they are more able to experiment and innovate. Noncharter schools would face competition for students from the charter schools. More important, the methods tried out in such settings would be given a trial run and then be ready for adoption by their public school cousins.

Traditionally thought of as a conservative measure with its reliance on the open market, choice has its proponents among the most progressive of educators. Deborah Meier, who began several choice schools in New York City's East Harlem neighborhoods, argues that choice may indeed be the saving grace of American public education. As she puts it, "Choice is a necessary but not sufficient part of a far larger strategy. Creating smaller and more focused educational communities, enhancing the climate of trust between families and schools, developing workable models of self-governance, increasing the heterogeneity of a school's population, and using pedagogies that respond to diverse learning styles and student interest are all factors that current research suggests correlate with improved school outcomes. All of these are far easier to accomplish in small schools of choice."*

In my way of thinking the most powerful thing to come out of the campaign for choice and charters is the ringing endorsement both these movements bring to small schools. Virtually all charter and choice schools reflect most of what I argued for in chapter 3. They are small, personalized, and built around getting to know every student well. They have fewer administrators, closer contact with parents, and a student body known personally by the school. The movement to such schools and the intense competition to get into them speaks volumes about how the American people want us to build educational communities.†

I admit that at times I have imagined the school I would like to create if charter schools were an option in this area. A small school, located somewhere in our beautiful Appalachian foothills, where students would spend part of the day under the tutelage of a teacher and the rest in our communities applying what they have learned. Students would graduate based on what they could demonstrate that they have learned, they would engage in an extended service learning program, and each teacher would be responsible for advising a small group of students through the entire experience.

But there are some questions that nag at me about choice and charters that become more pronounced when I think about it in our area—questions that for the most part revolve around the

---

* Meier, *The Power of Their Ideas,* p. 103. On the overall success of the school choice program in the district where Meier worked, see Seymour Fliegel and James MacGuire, *Miracle in East Harlem: The Fight for Choice in Public Education* (New York: Times Books, 1993).

† But, as Meier herself warns, "choice itself will not produce a single one of [these reforms], except perhaps a temporarily greater sense of ownership. It is a vehicle for allowing us to move ahead more efficiently, not a guarantee that we will do so" (p. 103).

issue of equity, fairness, justice. Is choice equitable for kids when *every* school is not a choice school? Is it fair to fund charter schools that students cannot attend? And why are we willing to settle for just a few good schools for a few kids instead of excellent schools for all kids?

We claim as a society to be committed to the equal treatment of all citizens. When it comes to schools, that means all of our children will have an equal opportunity to attend a good school. But will this be the case when we provide only some students the chance to make a choice or attend a charter school? If *every* school is not a choice, if *all* schools do not have the advantages that charter schools have, what can we say about the schools that take students who didn't choose or who didn't get in? Do choice and charters lead to a two-tier system where some students are fortunate enough to receive the benefits of such a plan while others just get what is left over?

As I mentioned earlier, our school district covers 190 square miles. In Ohio we currently have what is called "open enrollment," a form of choice where students in neighboring school districts cross district lines to attend another school. The simple problem with this plan is that a neighboring school may be thirty miles away! How does a student of limited means make such a trip? Does it seem fair that choice be limited to those with transportation? Or what about those kids whose parents might lack the educational background to keep themselves informed about the latest charter school in their district? Is choice fair to children when, because of circumstances they cannot control, only a few kids ever get to make a choice while the rest continue to go to what are thought to be less desirable schools?

In my way of thinking, and I hope it is every American's perspective, our children, each and every one of them, *deserve* a humane, engaging, and meaningful high school experience.* When we approach schooling as a marketplace, similar to selling automobiles, we will end up with a school system that resembles a shopping mall parking lot. Indeed, everyone in that lot is at the mall. But some are driving late model Ford Broncos, Mer-

---

* The best commentary I have read on the need to treat all children justly is Barbara Kingsolver's essay "Somebody's Baby" found in her collection *High Tide in Tucson* (New York: Harper Collins, 1995).

cedes Benzes, and Cadillacs; others are in relatively new Chevy sedans and Ford wagons; still others drive cars pocked with rust and calling out for a new exhaust system. For choice to be just, every school should be a Cadillac. While they might differ in programmatic emphasis, all schools would afford every student a high-quality educational experience. Anything less than that is not really choice, it's a sentence. There is nothing just about fixing up some schools so a few students can abandon struggling schools. Justice is only found when every school is so good the question a parent faces is not "Do I get to choose?" but "How will I ever choose?"

Site-Based Management

Obviously I believe in democracy. It shows up in the hours we take to make decisions as a faculty at FHHS and the engagement our students have in decision making.* In much of the recent school reform literature a great deal of emphasis has been placed on shared decision making in schools as a tool for school change. Usually referred to as "site-based" management or decision making, such strategies involve placing the power to make curricular, budgetary, personnel, and other decisions at the school level by the staff at that building. While plans may vary in the range of decisions given to the committee, the core agenda is to cut through bureaucracy and put power and control at the school site.

Obviously site-based decision making is a key element in building community. Schools that have the freedom to be flexible in how they meet their students' needs are more likely to have an engaging curriculum and policies that fit people rather than institutions. Placing decision making in the schoolhouse rather than the statehouse insures that the daily school experience reflects who the community is. Ending the one-size-fits-all approach to curriculum, discipline, texts, and teaching, site-based

---

* I am also proud to be associated with the Institute for Democracy in Education, the leading voice for holding true to the democratic mission of public education. See the Appendix for more information.

management holds out the possibility of schools as responsive communities rather than bureaucratic institutions.

Site-based decision making is not, however, a panacea. Just as with choice, when pursued as a single-minded strategy it has limitations that violate much of what should happen to build school communities. In particular, the site-based agenda often leaves unanswered questions around power and quality.

In communities power is widely shared. Indeed the agenda behind site-based management is power sharing. The argument is correct that the more you involve people in making decisions, and the more widely you share power, the more connected people will feel to the community. The problem is how widely power is shared in site-based decision making, as most of these plans rely on representation rather than participation. In every case a site-based *committee* is called for, usually a small number of teachers and the building principal, in whom decision-making power is vested. But what about those excluded from the process? What about parents? They may have one or two seats on the committee, but how do two parents speak for all parents? What about students, who seldom are offered a place on such representative bodies? For that matter, what about the rest of the teachers and staff in the building: how are all their diverse interests represented if not directly? Again, putting decision making at the site of the decision makes sense if the agenda is to build community; the issue is then to make sure that *everyone* at the site has a direct influence on the process.[19]

What disturbs me the most about the argument for site-based management is the lack of focus on the quality of student work. There seems to be an assumption that site-based decision making will improve student work, but this assumption is implicit. As I have repeatedly argued, the need for restructuring, the need to build high school communities, rests completely upon the agenda of helping kids do their highest quality work possible. There is no such guiding principle behind much of the argument for site-based management.

Couched in terms of "teacher empowerment" or some similar

---

[19] Marilyn Hohmann, whom we met earlier in this book, used a consensus model for decision making at her large high school. She can be reached at the Center for Leadership in School Reform, found in the Appendix.

slogan, the *assumption* seems to be that giving more local control will generate more quality. I do not believe this necessarily follows, as demonstrated by our own educational history in which federal intervention into locally controlled schools was required in order to insure adequate education opportunities for women, minorities, and the handicapped. To be sure, this intervention was often prompted by the good work of teachers and parents in opposition to a local school board. No doubt had these teachers and parents had more decentralized control even within their districts, the educational needs of these groups of students would have been met much sooner. However, the point I still want to make is that without an agenda of improving the quality of student work, site-based management can be just another way to delay the necessary work before us of transforming high schools into learning communities, as special interests get in the way of student interests.[20]

Student Achievement

I have not tried to tackle the issue of current student achievement for several reasons. First, I believe I have demonstrated that we could get better-quality work from our students no matter what the current quality by restructuring our high schools as learning communities. Second, we always want to do better, we just sometimes do not know what better is. I have worked to suggest what I think would be higher-quality student work and what our young people would be like if they did it. Third, we really do not know much about overall student achievement anyway, so I see little reason to debate it.

I know this third point flies directly in the face of what would be called conventional wisdom. For years we have heard how poorly our kids are doing in school. Report after report is issued

[20] As an illustrative point, in a school near us in a neighboring state a change in the daily schedule has been blocked by a site-based committee. This committee, which is elected, is made up of mostly senior faculty and department heads who currently have a reduced teaching load to take on administrative duties. Rather than risk losing such privileges, they are holding on to the current schedule even in the face of data which demonstrate students could do better work in a changed school schedule.

citing low test scores, international comparisons of student achievements, etc. Without much thought we believe all of these at face value and, rather than come to the defense of our children, accept rather uncritically that our kids are not doing a good job. We're wrong in doing so.

Perhaps the most rigorously researched antidote to all this pessimism is David Berliner and Bruce Biddle's work, *The Manufactured Crisis: Myths, Fraud, and the Attack on America's Public Schools*. In this work Berliner and Biddle do not deny that many of our schools are in deep trouble, especially many schools in poor rural or urban areas. However, what they do challenge is the notion that our children are doing poorly on tests. They debunk myth after myth, including that student achievement has fallen nationwide, that students are not as intelligent as in the past, and that we spend too much on schooling. Their argument, backed up by extensive research data, is simply this: "Americans are, of course, concerned about the performance of their schools. Such concerns are legitimate and should be encouraged. However, concerns about education . . . should be based on an honest and informed evaluation of available evidence . . . we shall use many data sources that lead to a clear but perhaps surprising conclusion—that, on average, today's students are at least as well informed as students were in previous generations and that education in America compares favorably with education elsewhere."[21]

Such a claim is certainly hard to swallow, especially after nearly a decade and a half of school bashing beginning with the oft-quoted *A Nation at Risk* released by the Reagan Administration in 1983. But here's an interesting observation: *A Nation at Risk* did not provide a single citation, research report, or reference. No studies backed up its claims that poor education was the reason that GM was struggling to hold off a wave of cheaper, better built imports. No evidence was given that the poorly educated American workforce was the reason U.S. business was relocating to those bastions of education such as Mexico. We simply accepted that it was our kids' fault for not doing enough math in fifth grade.

[21] David C. Berliner and Bruce J. Biddle, *The Manufactured Crisis* (Reading, Mass.: Addison-Wesley, 1995), p. 13.

There is something deeper at work here that leads us to accept the myths Berliner and Biddle so accurately discredit. It just seems all too easy to blame children for our failures as adults. Rather than fix problems, we try to fix schools and kids so the problems might someday go away. For example, long before public buildings were accessible to the handicapped, public schools were ordered to mainstream handicapped children. So it was when it came to rights for minorities and women. The nation as a whole has a drug problem. How to solve it? Mandate education programs. Our manufacturing base is dwindling as corporations move outside the country in search of low-wage, low-tax nation states. Our response is to insist kids score better on standardized tests.

Don't get me wrong—I'm not satisfied with the condition of our American high schools. But it is not because our economy is struggling (in fact, it isn't as I write this, so maybe teachers who were blamed for a poor economy in the early eighties should be praised for a good one in the mid-nineties). It is because we can do a better job of preparing our kids to be members of the communities in which we all live, through engaging them in high schools that are a daily experience in a learning community— the type of place we are building at FHHS along with thousands of other teachers, parents, administrators, and students around the nation.

APPENDIX

Resources for
High School Restructuring

Having finished this book, you are hopefully ready to begin rethinking your own school. This is the most important work, school by school transformation. Such work provides models and inspiration for others as well as the outlines of the legislative changes needed to allow restructuring to occur.

This is a daunting task. Your school may be the only one in the area to embark on such changes. Or you may be able to put your own twist on patterns tried in nearby schools. Regardless, change can be a lonely journey, and it always helps to have a few friends along.

The following resources include organizations that are happy to work with entire schools or individual teachers and parents. You will also find suggestions of other books, some of the best materials available today. Most of these focus primarily on high schools, but there is much of value here for middle and elementary school educators as well.

Organizational Resources

The Coalition of Essential Schools

The Coalition of Essential Schools
Box 1969
Brown University
Providence, RI 02912
401-863-3384
http://www.ces.brown.edu

The Coalition (CES) is made up of member schools pledged to put into practice a list of shared Common Principles. Probably the most powerful tool available for reconsidering what we do in high school, it is reprinted here in its entirety:

The Common Principles

1. The school should focus on helping adolescents learn to use their minds well. Schools should not attempt to be "comprehensive" if such a claim is made at the expense of the school's central intellectual purpose.

2. The school's goals should be simple: that each student master a limited number of essential skills and areas of knowledge. While these skills and areas will, to varying degrees, reflect the traditional academic disciplines, the program's design should be shaped by the intellectual and imaginative powers and competencies that students need, rather than necessarily by "subjects" as conventionally defined. The aphorism "Less Is More" should dominate: curricular decisions should be guided by the aim of thorough student mastery and achievement rather than by an effort merely to cover content.

3. The schools goals should apply to all students, while the means to these goals will vary as those students themselves vary. School practice should be tailor-made to meet the needs of every group or class of adolescents.

4. Teaching and learning should be personalized to the maximum feasible extent. Efforts should be directed toward a goal that no teacher have direct responsibility for more than 80 students. To capitalize on this personalization, decisions about the details of the course of study, the use of students' and teachers' time and the choice of teaching materials and specific pedagogies must be unreservedly placed in the hands of the principal and staff.

5. The governing practical metaphor of the school should be student-as-worker rather than the more familiar metaphor of teacher-as-deliverer-of-instructional-services. Accordingly, a prominent pedagogy will be coaching, to provoke students to learn how to learn and thus to teach themselves.

6. Students entering secondary school studies are those who can show competence in language and elementary mathematics. Students of traditional high school age but not yet at appropriate levels of competence to enter secondary school studies will be provided intensive remedial work to assist them quickly to meet these standards. The diploma should be awarded upon a successful final demonstration of mastery for graduation—an "Exhibition." This Exhibition by the student of his or her grasp of the central skills and knowledge of the school's program may be jointly administered by the faculty and by higher authorities. As the diploma is awarded when earned, the school's program proceeds with no strict age grading and with no system of "credits earned" by "time spent" in class. The emphasis is on the students' demonstration that they can do important things.

7. The tone of the school should explicitly and self-consciously stress values of unanxious expectation ("I won't threaten you but I expect much of you"), of trust (until abused) and of decency (the values of fairness, generosity and tolerance). Incentives appropriate to the school's particular students and teachers should be emphasized, and parents should be treated as essential collaborators.

8. The principal and teachers should perceive themselves as generalists first (teachers and scholars in general education) and specialists second (experts in but one particular discipline). Staff should expect multiple obligations (teacher-counselor-manager) and a sense of commitment to the entire school.

9. Ultimate administrative and budget targets should include, in addition to total student loads per teacher of eighty or fewer pupils, substantial time for collective planning by teachers, competitive salaries for staff and an ultimate per pupil cost not to exceed that at traditional schools by more than 10 percent. To accomplish this, administrative plans may have to show the phased reduction or elimination of some services now provided students in many traditional comprehensive secondary schools.

10. The school should demonstrate non-discriminatory and inclusive policies, practices, and pedagogies. It should

model democratic practices that involve all who are directly affected by the school. The school should honor diversity and build on the strengths of its communities, deliberately and explicitly challenging all forms of inequity.

CES publishes *Horace*, perhaps the best journal on school restructuring available today. *Horace* is free to faculties of CES member schools, and individuals may subscribe for a small fee.

The single largest conference on school restructuring is the Coalition's Fall Forum, held early in November. The Forum is open to the public and features teachers, principals, parents, and students explaining the cutting-edge programs going on in their schools.

Recently CES has decentralized its organizational structure and operates through centers located around the country. Information about school membership, connecting with a CES center, and subscriptions to *Horace* can be obtained by contacting the CES national office.

National Paideia Center

National Paideia Center
UNC-CH
Campus Box 8045
Chapel Hill, NC 27599
919-962-7380

Based on the work of Mortimer Adler, the National Paideia Center consults with teachers and schools on ways to bring a high-quality, challenging academic curriculum to all students. Recently the Center has striven to shed its perceived "elitist" image through working with poor rural and inner-city schools. In fact, plans are currently under way with the Center to incorporate their approach within all schools in one North Carolina county.

Of particular interest to those working on restructuring high schools are the approaches to instruction and curriculum the Center has to offer. Perhaps they are best known for their "seminar" style of instruction. To help all students use their minds well, the Center advocates and trains teachers in the use of a discussion method built around the examination of significant writings or pieces of art. Through having students scrutinize the work under the guidance of the teacher's questions, such discussions avoid becoming "bull sessions." Instead, students are drawn back to the text, asked to connect it with outside or previously discussed materials, and required to defend their reasoning publicly. I have seen firsthand at FHHS the power of such "Socratic seminars" in transforming teaching.

The Paideia Center has also begun to work with schools on the "what should we teach" question. The Center's belief is that *all* students, not just a few, should be taught a rigorous curriculum including exposure to the "classics" of modern civilization. How this works out in actual practice is something the Center is exploring with a wide range of partner schools in a variety of locations. The upshot of this work should be invaluable for any school that wants to tackle the issue of raising standards while simultaneously avoiding tracking and ability grouping.

The Institute for Democracy in Education

The Institute for Democracy in Education
Ohio University, College of Education
McCracken Hall
Athens, OH 45711
614-593-4531

Founded more than a decade ago by teachers who felt current reforms were both antiteacher and antidemocratic, IDE now has some two dozen regional offices across North America, Europe, and Africa. Taking seriously the words of the American philosopher John Dewey, IDE supports teachers at all grade levels who strive to hold their practice consistent with the democratic mission of public education.

IDE's primary focus is on direct service to teachers. Its journal, *Democracy and Education*, features the work of teachers applying democratic theory in actual classrooms. Additionally, the Institute holds an annual conference and provides workshops around the country in conjunction with regional offices.

The national office will provide subscription information and contacts with the nearest local offices and/or workshops.

The Kurt Hahn Center for Educational Activities

The Kurt Hahn Center
North Carolina Outward Bound School
2582 Riceville Road
Asheville, NC 28805
800-209-9773

For decades Outward Bound has been a leader in outdoor experiences that challenge individuals to learn more about themselves and their abilities. Built around four "pillars," self-reliance, compassion, physical fitness, and craftsmanship, each course is designed to inspire "self-esteem, self-reliance, concern for others and care for the environment."

The Kurt Hahn Center at the North Carolina Outward Bound School has been formed to work with educators to bring the organization's wilderness class philosophy to the schoolhouse. Named after the founder of Outward Bound, the Hahn Center offers courses for teachers as well as workshops at schools. The focus is on "expeditionary learning" which invites learners to overcome a challenge and, in so doing, develop more confidence in themselves as thinkers and problem solvers. While still in its infancy, the Hahn Center offers an excellent option for high school faculty members who want to rethink how they teach in order to more deeply involve students.

National Coalition of Education Activists

National Coalition of Education Activists
Box 679
Rhinebeck, NY 12572
914-876-4580

NCEA is "a multiracial network of parents, teachers, union and community activists, and others working for fundamental changes in local school districts." Past workshops have included sessions on community activism for school change and building school communities.

NCEA is also closely affiliated with the journal *Rethinking Schools*. Published in Milwaukee, *Rethinking Schools* has produced excellent theme issues on curriculum (such as their "Rethinking Columbus" packet) and school politics (recent issues have focused on school funding). Information on *Rethinking Schools* and with a wide variety of other resources can be obtained through NCEA.

Center for Leadership in School Reform

Center for Leadership in School Reform
950 Breckenridge Lane, Suite 200
Louisville, KY 40207
502-895-1942
http://www.clsr.org

Led by Phil Schlechty, CLSR works with leaders of schools and school districts who want to change how their schools do business. CLSR offers seminars and workshops on leading for change. But its most valuable work is building long-term relationships with districts through frequent site visits, seminars, and the providing of both human and print resources. Staffed by individuals with extensive school experience themselves (Marilyn Hohmann, formerly with Fairdale High, was referred to earlier), CLSR offers a real practitioner's approach to school change.

National Center for Restructuring Education, Schools, and Teaching

NCREST
Box 110, Teachers College
Columbia University
525 West 120th Street
New York, NY 10027
212-678-3432

In a field awash with all sorts of reports and commission findings, NCREST continually turns out some of the best firsthand accounts of school change around. Taking a predominantly case-study approach, NCREST reports provide valuable research on the effects of school restructuring. The Center's stated goal is to "bring together many voices: those of practitioners and researchers, parents and students, policymakers and teacher educators" and it does it quite well. In addition to issuing reports (write for a listing), it is also the leading clearinghouse for information on school restructuring efforts nationwide.

The Essential Library

This list of books and readings on high school restructuring is divided into two groups. The first four are must-have books for anyone seriously exploring restructuring a high school. They are written with compassion and heart, meant as much to inspire as to instruct. All of the authors have long histories of working for change in schools. If I could have only four books on my shelf—and sometimes you don't have time to read much more—these are the ones I would have.

To fill out any school-reform library include further readings that range from discussions of change per se to statistical information on public education. This list is my "second shelf" that provides the information needed to be effective in making change. All of these books are widely available and most of them I wish I had written myself.

The Top Shelf

Horace's Hope by Theodore R. Sizer (Boston: Houghton Mifflin, 1996)

This is the third book by Sizer tracing the work of the fictional teacher Horace to restructure his high school; the first two were *Horace's Compromise* (1984) and *Horace's School* (1992). (I'm cheating here, because I believe all three books should be read together, expanding the "top shelf" list just a bit.) Based on Sizer's decades of working in high schools for change, *Horace's Hope* sets out the parameters of what so many teachers wish for their schools. At once utopian and grounded in day-to-day practice, it can fail to inspire only the most cynical.

The Power of Their Ideas by Deborah Meier (Boston: Beacon Press, 1995)

The subtitle of this book says it all: "Lessons for America from a Small School in Harlem." Building on her experiences in leading what may be considered the best urban high school in the country, Meier shares her perspectives about the meaning of school. Each piece in the book tackles one of the tough problems we face in public secondary education and provides a progressive humanitarian solution that she and her staff have worked out in their own school. You laugh and weep along with her, and put the book down ready to change the world.

Redesigning Schools by Joseph P. McDonald (San Francisco: Jossey-Bass, 1996)

Joe McDonald is one of the best observers of schools I know. This book, based on his work with schools across the country for both CES and the Annenberg Institute for School Reform, looks at the daily experience of students in order to ask if we are doing what's right for kids. An argument and a strategy for "rewiring" the school is carefully presented, and it reflects not the cold eye of a researcher but the impassioned commitment of a former teacher and principal. A delight to read, this book causes one to question most everything we take for granted about school.

Revolutionizing America's Schools by Carl Glickman (San Francisco: Jossey-Bass, 1997)

A call for reclaiming the democratic mission of education, Glickman's work makes practical connections between schools and the American dream of life, liberty, and the pursuit of happiness. Beyond setting out our historic commitment to democracy and education, Carl provides activities to utilize in engaging in democratic school change. All of the ideas herein have been field-tested through his work directing the Georgia League of Professional Schools and can be applied in any school.

I should also note that this and McDonald's book are found in the Jossey-Bass Education Series, the best overall list of books on school reform.

The Second Shelf

The Manufactured Crisis: Myths, Fraud, and the Attack on America's Public Schools by David C. Berliner and Bruce J. Biddle (Reading, Mass.: Addison-Wesley, 1995)

Filled with statistics yet very readable, this book challenges the notion that our schools are not doing a good job. It helps redirect the focus of school-change work where it belongs: on the daily lives of kids in schools.

In Praise of Education by John I. Goodlad (New York: Teachers College Press, 1997)

What are schools for? Goodlad connects public education with democracy and presents an approach to building school community.

The Unschooled Mind: How Children Think and How Schools Should Teach by Howard Gardner (New York: Basic Books, 1991)

Gardner is the theorist behind multiple intelligences, the notion that we all learn in a variety of ways. He has written widely on the topic, but this is the volume I find to be most useful to teachers rethinking what and how they teach.

Successful School Restructuring by Fred M. Newmann and Gary G. Wehlage (Madison, Wis.: Center on Organization and Restructuring of Schools, University of Wisconsin, 1995)

Newmann and Wehlage and their team set out to look at what variables determine successful change in schools. Their answer: restructuring that focused on student work above all else. A useful study to keep any effort on track.

Inventing Better Schools by Phillip C. Schlechty (San Francisco: Jossey-Bass, 1997)

The leader of the above-mentioned Center for Leadership in School Reform sets out what it takes for leaders to rethink their schools. As with everything Phil writes, this is filled with down-home wisdom that most research reports lack.

The Human Side of School Change by Robert Evans (San Francisco: Jossey-Bass, 1996)

It isn't as easy as some folks make it sound. Evans walks us through the human needs of educators, parents, and students when confronted with change, and provides tools to make the transitions easier. Read this first before starting a change, and the unexpected confrontations that often accompany change can be avoided.

Breaking Ranks: Changing an American Institution (Reston, Va.: National Association of Secondary School Principals, 1996)

Short, fact-filled, direct, this report from the largest organization of high school principals is a mainstream call for reorganizing our high schools. Written by a panel of practicing school administrators, this volume cannot be ignored as "just theory." A valuable tool to use in convincing school boards or administrators that something should be done—the sooner the better.

Prisoners of Time: Report of the National Education Commission on Time and Learning (Washington, D.C.: U.S. Government Printing Office, 1994)

After you read this slim report, you will never look at our use of time in high school in the same way again. Drawing both from studies of the current use of time and from alternative models, this report provides ways to put time at the service of learning rather than allowing learning to be controlled by the clock. Another excellent tool to use in convincing local educational leaders of the need for immediate change.

Of course there is so much more to read, but the time is for action. Fill your shelves with these books and let them lead you on to others. But don't let reading get in the way of acting. Go out there and do something, today, for your children, my children, our children.

Index

37´
W